Marginality in Philosophy and Psychology

Marginality in Philosophy and Psychology

The Limits of Psychological Explanation

George Tudorie

BLOOMSBURY ACADEMIC
LONDON • NEW YORK • OXFORD • NEW DELHI • SYDNEY

BLOOMSBURY ACADEMIC
Bloomsbury Publishing Plc
50 Bedford Square, London, WC1B 3DP, UK
1385 Broadway, New York, NY 10018, USA
29 Earlsfort Terrace, Dublin 2, Ireland

BLOOMSBURY, BLOOMSBURY ACADEMIC and the Diana logo
are trademarks of Bloomsbury Publishing Plc

First published in Great Britain 2022

Cover image: The miracle of the speaking infant, by Titian. 1511 © Photo Archive
Messenger of Saint Anthony, Padova, photo by Giorgio Deganello

Photo by Giorgio Deganello / Photo Archive Messenger of Saint Anthony

A catalogue record for this book is available from the British Library.

A catalog record for this book is available from the Library of Congress.

ISBN: HB: 978-1-3501-5512-1
         ePDF: 978-1-3501-5513-8
         eBook: 978-1-3501-5514-5

Typeset by Integra Software Services Pvt. Ltd.

To find out more about our authors and books visit www.bloomsbury.com
and sign up for our newsletters.

To David, Ceci, and Dida.

Everything is on a reduced scale here in the Polar regions;
we can't afford to be extravagant.

Amundsen

Contents

Figures

Acknowledgments

Behind this book is my own tale of two cities, and a year of magical thinking, a plague year. The debts that I acknowledge below run deeper than the writing of a book.

Toward the end of 2019, and especially in the first months of 2020, I began working on the project Bloomsbury had so generously accepted. I had just completed a teaching semester in Bucharest and finally had the time to revisit my PhD thesis (Tudorie 2013), on which this book is based. Early in 2020 I was back in the library of the Central European University in Budapest, my *alma mater*, overlooking a gray Danube through the canyon of Vigyázó Ferenc street. I was expecting an auspicious year. That spring, I was to become a father. And I was rewriting my thesis into a book. One benefit of making plans is that one can later reflect on their, and one's own, fragility.

Needless to say, things did not go as I expected. But that this book exists at all is testimony to the support I had. My gratitude goes first to Colleen Coalter, Becky Holland, and Suzie Nash at Bloomsbury, who patiently helped me navigate the path from proposal to final manuscript. I also want to thank the three anonymous reviewers who evaluated the manuscript at various stages, made helpful suggestions, and were anachronistically kind in their criticisms.

My main debt for the work that eventually took the form of this book is to the Central European University, which by now has been forced to move to Vienna by the whims of an autocrat. The CEU Philosophy Department that I knew was mostly a Central- and Eastern-European melting pot. I was very fortunate to have been part of it. Hanoch Ben-Yami, my doctoral supervisor, restored what could be restored of my confidence, something that too few supervisors do. I am afraid that in terms of philosophical enlightenment there was not that much that he could do. Be that as it may, to the inadequate and sometimes obstinate student that I was Hanoch truly was a *Doktorvater*.

I also want to thank my friends and colleagues at the National University of Political Studies and Public Administration (SNSPA) in Bucharest, my employer, for their constant support and patience. Their kindness meant that I had the unusual comfort of time to work on this project. I like to think that some of the lessons I learned in this context will translate into being a better teacher.

Some of my debts are both intellectual and existential, and they go back to a dusty town in devastated 1990s Romania. A number of extraordinary teachers, beginning with my mother, shaped my thinking and my writing. I need to mention at least the late Emilia Cambeşteanu, Titi Damian, and Grigore Spermezan. Sharing at least in part my roots, lifelong friends supported me when it mattered most. Thank you, Cristi Petre, Marcela Jalbă, and Dan Mihăilă!

I do not know how to thank my family, they're too close, as it were, for this echo to be properly heard, but I'll live with both the awkwardness and the cliché. This book is dedicated to them—to David, Cecília, and Dida.

Introduction

Toward the end of the eighteenth century, just a few years before the Revolution, the surgeon and wax modeler Pierre-André Pinson, who worked for the anatomy lab of the Duke d'Orléans, produced a composition representing a fetus at about five months (figure 1). The unborn child rests on a wooden plate, the umbilical cord still connecting it to the placenta, which is positioned at a distance to its left.

Pinson's model is an instance of what was by then a coherent and macabre iconography involving the unborn,[2] part of the larger theme of *memento mori* or *vanitas*. As in other such works—some involving real human remains—it is the pose given to the fetus which makes the model truly disturbing. Uncannily, the child is lying on its right side, the right arm flexed and supporting its head, the left arm fully extended, the legs also extended and softly crossed. A paradigmatic melancholic pose, instantly recognizable to anybody remotely familiar with one of the oldest tropes of European art.[3] Philippe Comar comments:

> The melancholic posture given to the fetus in this case [...] seems to express the bitterness of the anatomist who, while perfecting his ability to describe the human body, still remains unable to understand its constitution and development. It is a kind of "pre-biological" melancholy. Knowledge of anatomy is mute about life, for it is only knowledge of the corpse.
>
> (Comar 2005)[4]

This is a book about an analogous kind of bitterness (*dépit*), one which shares a number of philosophical reflexes with the drive that made the old biologists search for the inexplicable spark of life, to paraphrase Collingwood, "at vanishing-point" (1992, 227). Much as the riddle of *life* haunted the philosophically inclined biologist, the mystery of *mind* became the make-or-break bet of the psychologist. To a certain extent, this was a bet that human minds were indeed mysterious, and that therefore adequate explanation was long overdue. The

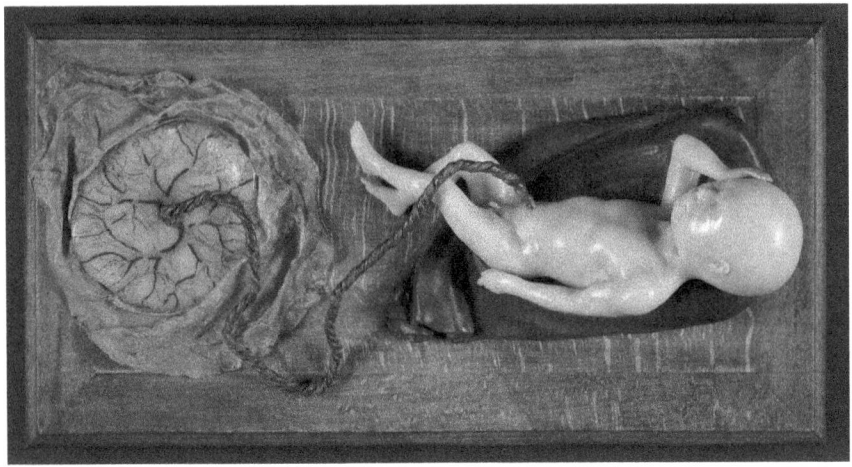

Figure 1 Pierre-André Pinson, *Foetus de cinq mois avec son placenta, c.* 1780 ©
Muséum national d'histoire naturelle, Paris.[1]

emergence of psychology as a scientific discipline and its obsessive quest to
emulate the successful natural sciences is, at least in part, the story of frustrated
attempts to study the mind, as it were, "anatomically." If biology has for long
been in the position of putting aside worries about the evasiveness of life,
psychology, even in its recent history, has been more prone to hesitations about
its subject matter and method. As a first determination, what is explored here
is this endemic fragility. Why is it so with psychology? Perhaps mind *is* more
mysterious or resistant to scientific investigation. Or maybe its slipperiness is
persistent for other reasons—reasons that tend to be ignored or downplayed
once the investigative machinery of the psychologist is set in motion. I should
note that these are not exhaustive or mutually exclusive hypotheses.

This first glance is evidently too wide for a workable book-length project.
Questions as those suggested above will immediately explode into countless
threads expanding not only into specialized subject areas—say, the philosophy
of psychology—but also into the past and current intellectual landscape.
Psychology has not been a stranger to public affairs or the arts, for example.
It has been in the vicinity of moral panics with ideas such as *brainwashing* or
schizophrenogenic mother, and it has also paraded promises of socially engineered
utopias, notoriously with public figures like Skinner, but also in more recent
guises—think *effective altruism* and the like. Given this predicament, the most
that can be attempted here is to contribute to an answer indirectly and within a
narrow field of view. *Indirectness*, because, while informed by larger worries, this

essay cannot in any sense dissipate them. At best, it will work *against* the idea that lessons learned in certain areas of the study of mind are generalizable, that they carry over by default to all other regions. If this is right, and since this book itself is focused on a few fragments of psychology, the most that can be learned about other fragments will be in the negative: how things should not proceed. *Narrowness*, because from a large number of possible perspectives this one amounts to a drastically circumscribed view point—the margins of psychology, in a sense of "margin" to be explained shortly. While comparison, connection, and example will be privileged instruments in the following, there is no attempt to systematically compare this perspective or location with others.

Let's then come closer to the subject matter at hand. What is meant here by "margins of psychology"? The paradigmatic human subject in psychology is the typical human being: mature, in possession of at least one language, reasonably competent in the social and cultural matters characteristic of her position in the world, more or less normal relative to the standards of the community to which she belongs. Admittedly a loose description in an endlessly problematic language, but this is a claim not about, say, the statistical fact of the matter in psychology (e.g., number of publications on such topics) or even the factual history of the field (something like Kuhnian paradigmatic problem). It is an observation about the central position occupied in psychology, as landmark and *measure* of things, by the concept of a normal person. It is not, to be clear, that psychologists work on anything like the "problem of the normal person," but that they work in a field organized by this concept, with explicit or implicit expectations about what people do or would do, what they think or would think—and so on. This central anchor determines a series of peripheries or margins.

To begin with, since humans are a kind of animal, one margin is that of the *non*human: extinct species of the genus *Homo*, animals, machines, possibly aliens, improbably gods and angels. From this amalgam, psychology may be expected to have something to say about at least those agents we are familiar with. And, of course, it does—whole branches deal with animal psychology, which has a long and respectable history, and, more recently, with evolutionary theorizing, machine intelligence and human–machine interaction. And if there are exobiologists despite the current lack of evidence about extraterrestrial life, there may as well be exopsychologists.

In addition to these nonhuman vicinities, there are differences *interior* to our species. One such fault line is that which we may call "anthropological." Different cultures and times may have their own mindsets, and these, while mutually understandable, may not be reducible to something unitary or more fundamental. Some such dissimilarities are to be lived with, and this may or may not be something psychology needs to pay attention to.[5] Even if it turns out that anthropological (or cultural) difference in some sense impacts the realm of psychological phenomena, this is not the kind of difference that determines the notion of margin aimed at in this book. To anticipate, a difference counts as anthropological to the extent that it is an expression of a *culture*, in other words, if it qualifies a more or less functioning community. As such, it will be at least in principle open to a public process of understanding, reconciliation, or translation which may or may not involve psychological elements. Cultures may be marginal *relative to a view point*—a coda all should constantly remind themselves of—but a culture cannot be *psychologically* marginal in the sense which is relevant here.[6] The dangers of exoticism have been experienced not only by Western art but also by Western social-science. A culture which as a matter of principle cannot be understood is a contradiction in terms; a psychological subject endlessly resistant to interpretation is not. This takes us to two further fault lines.

Age and the process of ageing matter greatly to humans. This determines yet another kind of internal difference. Human beings are born extremely immature and they need a long time to develop, and to learn their way in their surroundings, notably those of their culture. Humans are also special in the way they age and face death. It is not therefore unreasonable to expect that different age groups—infants, children, adolescents, adults, the old—may have significantly different psychological traits, and may have to be approached with specific lenses. Indeed, this has been one of the most powerful engines of specialization in psychology. Developmental psychology, somewhat analogous to pediatrics in medicine,[7] is an example of such a project.

A special case of the array of differences determined by age is that which separates those who have entered language, culture, and society from those who have not. Leaving aside the miseries of old age, and mental illness, this distinction—which is, of course, one of degree—concerns mostly young children. It takes years for human children to acquire the rudiments of language and culture; for the first few months of life even the rudiments are missing. This, as we will see, turns out to be a contentious claim. And it is here that we face the first instance of psychological margin in the sense intended in this book. The beginning of life for the human being does not overlap with the beginning of characteristically human life, which, generically speaking, is that of reciprocal understanding. The question in this context is how to illuminate the interval—perhaps just a few months wide—in which the young child is neither in nor completely out of the interpretive conceptual net in which those around her are at home. A prefatory question to this one, given recent, and not so recent, psychological theorizing is the following: *is* there such an interval?

The case for mapping a marginal area in the case of infants is perhaps counterintuitive, given both natural and theoretical inclinations. We gladly see ourselves in our children. Opposite dispositions must be kept under control in what regards another source of distinction within our species: departure from typicality in adults. Being normal is a dubious distinction, but human cultures seem to have always been able to recognize that all people are different, and then some are not just different, but bizarre and unanchored from the familiar facts of common life. Mental illness, though historically one of the main interests of psychological study, is a psychological periphery in the sense of being recognized as deviation from a tolerable interval of variation—as *exception*. To be clear, being atypical or mentally ill can take many forms; method may overlap with madness, or may seem entirely absent from it. The cases which are of interest here are the latter, essentially instances of psychosis (delusion being the defining symptom thereof). Psychotic mental illness, then, constitutes the second case of psychological margin to be discussed in this book. It, too, is a type of situation in which regular interpretive concepts waver, which, I will argue, makes them unusable for psychological theorizing. Psychosis is certainly not continuous with early childhood, the research territory suggested above, but some parallels concerning attempts at explanation are nonetheless possible.

We can now draw a line and sketch an initial characterization of the notion of margin relevant for the aims of this book. The marginal is not simply different or distant from the paradigm of the normal person. What isolates individuals we can consider marginal in the intended sense, what makes them special, is precisely their isolation from the surrounding culture and its affordances of meaning-making. The nonverbal infant and the (psychotic) madman, though in vastly different predicaments, are *almost* outside language, community, and culture; these human beings come in and out of view at the horizon of (psychological) intelligibility. The first is not yet at home in it, the second no longer. This confronts us with a problem of understanding, which is not a new problem, but which has renewed relevance given the attempts of psychology to say something illuminating about such subjects. At the root of this problem is the tension between (psychological) intelligibility, which depends on public and culturally embedded practices and concepts, and the limitations of the infant and the madman, who cannot act as parts of the open and structured world which makes understanding possible, even if they are not completely foreign or detached from this world. This tension destabilizes explanatory discourse, to the extent that it is rooted in our common interpretive practices.

One worry should be answered early on. Why should a problem of (psychological) *intelligibility* determine a notion of *psychological* margin? Psychology is not hermeneutics; it has fought hard not to be any kind of philosophy. And psychology's aspiration of becoming a natural science was at the same time a doing away with issues of sense-making and intelligibility, wasn't it? No matter. The cases designated above as margins obviously belong to psychology in the sense that they have a place in the history of the field. Moreover, circumscribing them in terms of intelligibility holds, since the science of psychology, despite its self-image, continues to depend for its explanations on ordinary psychological concepts such as *thought, intention, reason, decision, motive,* or *belief.* These concepts, even when regimentation is claimed, even when they are disguised in jargon, are inherently correlated with the possibility of understanding, with there being intelligible thought and action, and with the respective practices of sense-making. This correlation means that the applicability of said psychological concepts will wax and wane with that of intelligibility and understanding. A margin of understanding will ipso facto be, in this sense, a margin of psychology. There is in fact more in the decision to call these cases *psychological* margins, but things should become clearer as we proceed.

It should now perhaps seem less arbitrary that Pinson's wax model stands at the beginning of this book. We there have, fused in one representation, the unborn and the (melancholic) madman, the before and the beyond of recognizably human life. What joins them, however, is not the fact they are in some sense *in*human (to curb early any ethical worries). They are human and among other humans—indeed, usually cared for. What brings them together is nonetheless a form of loneliness, which only language and the intelligible society of others can extinguish.

With this visual metaphor in the background, let us now observe what the notion of psychological margin, so understood, does. Essentially, the concept allows for a second, and more precise, determination of the questions raised at the beginning. Psychology mixes a number of traditions, and these traditions are, in part, views about the nature of psychological *explanation*. Our problem becomes this: what kinds of explanation are adequate if one aims at investigating the *margins* of psychology? But even this formulation goes somewhat beyond what is attempted below. It suggests that explanations will be offered, which is not the case. What will be proposed, rather, is a criticism of an explanatory strategy which does not work in marginal cases, but which seems to be a constant temptation in psychology. The question, then, takes the negative form: what explanations are not helpful at the margins? Phrased like this, the problem is not one of excluding arbitrary possibilities, but one of qualifying or opposing actual research programs, and especially their philosophical presuppositions. So perhaps one should be satisfied with putting things in this form: *this* does not work, does it?

What does not work, then? The main target of the criticism that will be developed in the following is the attempt to use patterns of explanation typical of cognitive psychology in order to account for the early development of human social and communicative abilities on the one hand, and for some symptoms definitive of psychosis on the other. By "cognitive psychology" I will generally refer to the kind of psychology for which the metaphors of mind as computer, and of thought as computation are canonical. Even if I will proceed by way of example, it should be stressed that the target remains a kind of explanation. That is to say, skepticism is only incidentally placed over one or other research program in psychology; its proper object is a *philosophy* of psychology.

Cognitive psychology emerged as a reaction to behaviorism's hostility toward mentalistic theorizing. As such, it attempted to rehabilitate through regimentation regular psychological concepts—the stuff of everyday interpretative practices, which has also more or less been the bread and butter of pre- and non-behavioristic psychologies. On this, the position taken here is rather unoriginal: cognitive psychological explanations misuse regular psychological concepts. This often does not make much of a difference if, as it were, these concepts benefit from their being already embedded in an interpretive practice and are therefore able to take care of themselves—to preserve their force to illuminate human action and thought even when presented as technical jargon. The more original part of the criticism is supposed to be this: at the margins of psychology, the misuse of psychological concepts does make a difference: regular notions are displaced from their domain of application and, because of that, they have intermittent traction and offer little insight; the appearance that they, instead, do scientific work—that they act as instruments of *discovery*—is an illusion. Also an illusion, an even graver one, is that, as regimented concepts applied in marginal cases, they offer insight into the origins, history, nature, or meaning of the *regular* concepts applied in *regular* circumstances. I will come back to these two mistakes in the final lines of this Introduction.

This criticism is an instance of a more general one. Whenever the regular psychological concepts have been so used—and they have, for example, in psychoanalytic accounts of psychosis[8]—analogous mistakes have been made. This possibly more interesting comparative approach is only minimally developed in this essay. Even if a variety of examples—including some quite distant from cognitive theorizing—constitute the scaffold for the case defended here, it does not amount to a systematic treatment.

There is also a larger context for the critical analysis that I propose. This is the aura surrounding the idea that psychology, in its growth as a scientific discipline vulnerable to all kinds of reactionary attacks (e.g., this one), should try to unify its field and method. Computer-cognitive psychology is just an instance of this larger current. Psychological explanation, in consonance with an image of what a natural science should look like, must be *one* (uniform) recognizable kind of thing; perhaps a match for the putative "physical explanation." This is injustice psychology does to itself. One comparison that will recurrently appear in the examples discussed here is between psychology and medicine. Like medicine, according to this suggestion, psychology should make peace with its past and present diversity, in both theory construction and practical application. This, it seems to me, is a far more adequate image to have for psychology, both in terms of a historical, retrospective look, and in terms of the constant plurality of the field. It also has the advantage of qualifying any overoptimistic or dismissive claim about what a particular kind of psychology is or is not able to explain; it should as such keep both optimism and skepticism under control.

To move now to the issue of method, this essay does not present, defend, or explore a formal argument, in the sense of aiming at a proof. It seems unlikely that the area investigated here would allow for that, except by artifice. The book proceeds, rather, by amassing evidence in what is hoped to be a nonarbitrary fashion. What organizes the examples collected here is a set of ideas which I briefly describe below, and to which I return rather frequently throughout the book.

First, the distinction between the study of human beings as natural objects and their study as rational and cultural beings is one which crosses rather than circumscribes psychology. This means that the traditional distinction between explanation and understanding is one to be lived with within psychology. A permanent methodological insecurity need not follow, if philosophical slips and ideological ambitions are kept in check. What "psychology" means is left to the (local) interests of psychologists, much like in other fields.

Second, the obsession of psychology to do away with philosophical worries emanating from the fault lines just mentioned is misplaced. They are important and there to stay, at least in the form of recurrent temptations and mistakes. At this point in our history, most of us, I suspect, carry miniature versions thereof in the puzzles of our reflection on self and others. It should not be *too* surprising that psychology has been torn between becoming more like the natural sciences or more like the humanities. But perhaps a better strategy would be to say that similarities should depend on what, or rather whom, one tries to explain.

Third, it matters how the dominant current that pushes psychology toward a natural-scientific ideal is opposed. The margins of psychology in the sense sketched above constitute a region in which this ideal can be *demystified*, not demolished. This is so, because it is precisely in the marginal cases that the ideal truly begins to have a point. The web of understanding naturally comes apart at the margins and one cannot mend it from the outside, or transition seamlessly from it to the crystalline structure of explanation. Approaching opacity shakes us and our certainties, and a turn to explanation will be felt. But this may help the central regions of psychology to be less dependent on the natural-scientific ideal, less puzzled by the transparent powers of the reasonable person.

Fourth, this perspective has obvious connections with a long tradition that has distinguished between nature and culture, and between a psychology of reason and one of passions. But this does not mean that now, as then, these distinctions are very helpful. Nature does not abruptly begin below *x* months of life, or at the gate of the psychiatry ward. Passions are sometimes highly conventionalized, and often, in the Hegelian manner, engulfed by the cunning of reason. One is not pointing here at something *alien*, inscrutable, or mute. The difficulty faced at the margins of psychology is paradoxical: the distance perceived in one's vicinity, the hesitation irrupting within certainty, the inescapable struggle with the barely expressible.

Fifth, what should be understood by psychology's *turning* to natural scientific explanation at its margins is not abandonment or judgment about moral status or human essence. It is the recognition that its regular concepts, which just are, or are derived, from the public regular ones, cannot, as it were, *decide* marginal cases. It is not that they are blind or strictly inapplicable at the margins. But we, the psychologist here included, have a limited grasp of these cases, and it cannot be made firmer by stretching the relevant concepts. If anything, the grasp is thereby diluted. What psychology could do here is to extend our ability to deal with these cases by acting according to its ideal—truly as a concept-introducing science. As in, say, working with high-dimensional objects, questions of grasp or understanding may remain moot, but this will not detract from the enterprise.

Let me conclude this Introduction with a chapter-by-chapter walkthrough. The book begins with a discussion of the predominant philosophy of psychology at work in current computational cognitive-psychological models. While the reader may have formed an expectation by now that I will be critical, it is quite important to take note of the historical path that made this way of thinking the norm, and also of its undeniable strengths. I will return, in the context of this analysis, to a more detailed sketch of the notion of psychological margin.

The second chapter provides a partial view of the historical path mentioned above. It documents the persistent idea in the philosophy of psychology—as practiced by psychologists themselves—that psychology is a young natural science which advances by discovery. As all such enterprises, the science of mind begins in familiar areas and it evolves toward uncovering more and more *un*familiar territory. Its progress is seen initially as dependent on the exclusion of conceptual worries, including the one about the link between the notion of mind and that of understanding. More recently, progress in psychology is described as capable of (dis)solving such conceptual difficulties with scientific tools. This perspective survives otherwise radical theoretical changes (the rise of behaviorism, for example), and it is this conceptual continuity underlying discontinuities in explanatory models that is of interest here. The discussion proceeds from canonical figures such as Mill, James, and Watson, to Köhler, and then to a few influential cognitive psychologists from the recent past, such as David Marr, or currently active, such as Susan Carey.

The story of progress in psychology has been opposed from a number of directions, and this counternarrative of resistance is the ground from which this book, too, has grown. I will discuss three critical threads, merely gesturing at others for reasons of space. This part of the book begins in Chapter 3 with a source of resistance that can be generically called "the humanist tradition." It aimed at keeping the study of mind—under the name of "psychology" and sometimes under other labels—within the human studies or *Geisteswissenschaften*. The examples discussed in this context are Dilthey and, on a separate note, Collingwood. They both found an engagement with psychology unavoidable, even if their main aims were elsewhere. Given that with these thinkers one arrives in the vicinity of philosophical reflection on the epistemic status of history, the chapter includes an incursion in mid-twentieth-century philosophy of history, Gardiner and Dray being in this case the protagonists.

Another source of opposition to the narrative of psychology's ever-ascending scientific trajectory is that illustrated by Wittgenstein and the thinkers he inspired in philosophy and in the social sciences. This is a vast and unequal landscape, and I present some snippets of it in the fourth chapter. From the numerous threads involved in Wittgenstein's remarks on psychology, I will focus on two examples—the notes on Frazer and those on James's Ballard respectively. They help clarify the distinction between what I have called above "anthropological" and "psychological" differences and senses of margin. Toward the end of the chapter I comment on the problem of the "logical alien," which has been given prominence in the so-called new Wittgenstein scholarship.

Another angle of attack has at its vertex the concept of logical space of reasons, developed as a critical instrument against "the myth of the given" by Sellars and then by Brandom and McDowell. The latter's framing the analysis of human reasoning powers as "second-natural" is particularly relevant, and the fifth chapter of the book builds mainly on that insight. I suggest that it can be seen as convergent, given the aims of this essay, with the critical perspectives mentioned above.

What these threads offer is a picture of partial overlaps that should help characterize a sensible notion of margin and its relation to the larger preoccupations of psychology. Here is a brief sketch of this picture: There is, first, a defense of the autonomy of psychology as *Geisteswissenschaft*, an enterprise which is largely descriptive in nature, which progresses not by discovery, but by amassing and evaluating examples, and whose method is understanding (*Verstehen*) rather than mechanistic explanation. This is at best a partial picture of psychology, and it does entail anachronisms, but I will suggest that Dilthey's claim that it is essential to the "central regions" (1977, 28) of psychology stands. It may also make sense to at least raise the question whether one can think of some problems of psychology as specific to a *historical* science (think geology rather than physics as model).

In the second step, I propose that we turn to Wittgenstein to discuss his remarks on Frazer's *Golden Bough*, and his criticism of James's claim that there are unambiguous cases of sophisticated thought in the absence of language (Ballard's autobiographical report is the evidence mentioned by James and rejected by Wittgenstein). According to Wittgenstein, Frazer exemplifies the mistake of thinking that cultural difference amounts to savagery. A whole group, given one's local standards and illusion of holding the moral high ground, may appear mad, doing things, as it were, blindly. That is, there may seem to be no point in trying to interpret their doings as one would with one's own group. But to succumb to this perspective would be a mistake. By now, noticing this mistake in the history of social scientific theorizing has become a trope, and a cleansing ritual. But it is not redundant to look again at Wittgenstein's notes, and to focus on the basic nature of the error. The very presence of what unmistakably amounts to culture gives interpretive concepts traction. Wittgenstein rejects, to use the terminology suggested above, the assimilation of anthropological difference to psychological difference.

What psychological difference may look like and what its impact may be we see in the case of Ballard, a deaf-mute who claimed having contemplated metaphysical issues at a time when he had at most a very rudimentary ability to sign. Wittgenstein discusses this case as presented by James, and he aims at rejecting Ballard's story as an instance of *remembering*. The moral of the case, given the context of Wittgenstein's philosophy of psychology, is, however, quite general. In a marginal case, such as Ballard's, regular psychological concepts (*remembering* is but one example) become unstable, and this cannot be compensated by treating the concepts as items in a technical jargon. It is inherent to serious psychological difference to disrupt psychological intelligibility, given that the latter is forged in everyday interpretive practices. This is not a comfortable view to contemplate, and not only for obvious ethical reasons—an issue to which I return a number of times in the book, including here.

There is in Wittgenstein a theme that needs to be mentioned, if not fully addressed, in this context. This is the problem of the "logical alien," that is, the question if there could be thought that contradicts basic logical laws. If this question is given a *psychological* reading, then it may seem that the problem of the logical alien overlaps with that of the psychologically marginal. Isn't logically alien thought simply another name for madness? This—the psychological reading—would be a misrepresentation of the problem. The logical alien confronts us with an apparent puzzle about thought as a *logical* notion. The logical alien, accordingly, is not a main character of our tale. Taking a proper distance from this puzzle is not, however, a trivial matter, and therefore some comments are in order.

The third source of resistance, as announced, starts from the suggestion that citizenship in the space of reasons comes as a matter of *Bildung*, of being cultivated within a language and a tradition which become, in McDowell's words, "second-natural" (2000, 84). As in Wittgenstein's, in this perspective the concepts which matter here—*thought* and *intention*, *belief* and *understanding*—are seen as anchored in nonarbitrary public practices. Moreover, they carry normative loads: beliefs are more or less justified, understanding implies the possibility of misunderstanding, intentions can be judged by their reasonableness, thinking may have or lack accuracy or perspicacity. These concepts, thus illuminated, suggest aiming at a standard, or having criteria in view, and this should calm naturalistic excesses without inviting in any kind of supernaturalism. In the context of this book, taking this road means consolidating skepticism about projecting the relevant concepts to regions where standards and criteria are out of place.

Put together, these criticisms should help clarify the benefits and costs of applying regular psychological concepts, including the benefits and costs induced by using them in theories that aim to illuminate the margins of psychology. The suggestion in the following will be that such theoretical offensives gain us little. Cognitive psychological theorizing, like that emanating from older schools of psychology, is on thin ice when it treats the margins as "more of the same" by applying unexceptional concepts in exceptional circumstances. The pretensions that, in so doing, we learn about what concepts such as *intention* or *belief* signify, or about their origins, are without fundament.

The picture presented in the first five chapters is not intended to exhaust the subject matter, but to orient the view. Ideally, the samples that are discussed will act as a lens, providing focus. We will be reminded that some mistakes we have made before, that some temptations are perpetual, and that we have *long* had better ideas than what gets periodically paraded as a revolutionary view of human nature. The remaining three chapters of this book are placed in this general perspective, but, being so located, they also carry their own agendas, because they deal with cases and theories that have substantial differences.

The sixth chapter is focused on the explanatory machinery that has been thrown at early human development, specifically on the way the first social achievements of young children are explained. Historically, Western culture has often enough portrayed children as smaller-scale adults, and not only in the literal sense of portrayal, in the arts, but also when theorizing about what children are, and how they should be treated. It is important to avoid that mistake, even in its sophisticated contemporary travesties. Here, this background commitment, which has the potential of skewing explanations, is seen as an instance of assimilating psychological margins to the paradigm.

The chapter provides historical context and a series of analogies, then moves to a critical assessment of a major theory of development in current psychology, that assembled in the last decades by Michael Tomasello and his students. This model of the incipient cooperative and communicative aptitudes of the pre-linguistic child has been very influential in both philosophical and cognitive scientific circles, and it is important to know whether this reception has been wise. Even if the theory will be discussed in detail, the aim is to reveal its philosophical commitments, and to show that they are misplaced. I should note that other theories in recent developmental psychology could have been discussed in a similar manner.

Tomasello's model is currently centered on the notion of shared or collective intentionality. This notion has not at least initially been a technical or special concept of cognitive-developmental psychology, but one borrowed from the philosophy of action, initially from Searle, and then, increasingly, from the work of Michael Bratman. The essence of my criticism is that this relocation does not result in a novel scientific notion or in a change of meaning, but in a mock concept of null explanatory value. Admittedly, this is harsh, but it is high time, it seems to me, we curbed the enthusiasm of the cottage industry of collective intentionality explanations of most of the interesting early developmental achievements.

The seventh chapter raises doubts that to some extent are analogous to those anticipated above in the case of psychotic mental illness. While most of us are familiar with young children, madness is a different story, one of selective blindness, rejection, shame, stigma, and self-imposed isolation. Familiarity is thus not assumed, nor is it assumed that a brief orthodox description following current psychiatry or the psychiatry of yesterday would do. The chapter compensates by sketching two portraits, and the theories of psychosis that were attached to them. The aim is to have in view *what* is being explained by various theories of psychosis, and how it has been done.

One portrait is that of Daniel Paul Schreber; it is built on his extraordinary autobiography, and it is presented in parallel with Freud's speculations about this "patient" he never met. The other character, one who is far less known, is called Leon Gabor (not his real name), and he speaks through the extended notes collected in Milton Rokeach's study *The Three Christs of Ypsilanti*. Both these cases are exceptionally well documented. Schreber is an astonishing writer, and intervention on his manuscript before publication meant deleting rather than changing stuff. The text is authentic madness. As for Gabor, Rokeach spent two years with him and the other Christs, during which he saw them almost daily. The quoted transcripts provide plenty of firsthand material.

The theories that shadow these two tragic men belong, by now, to history. Freud supposed that Schreber was a repressed homosexual, haunted by a dominating father figure. Rokeach, not himself a psychiatrist, toyed with the "schizophrenogenic mother" theory, which was academically kosher in the early 1960s. Both these psychological—psychoanalytic, to be precise—models of psychosis played the card of intelligibility. They constructed a perspective in which what the psychotics said and did began to *make sense*, given their *circumstances*. Psychoanalysis is gone, but this explanatory strategy is still with us. It is exemplified by cognitive-psychological theories of madness.

The chapter focuses critically on such a theory, or rather family of theories. In the early 1990s, Christopher Frith proposed a theory of schizophrenic symptoms which explained them as consequences of a general breakdown of the system which normally supports "theory of mind" abilities. With this move, Frith effectively equated schizophrenia with late-onset autism, since a theory of mind account of autism was at the time fashionable in cognitive-developmental psychology. The fact that by definition autism excludes psychosis was brushed aside. Explanation proceeded by speculating about the impact of deteriorating theory of mind abilities: surely other people should seem menacing, as it happens in paranoid delusions, when one is *no longer* able to fathom what they are up to. This pattern of explanation assumed that the psychotic individual reacted as *anybody* (i.e., a *non*psychotic person) would, given the circumstances. This amounts to an assumption of intact insular rationality, and as such it is untenable. One does not explain *ir*rationality by calling it alternative rationality without begging the question.

With the theory of mind model of autism losing ground, Frith's theory of schizophrenia also lost traction. But the idea that there must be *some* causal-explanatory connection between psychosis and defective theory of mind continued to be influential. For more context and contrast, the chapter includes a brief discussion of the radically antipsychiatric cognitive theory of psychosis proposed by Richard Bentall. Even if he is critical of Frith, Bentall shares the idea that psychosis is to be explained by showing it to be ultimately intelligible.

The large-scale analogy to the previous chapter on developmental psychological theorizing can be thought of in the following terms: trying to explain psychosis by drowning it in "the ordinary miseries of life" (Bentall 2010, 40) until it looks understandable is an instance of assimilating the margins of psychology to its paradigm. Perhaps this chapter could also be judged in separation from the larger agenda of the book, though this would be much harder than in the developmental context. Madness brings the question of ultimate intelligibility *acutely* into focus.

This last note is important. The sixth and seventh chapters of the book are not symmetrical. Seeing young children and psychotics as psychologically marginal does not mean that they are marginal in the same sense, or, as it were, in the same direction. The mad, like other brutalized populations, have often been considered childlike. This is a step one should not take again.

Childhood is not abnormality or sickness. Children are nurtured into becoming what their culture demands; they are from the very beginning drawn into the social world, though for some time they might not be aware of it. Assimilation in their case is anticipation. This essay does not dispute the obvious—children are born on the doorstep of our world. They are not outside that world; but neither are they yet in. We project ourselves in them, and this is *eventually* vindicated.

It is a different situation with the mentally ill. These are people who, in the serious cases, have lost a world, which is everything one *can* lose. The sense of being at the margins has immensely stronger connotations in their case, and the ethical problems of dehumanizing what seems a permanent human possibility are insurmountable. But precisely because of its historical stature and continuous scandal, psychosis allows for a clearer view of assimilation at work. We project the mad *back* into us, into a world that, as if by choice, is no longer theirs.

The directions of assimilation are distinct not only in the sense pictured above. In both the developmental and the clinical cases two *kinds* of assimilation are at work: (i) as already discussed, there is illumination of the margins as *more of the same*. One claims to be able to apply the same concepts in the same way; the margin is colonized. I *remember* how my book proposal was received at Bloomsbury; Ballard *remembers* his pre-linguistic thoughts about the origin of the universe. But (ii) there is also a sense in which the margin is seen as illuminating (vs. being illuminated by) the paradigm. This happens usually in the context of a "reverse-engineering" story.

The "understanding" of belief by three-month-olds and the delusional "beliefs" of schizophrenics are presented as *rudimentary* understanding and *broken* belief, respectively. If one modeled *those*, then one would ipso facto learn something about understanding and belief—that is, about their *familiar* instances. Since one is already familiar with understanding and belief, it is expected that one would learn something yet unknown, something waiting to be discovered: what is the *origin* of these concepts, what is the cognitive and neural *machinery* underlying the relevant abilities, and so on. The crucial step here is to assume that the first kind of assimilation already works—that "understanding" is a scaled-down version of understanding, that "belief" is a kind of anaerobic belief, metabolically adapted to adverse circumstances.

Both kinds of assimilating are conceptually bankrupt, but the differences between them should be observed. They are not equally represented in the developmental and the clinical case, though both are present in both scenarios. This is because reverse engineering is usually focused on breakdown. This strategy means in practice that madness is asked to explain reason, the exception the rule. An ironic distortion of Erasmus's classical metaphor.

With all these differences noted, what the reader will find in the following is nonetheless a fragment from the family album of an odd *couple* with a long cultural history, child and madman. To use a canonical example, Foucault documents, in his *Histoire de la folie*, not only a *terminology* that often designated demented persons as "returned to childhood" or "in a second childhood" (Foucault 2006, 81)—(*en enfance*) (Foucault 1972, 95), but a certain persistent disposition to conceptualize madness as childhood. For instance:

> For this new reason that reigned in the asylums, madness was less an absolute form of contradiction than a minority status, an aspect of itself that had as yet no right to autonomy, which could only exist grafted onto the world of reason. Madness was childhood, and at the Retreat, everything was organised so that the insane might be treated as minors.
>
> (Foucault 2006, 489)

Or:

> Judges follow the same reasoning when they refuse to see the actions of a madman as a crime, and when deciding on placing him under guardianship always suppose that madness is only a temporary incapacity, the soul being no more affected here than it is inexistent or fragmentary in the child.
>
> (Foucault 2006, 209)[9]

Before we have a look at the exhibits, I should ask patience from the reader, because assembling the pieces of this story will be slow-paced. My choice of medium and approach cannot result in proof, but I hope it does eventually provide a vantage point from which to weight promises of understanding mind, past and present, and to exercise reasonable doubt. What follows is both an engagement with contemporary ideas, and a deliberately anachronistic mosaic, since I think that in reflecting on psychological explanation at the margins of psychology we need to remember rather than rethink.

1

Against Cognitivism

I

Writing about the multifaceted legacy of Jerome Bruner, Clifford Geertz has us contemplate the centrifugal history of psychology. Beyond the predictable disagreements of a formerly young science, one can hardly miss a certain tendency to walk on incongruent theoretical paths. This sometimes happens at the same historical moment, or in the same person, Bruner himself being such an example. Geertz nods to Pirandello: From the outside at least, psychology

> looks like an assortment of disparate and disconnected enquiries classed together because they all make reference in some way or other to something or other called "mental functioning". Dozens of characters in search of a play.
>
> (Geertz 2001, 19)[1]

That this picture is only available to someone who is not captive to the problem, or the apparent problem, of claiming a unitary domain for psychology—in other words, of circumscribing the mental—will not be surprising. But, in only being fit for so serene a person, the image probably downplays the inside perspective of those who staged one or another volte-face in this field, and the substantiality of the stakes. The pressure to uncover a common dialect in the Babel of psychology has been real, and a part of the quest for scientific citizenship. Consonantly, psychology has suffered not only ruptures but also revolutions. It is not only that people decided to go their own way in their research and manner of describing and explaining findings, as one would, perhaps, in the humanities; parties have repeatedly argued that their way was *the* way of getting things right for everybody doing psychology.

As if echoing Ryle, who compares psychology with medicine—"the name of a somewhat arbitrary consortium of more or less loosely connected inquiries and techniques" (1949, 323)—Geertz suggests that, with Bruner turning psychology cultural, one arrives in the vicinity of anthropology—the "other hopelessly miscellaneous and inconstant science" (2001, 23). Perhaps, but one need not remind oneself of Bruner's own lament at the beginning of *Acts of Meaning* about the fragmentation of psychology (1990, ix–x), or of his earlier career as a founder of the cognitive revolution, to understand that psychology does not seem to be comfortable with such a self-image. As chromosomes during cell division, this uneasiness becomes visible at times of change. For example, the two major turning points in twentieth-century academic psychology[2]—the behaviorist movement, which dominated the first half of the century and which at the end of the 1940s was still considered revolutionary by Ryle (1949, 328), and the cognitive revolution of the 1950s—have both been immodest in scope.

In the case of behaviorism, we tend to recognize this as a mistake. We also recognize that one characteristic way in which immodesty manifested itself was philosophical speculation. Here, I am not only referring to the pointless attempts to translate all suspect vocabulary in behaviorist newspeak. Hawkish dispositions are also exemplified by the formulaic rendering, "solving," or rejection of classical topics (thinking, learning, deviance, human nature), by pop-science campaigning, or by the "deduction" of overly ambitious sociopolitical consequences from one's psychology.[3] This philosophical halo has since evaporated, as few people continue to think that the rigor of behaviorism simply is scientific rigor in psychological clothes. There are standards of scientific respectability that a research program has to meet, and this often is an issue worth discussing, but one of the clearest signs of conceptual hubris is the parading of candidate scientific commandments as religious relics. The significance of this should not be obscured by the inevitable messiness of empirical research. Perhaps no scientific program can live up to its own rhetoric, but in the case of behaviorism the rhetoric itself should be—and has been—the subject of legitimate worries. The philosophical halo inherent in this rhetoric was symptomatic for the mutation of the behaviorist research program into an ideology of the mind.

If this summary and unexceptional diagnosis of what went wrong with behaviorism is correct, what can one say about the kind of psychology which emerged after the cognitive revolution? To continue with the language I used above, has cognitive psychology been not only a critique of behaviorism, but also a successful critique of ideology? In asking this question, I propose to contribute to an ongoing argument to the effect that, in the wake of the cognitive revolution, the now-dominant conception of the mind has itself become an ideology. The core of this ideology (which we might call "cognitivism") is the computer metaphor as a model for mental states and processes, *and* the idea that the language of psychology is to be made explanatorily good by being shown to be, at bottom, a language of computation. More recently, this language is thoroughly colored by the attention given in the field to neural loci where said computation presumably takes place, but this does not change the nature of the problem. Like behaviorism, cognitivism *unifies* the mental by providing a criterion for it (computation), but unlike at least some strands of behaviorism, cognitivism also *reifies* the mental by requiring computational substance from its explanatory terms. We recognize mental phenomena by the fact that they are computational phenomena involved in the control of behavior; what people call, for example, "belief" qualifies as mental because it can be given a computational description (unification). Moreover, belief *is* such and such a computational pattern (reification).

In the cognitive sciences, this view is, more or less, the foundation of the administrative jargon, and it is taken to express a scientific breakthrough, indeed, the definitive mark of doing away with the dogmatism of behaviorists. While acknowledging at all times the progress made in psychology in the last decades, the areas most involved in the cognitive sciences here included, I think it is a mistake to associate this progress with cognitivism. Cognitivism is in fact a source of confusion in thinking both about explanation in psychology, and about the folklore of the mind that has been organizing our lives since forever. As with the behaviorists, or with Freud, a Copernican revolution has not taken place in psychology, advertisements to the contrary notwithstanding.

Now, even if this is true, we need to start by recognizing that we are far from such an accepted diagnosis for what followed the cognitive revolution, although the idea of ideological continuity is not particularly original.[4] Even the worries expressed by some of the very people who founded the cognitive sciences in the 1950s, such as Bruner (1990) or Chomsky (2000), remain peripheral. Philosophical criticism seems even less influent. There have by now been numerous such warnings, involving very different threads of thought, from Searle's rejection of the syntactic engine metaphor (e.g., 2003a), to Putnam's change of mind about functionalism (e.g., 2001, especially chapter 5), or to the criticisms on Wittgensteinian lines put forward by authors such as P.M.S. Hacker (e.g. 2007) and Stuart Shanker (1998). These criticisms do not all carry significant bite, perhaps, and may be plagued by problems of their own. But added to inside worries they should give some pause to the idea that the computer metaphor is a particularly illuminating stance on what minds are. Philosophical worries, especially when expressed by practicing scientists, should not share the fate of philosophy as a discipline—often quietly escorted to the corner of the formerly reputable, but now silly, seniors.

This barrage of skepticism, one should note, cannot be uniformly assimilated to (and dismissed as) that which naturally fits those who conceive of psychology as closer to the social sciences and even to the humanities than to physics or biology. Predictably, cognitivism could not be considered an authentic renaissance of the mind from such a perspective, as we will see later in the book. But clearly one need not agree with this softer view of psychology and the unsurprising opposition to the mechanization of the mind which it has generated to be critical of cognitivism. Let psychology be as natural a science as it pleases; one can still resist the idea that psychology is scientific *to the extent* that it is cognitive in the sense of mentalistic *and* computational. This criticism which originates, as it were, closer to home is more damaging. Nevertheless, for the regions of the academic world that are the inheritors of the cognitive revolution this does not seem to be a time of insecure self-reflection. Maybe the thought is that, since the mind returned to the scientific picture, resulting psychologies are immune to the ills of behaviorism. Part of this may very well be true, but attention is needed to the part which is not.

One way to give credibility to the view that there should be parallel worries about the behaviorist and the cognitivist attempts to explain everything mental with a single set of tools is to notice that some of the more excessive claims of behaviorism were not results of the specific posits of this school, but of a deformed, and historically endemic, image of what counts as science—of what psychology should strive for. If physics is the science of everything physical, whatever that may be, then psychology should be the science of everything psychical, whatever that may be. If physics aims to explain everything physical in terms of particles, elementary forces, and so on, then psychology should explain everything psychical in terms of whatever the psychical equivalents of particles and forces may be.[5] The point then is not that the cognitive revolution failed in its attempt to reverse the specific misconceptions of behaviorism, but that it inherited, like behaviorism before it, a hollow ideal. The revolution was not, in this sense, revolutionary enough.

It is telling that, if radical behaviorists felt they had to ostracize the "mental" for not being scientific, Jacobin cognitivists arranged for its return, but only with the naturalization appropriate for an alien. This embarrassment deserves, perhaps, more therapy than it has received, and it is unnecessary. Nothing tragic should follow for psychology if the mind unravels, if it turns out to be different kinds of things which we understand in various ways, not all of which, to say the least, are compatible with the explanatory language of cognitivism. The unity of the mental, like that of psychology, has always been, after all, illusory, and a sign of *mauvaise foi*. If I am not mistaken then, we continue to be in the position of warning that the appetite for theorizing about everything mental in one move constitutes a symptom of philosophical addiction rather than scientific virtue.

The existence of many traditions within psychology is itself the proximal antidote of grand generalizations and a proof that even the best ideas and the most convincing explanations and analogies do not naturally extend to all mental phenomena. Important differences, for example, can easily be found even among the various approaches to the mental life of typical, mature humans—psychology's paradigmatic[6] subject matter. Consider, for example, the important differences between social psychology and the schools of cognitive psychology focused on the isolated individual.[7] *Cognitive dissonance* (Festinger, Riecken, and Schachter 2008) and *the magical number seven* (Miller 1956) were born in the same year (1956), but they do not belong in the same conceptual habitat. Nor is it obvious that there should be a hierarchical relation—reduction, analysis—between such concepts. Manifestos aside, it does not add much to the discussion to ask which kind of concepts (or which branch of psychology) is more fundamental. This only becomes a problem if one starts by stipulating that the mind *must* be, for all intents and purposes, a computer, or a neural network, or an electrochemical engine. But this is to get things upside down, since, as a matter of historical and conceptual fact, we do not start, even in psychology, with a regimented concept of the mental. The mental is already in front of us, as a matter of our nature and socialization. We need psychology to study it, not to identify it.

It is enough to accept that the fragmentation of psychology is neither accidental, nor a pubertal detail, to be en route to a criticism of cognitivism which may even prove constructive. To confront cognitivism head-on would be a mistake, and in more than one sense. One should not get carried away by a certain natural weariness about a discourse that happens to be dominant at a certain moment. There is a legitimate task of exposing the limits of received wisdom, but this goal should be accomplished with discernment and charity. It would be a grave error to think that one can sort decades of research into valuable and worthless with a few conceptual remarks. Here, the aim will be to erode those philosophical commitments which I consider ideological—a *way of talking* about findings, not their authenticity, will be the eventual target.

A partial and contextualized engagement is, in practice, unavoidable since objections need to be specific, even if their systemic significance is what interests us most, and since different regions of cognitive psychology have been made more or less vulnerable by cognitivism. It leads nowhere to measure a colossal theoretical edifice with an overstated disapproval. Moreover, even if there is some sort of urgency in being lucid about the dominant psychology of our day, it should not be forgotten that it is a general tendency to reify and unify the mental which forms the horizon of this criticism. The commitments in question embody philosophical dispositions that have affected psychology throughout its historical development. This is why, in the following, time will be spent describing at least in part the intellectual past of the puzzles we face today. They are not new.

II

History, then, will be our ally in the effort to emphasize the plurality of psychology. As in most situations, a historical investigation might be the best one can do to illuminate the present. Here, however, I will only be able to offer a fragmentary historical overview. Most of the weight of the criticism must rest elsewhere, in how these fragments are put to use. One can capitalize on there being, and there having been, many kinds of psychology in more than one way. Geertz's ruminations, to which I gestured above, constitute one such example. In the following, I propose to rely on what may be called a "topological" argument.

The fragmentation of psychology preserves some of the pre-theoretic fault lines of its subject matter. In the Introduction, I prosed the following perspective on this fragmentation: there is an equator of psychological preoccupations—the typical, mature, socially competent human being—and there are also marginal regions. Our self-understanding is grounded in our life at the equator, in our familiarity with, or being at home in, our social universe. Making sense of what people do and why, of what they say and think, begins here, in the ordinary. The concepts that allow for understanding others and ourselves—belief, intention, motive, and so on—belong in this social environment; they are given meaning by being regularly used as part of familiar and shareable practices: interpretation, answering questions, prediction, giving reasons, finding excuses, and so on.

As we move further away from the ordinary, none of the above can be taken for granted; we arrive at the margins of psychology. The margins are to a certain extent a matter of context. The notion, as already explained, is meant to capture a *gradual* erosion of confidence or transparency in making sense of others; it does not carry an ethical judgment. The figures of the infant (not yet fully developed human) and of the madman (beyond shared human life) can be safely situated in these outer regions, but they are not, by far, the only such examples.

This is a geography psychology inherits from the nonscientific world essentially due to the fact that it takes over the conceptual repertoire of the "folk." The common psychological parlance or "folk psychology," even if notoriously laissez-faire in use, is mainly about what typical adults feel, think, or do—and why. Of course, we talk in mentalistic terms even when we are quite far from the paradigm, and this includes our reflections on the mental lives of small children and of bizarre fellow humans, as well as those about more distant characters, such as other animals, machines, and the inhabitants of philosophical thought experiments. But even if we do ordinarily talk about all of them in "folk psychological" terms, we cannot claim the same degree of confidence as in the case of typical, mature individuals. Puzzling situations are to be expected, since they come with the territory. We know full well that the soil can suddenly turn slippery, that we can exceed at any moment the explanatory grip of everyday discourse. We thought the child was scared of the dog when she ran, but now she hugs it; well, who knows what she thought. We cannot ask the child and, even if we could, if she is very young, we would not consider her report *decisive*. The question is if anything *else* can help settle the case. The notion of margin should also capture the claim that this question must be answered in the negative.

The idea of the gradual erosion of folk psychological explanations (or simply put of understanding), at least in the case of bizarre behavior, has been on the philosophical agenda, notably on that of the radical interpretation/translation literature, and also on that of the eliminativists (Stich 1983, Churchland 1996). It has been observed, for example, that our interpretive capacities eventually break down when facing behavior that cannot be assimilated to any rational paradigm we recognize. Or that the impotence (and perhaps the indifference) of folk psychological "theorizing" in the case of mentally atypical individuals is evidence as to its being a terrible theory of the mind. I will try to put the idea to a different use.

To the extent that we are successful in the remote regions, according to these threads of literature, we manage to illuminate them as "more-of-the-same." So, for example, we impose our logic upon the native, as Quine[8] has it, or we hope for a mature science of the brain[9] that will explain behavior *both* typical and atypical, *both* verbal and infraverbal, as the eliminativists repeatedly advised. This "more-of-the-same" picture does a poor job when it comes to conceiving *serious* psychological difference. For example, there is little reason to think of mental illness as a kind of *anthropological* difference, à la Quine. And, contrary to what Churchland and Stich have argued, the infant and the madman are *not* best seen as falsification instances for an alleged folk theory of the mind.

The interesting characteristic of the psychologically marginal cases is that they force a divorce between the folk and the psychologist. If, in the case of typical, mature individuals, both the scientist and the folk are quite confident about their explanations, in the case of, say, individuals who behave exotically, the folk can be pragmatic about explanatory failures, whereas the scientist cannot. A psychologist cannot say, "I thought it was his failure to correctly represent others' intentions which made him paranoid, but perhaps it was not, I cannot really tell, this individual is really strange." The commoner will, in the face of mystery, label someone bizarre and live with it, while the psychologist must tell us *why* that person acts strangely. At least the first half of Ryle's dictum is true: the psychologist's task is to tell us why we are deceived.[10]

The current physiognomy of this divorce is a result of the cognitive revolution. What we observe nowadays is not the separation decreed by behaviorists between scientific psychology and folk babble, and it is not simply a disagreement about the scope of psychological explanations. Part of what it meant to bring the mind back in the scientific picture was to rehabilitate, through regimentation, the terms of the everyday psychological language so that it became once again legitimate to theorize in terms of beliefs and intentions, emotions and moods, memories and character traits. As Stephen Stich notes, this outlook seemed to close the gap between the scientific and the manifest image of the mental. But the very means of closing this gap—"[t]he use of [the] workaday 'mentalistic' folk vocabulary [as] one of the hallmarks of the burgeoning field of cognitive science" (1983, 5)—produced, in the marginal regions of psychology, the rupture I have described.

To say that scope is not the main issue in this context may seem strange. It would be wrong, however, to focus on scope, that is, on the idea that in current cognitive science, as in some of its intellectual precursors, the use of folk psychological terms is extended to areas previously *not* covered by such explanations. This is strictly speaking false, since those areas—for our purposes, early development and serious mental illness—*are* covered. As already said, in everyday contexts there is little timidity—though also little certainty—in speculating about the psychology of infants or madmen. The divorce then is not fundamentally about scope, but rather about the way explanatory terms are used in marginal contexts.

This is not to claim that in abnormal or developmental cognitive psychology explanatory terms are used in a peculiar manner. On the contrary, it is the insistence of using a uniform explanatory vocabulary that, added to these special contexts, generates the oddness. If one proposes to discern whether something has gone wrong conceptually in current cognitive psychology, a good strategy is to try to explore the sources of this oddness.

III

Let us begin by returning to a contrast already mentioned above. In the case of typical adults, the use of the everyday psychological vocabulary to construct scientific hypotheses has produced a rough overlap between the "naïve" and the cognitive scientific discourse. The explanations, if not always the findings, of this kind of cognitive psychology have, accordingly, an air of *familiarity*. People act, think, and feel because they see, believe, prefer, or remember things. They see others as trustworthy or threatening. They try to achieve goals without spending too much time and energy. What one should note is that the overlap and the familiarity may mask—indeed, that they often do mask—the different conceptualizations at work in the everyday as opposed to the scientific/technical discourse. Even when the cognitive scientists do not work with an explicitly regimented set of mentalistic concepts, they seem to work *expecting* such a set of concepts to be available. The availability of these concepts is seen as a likely consequence of the overall progress of the sciences of mind and brain. In any case, we are given interpretations of findings in mentalistic terms *as if* these were terms of art.

No such further legitimacy is needed by the folk. Where the folk will be happy with accepting that people act because they have goals, the scientist will add, for example, that goals are in fact internally represented informational states with an attached galaxy of computational roles. By attaching this coda, the psychologist provides an explanation of the folk platitude, of *why* people act on goals, and, to generalize, of *why* "folk psychology" works when it does. Since we already knew that people try to achieve their goals, the merits of this schematic psychology stand *in the coda alone*. However, since the folk and scientific explanations overlap at the level of people acting on goals, that is, since an explanation is in any case provided, it may be difficult to evaluate the merits of the scientific proposal in isolation. I am not assuming, in saying this, that the "naïve" explanations are scientifically adequate; the point is that they are explanations nonetheless, and that, as it is often remarked, they strike us as natural. For example, is the explanation that the politician voted against the proposal *because she formed the goal to block the proposal* convincing because the scientific view of goals is correct, or because the term "goal" inherits its explanatory force from its everyday use? This kind of question is further complicated by the fact that the two possibilities need not be exclusive.

As we move away from the paradigm of typical, mature individuals, however, the overlap between the folk and scientific manners of explaining behavior breaks down. In these regions, as suggested above, there is a sense in which everyday interpretation can, while scientific psychology cannot, turn to pragmatism. (Perhaps one can better express the point by saying that in these cases it becomes clearer that the folk need not *turn* to pragmatism, since it has *always* been pragmatic about such issues.) Here, the scientific counterparts of the folk concepts are no longer in the position described above of explaining why everyday explanations work. At the margins of psychology, the scientist faces the harder task of showing that her theory of why "folk psychology" works is ipso facto a theory of why, by the scientist's standards at least, folk psychology does *not* work.

The driving idea of the criticism that will be gradually built in the following may now be expressed in a clearer way. Cognitivism does not provide us with illuminating accounts of mental phenomena that are distant from the paradigm of typical, mature psychology. This is because, at least in these contexts, cognitivism misuses the explanatory terms of the everyday psychological discourse. This can be shown by noting that there is a divide between the "naïve" and the scientific explanatory customs in marginal cases, and by arguing that the language of cognitive psychology does a poor job at illuminating these cases. Whatever its merits and faults, the view of the mind that we have inherited from the cognitive revolution is not a general psychology. At least marginal cases, as described here, constitute explanatory *niches* that seem to require other—perhaps biological— kinds of illumination. Set in the proper historical and conceptual context, the philosophical tendency to focus on a single metaphor of the mind (computer/ computing) manifest in current cognitive psychology may be shown to be an old mistake that has already been confronted, save for the jargon, a number of times. Let us now turn to building up such a contextualization.

2

Manifest Destiny in Psychology

I

The story told in this book is critical, but I would very much like it to be read as sympathetically critical. Like most reasonable people I know, I place many hopes in scientific progress, I admire the heroes in the improbable and happy chain of events which is the history of science, and I have little patience for anti-scientific diatribes and for anti-intellectualism in general. If in this chapter I question a narrative of progress, it is because I think critical reflection strengthens the position of science as self-repairing structure. Moreover, to move closer to the subject at hand, it could be argued that the philosophical dead ends which I think one can observe in certain threads of psychology have come with the territory. The retrospective look which follows begins from afar to signal the enduring attraction of the idea that an advanced science of mind will get us, as it were, *through* some of the conceptual puzzles related to our self-understanding, and perhaps even constitute the foundation of a more comprehensive humanism. What I think should be said when faced with the various avatars of this idea is that the puzzles are here to stay.

We can start by considering an important motive *not* to accept the claim that the areas of human life I termed marginal or peripheral will be poorly mapped if one persisted in using a psychological vocabulary which is definitive ("constitutive" is perhaps a better word) of the paradigm. A characteristic way of arguing against this view is precisely what I alluded to above: telling a story of progress. Parallel to its relation to the nonhuman world, humanity enters history with a limited self-understanding (think: mythical, ambiguous, vague, contradictory), which then gradually expands, especially when this effort becomes regimented in the scientific enterprise. If there is no principled reason why we cannot know forever more of what is not us, then why should there be a reason to draw the borders of what we know about ourselves, specifically about our mental lives, at any other place than the (biological) limits of our species? To think there could be such a reason is to have the obstinacy of remaining in the mythical and the vague.

This idea of progress in understanding ourselves, it should be noted, has a degree of specificity. It is not, for example, very close to an image of growing empathy and increasingly refined reflection. What is central to it is the notion of *discovery*. We look at the skies and see gods and heroes; the maladroit astronomers of Swift's floating island of Laputa are familiar with two satellites of Mars, but it is all fiction, of course; then, as our ways change and science enters the picture, one day we truly discover the satellites of Mars. Similarly, we speak of what our fellows fear or desire, of the purpose of their actions, of our own aims and motives; but one day we discover what fears, desires, and motives really are. It is as if in the realm on the mind, too, one moved from Swift's speculations to Asaph Hall's[1] discoveries. Once we arrive at this stage, other, perhaps less pressing, questions can begin to be settled: mysteries of origin, evolution, or genealogy, oddities related to limit-cases and travesties, puzzling similarities and differences that used to destabilize conceptual systems and pushed the imagination in all directions. Here one has in mind the ambiguous cases of old: animals, machines, angels, primitives, babies, madmen, Martians.

Without further qualifications, it is too easy to say that the parallel between the progress of science and that in the knowledge of human affairs is misleading—*or* to accept it as the safest bet when it comes to understanding ourselves. A number of fault lines, not just one, dividing science and its discontents, cross each other in this region without determining an overall pattern. But if progress is understood essentially in terms of discovery, then the comparison illustrated above is one we should regard with caution.

It will matter how this caution is expressed. The difficulty that confronts one here is not that of constructing a case for skepticism about the notion of discovery in the study of mind. Even if unfashionable, a redoubtable tradition—that which insisted, in various ways, on the autonomy of the *Geisteswissenschaften*, psychology here included—is immediately available for such a project.[2] The difficulty, rather, as illustrated by the tradition, is to keep skepticism, once raised, under control. Global mistrust of psychology generated by conceptual observations should count, until further notice, against such observations themselves. The point of paying attention to the margins of psychology, again, is to note the *gradual* erosion of certain explanatory strategies. This is to say that the resilience of other strategies available to psychology, or of the same strategies used in different contexts, is not thereby called into question.

A nuanced critique of the notion of discovery in psychology suggests itself once we start reflecting on what happens explanatory-wise at the margins. This is, on the one hand, where discovery seems most needed in order to settle puzzles and dissolve hesitations. This is also, on the other hand, where we are constantly tempted to "discover" that there is nothing fundamentally novel or different going on—that discovery was not needed after all. It is worth focusing on this paradox if we are to resist, within reason, the idea of progress in psychology.

We begin on the positive slope of the paradox, by contemplating the rebellious optimism that periodically infects if not psychology proper, then its self-reflection and the image it presents to the lay public. As a matter of both historical legacy and recurrent conceptual difficulties, psychologists have felt the need to establish—and then defend—the scientific credentials of their trade. This has meant not only developing an obsession for imitating the methods and discourse of the natural sciences, specifically a hypostatized and not always accurate version of physics, but also a complementary obsession for distancing themselves from areas of philosophy dealing with mind and action. Austere naturalism was to be cultivated, metaphysical fog and presumed reactionary attempts by philosophers to reabsorb psychology resisted. Let us go through a few examples, beginning, given that we first drop anchor in the first half of the nineteenth century, from within philosophy, and then moving to psychology proper.

II

When he begins the last part of his *System of Logic*, which he devotes to the moral sciences, Mill places it under the blessing of an overly optimistic Condorcet. Mill is about to present a case for extending his conception of methodology from the relative limpidity of the natural sciences to the murkier waters of the sciences of man. He is aware that a vision which sets this latter region of knowledge on the same foundation as any other scientific enterprise will face skepticism.

> At the threshold of this inquiry we are met by an objection, which, if not removed, would be fatal to the attempt to treat human conduct as a subject of science. Are the actions of human beings, like all other natural events, subject to invariable laws? Does that constancy of causation, which is the foundation of every scientific theory of successive phenomena, really obtain among them?
>
> (Mill 1872/2006, 835)

In the early chapters of this part of the book, Mill refers, politely, to the "controversy" that surrounds the issue, notably the "celebrated" (1872/2006, 836—chapter II) one about the freedom of the will. But Mill, with and without reason, has little time for this kind of skepticism. By chapter III, the resistance is diagnosed as "confusion of ideas" (1872/2006, 844), and, when he is done, by chapter VI, where he moves to discussing social science, the controversy turns out to have resulted from "prejudice" (1872/2006, 875). The quote from the last chapter of Condorcet's *Esquisse* is thus only fitting.

Having painted a ladder-like image of the progress humanity made from its dawn toward liberty, civilization, and knowledge, Condorcet speaks, in the last chapter of his sketch, of a future of even greater and unstoppable evolution. He thinks he is entitled to his sunny forecast, since knowledge of human beings and of their social and historical world is a species of scientific knowledge, that is, one based on laws which can be discovered and which can generate reliable predictions. Condorcet is not, accordingly, expressing his heartfelt hopes, but *calculating*. The question he asks below is merely rhetorical, as only a mind opaque to the *lumières* would think there are reasons to resist optimism:

> The only foundation of faith in the natural sciences is the principle, that the general laws, known or unknown, which regulate the phenomena of the universe, are regular and constant; and why should this principle, applicable to the other operations of nature, be less true when applied to the developement of the intellectual and moral faculties of man?
>
> (Condorcet 1795, 316)[3]

While Condorcet takes for granted that this principle of uniformity holds, and spends the reminder of his text describing a world enlightened by the ideals of the French Revolution, Mill actually argues for the principle of uniformity (or unity of science, to use the common designation) by constructing a logical architecture for the sciences of human nature and of society—a vehicle of assimilation that integrates them in the overarching methodological edifice of science-without-qualifications. It is difficulty generated by complexity, not kind, that separates mind and its products—notably society, which crowns the hierarchy of complex objects—from other subject matters. Everything needed to study it, in terms of method, Mill tells us, has already been laid out in discussing the ways of the natural scientific enterprise:

> In substance, whatever can be done in a work like this for the Logic of the Moral Sciences, has been or ought to have been accomplished in the five preceding

Books; to which the present can be only a kind of supplement or appendix, since the methods of investigation applicable to moral and social science must have been already described, if I have succeeded in enumerating and characterizing those of science in general.

(1872/2006, 835)

What is left to do is a bit of detail housekeeping at the level of the "appendix," so that, on the one hand, existing psychological concepts are shown to be recoverable by a proper science, and, on the other, residual "metaphysical" frictions are eliminated. In what concerns the first goal, we are presented with a twofold structure. In the study of the individual mind, Mill sees "the experimental science" of Psychology (1872/2006, 872)—which more or less follows the "practical knowledge of mankind" (1872/2006, 848, 861) or the "common wisdom of common life" (1872/2006, 864)—as legitimate only since its "empirical laws" (1872/2006, 861) are to be eventually vindicated by "the general laws of the causes" (1872/2006, 867) belonging to Ethology, "the deductive science" (1872/2006, 872). Roughly, and to use one of his own analogies, Mill's Ethology[4] is to his Psychology what Newton is to Kepler. Which is to say that not even this division of labor counts as pathognomonic of the moral sciences; it simply is a characteristic of studying complex phenomena. Often, even in cases where a small number of well-known causes determine phenomena, as in astronomy, empirical laws are not strictly speaking true. Psychology, in any case, is not in a worse position then, say, meteorology (1872/2006, 844). What anchors it firmly in the realm of science is the availability, in principle if not in practice, of universal causal laws:

But in order to give a genuinely scientific character to the study, it is indispensable that these approximate generalizations, which in themselves would amount only to the lowest kind of empirical laws, should be connected deductively with the laws of nature from which they result; should be resolved into the properties of the causes on which the phenomena depend. In other words, the science of Human Nature may be said to exist in proportion as the approximate truths, which compose a practical knowledge of mankind, can be exhibited as corollaries from the universal laws of human nature on which they rest.

(Mill 1872/2006, 848)

Distrust of psychology's mundane concepts needs to be settled *somehow*; if not by reduction or elimination in favor of physiological terms (which Mill explicitly rejects as a mistake even "in principle" [1872/2006, 851]), then by assimilation to the familiar logic of studying planets, weather, or waves. That this pressure to do *something* about the regular concepts is accepted as legitimate—that it is considered obvious—is a crucial step in Mill's project.

There is then the delimitation from philosophy—performed, as it happens, via a philosophical argument. Mill seems to think that in the given context his role, just as Bacon's in his, is not to actually construct even the rudiments of the envisioned sciences, but to block skepticism issuing from philosophical anxieties. Thus, before presenting the structure sketched above, his first move is to neutralize the traditional philosophical worries about the compatibility of a determinist-causal world with the freedom of human action and thought. It is not the substance of this preemptive attack which is of interest here, but the very fact that it is there, and the role it performs. The role, as already suggested, is to uproot stubborn philosophical undergrowth in order to make the parcel roughly circumscribed by the ordinary psychological concepts legitimate and apt for scientific cultivation. In different guises, the suspicion Mill tries to dissolve will be perceived and dealt with, politely or brusquely, again and again. We will see the ritual evolving in the next samples.

III

It was just over a decade since the official recognition of Wundt's laboratory by the University of Leipzig in 1879 when James published his didactic attempt to lay down *The Principles of Psychology*. The influence of the book burned quickly in the larger conflagration that consumed introspective psychology, but it remains an obligatory presence in the history of the field.[5] That is not, however, the reason for it being present here. The *Principles* is a monumental work in a peculiar way— not primarily due to its colossal size, but because of its kaleidoscopic nature. Such a vast collection has constituted an endless source of reflection. It is also a collection which documents with a remarkable transparency hopes, hesitations, and mistakes which we seem condemned to repeat in the study of mind. Going through some of the topics James discusses is strangely reminiscent of a number of current debates. In this context, the same two directions of thought that we saw in Mill will occupy us: the undiscriminating anchoring of psychology in the realm of natural science—with the usual footnote which excuses the resulting awkwardness by referring to its young age; and the extirpation on any "metaphysical" doubts about the subject matter or status of psychology, which leaves a clean tissue of scientific problems within psychology, and exports all the residual messiness to where it naturally belongs—with philosophers.

Unlike Mill, who sees things, as it were, from above, James begins *in medias res*. Psychology, after all, has been in place for some time when he writes and he is busy presenting and debating an already considerable amount of theory and experimental results. When it comes to the status of psychology however, things are quite clear. The *Preface* notes that "the point of view [is that] of natural science throughout the book"—even one which is "strictly positivistic," though the latter is open to future revision, as in "physics and the other natural sciences." Moreover, the aim is to establish lawful correlations between phenomena— notably those "ultimate laws" which link the mental with "brain states" (James 1890/1983, 6). The correlation of conscious activity with brain physiology is, at least declaratively, the bread and butter of psychology. Beyond the opening niceties, it is the object of study (scope) and its methods that confirm the identity of psychology as an ordinary scientific enterprise.

Thus, the first chapter begins by defining psychology as the study of "Mental Life" (1890/1983, 15),[6] and then progresses toward a principled circumscription of that territory. This is done via a test for inclusion in the psychological realm— the presence of purposes which drive behavior in a flexible manner: "*The pursuance of future ends and the choice of means for their attainment, are thus the mark and criterion of the presence of mentality* in a phenomenon" (1890/1983, 21—emphasis in the original). This is admittedly vague—what should one say, for example, about "mechanical" performances that nonetheless strike one as purposeful (think of heliotropism in plants)? After all, one sees function and teleology everywhere in the living world, and perhaps beyond; should mind accompany them always? It is quite clear that James does not think that such questions are pressing for psychology proper, or threatening for a naturalistic approach:

> It is better not to be pedantic, but to let the science be as vague as its subject, and include such phenomena as these[7] if by so doing we can throw any light on the main business in hand. [...] [W]e gain much more by a broad than by a narrow conception of our subject. At a certain stage in the development of every science a degree of vagueness is what best consists with fertility. [...] I shall therefore feel free to make any sallies into zoology or into pure nerve-physiology which may seem instructive for our purposes, but otherwise shall leave those sciences to the physiologists.
>
> (1890/1983, 19)

Note that this is not a gesture in the direction of psychology being an explanatorily plural field, though James comes close to that when he announces "sallies" in neighboring disciplines. The point remains that vagueness is a temporary obstacle on the road to mature unity, an accidental defect excusable by psychology's young age.

What begins as vagueness, however, deteriorates soon enough into something unambiguously confusing. To block the overlap between "mere outward teleology" and mentality, James presents his criterion for mentality at work in a series of experiments with increasingly mutilated frogs. What shows that his criterion does well is the availability of such presumably fruitful *empirical* questions as: is the spine of a headless frog a proper target for attribution of mental life? Surely, if the spine can *choose* between commanding a movement of the left versus the right leg (depending on which of the legs is amputated) to wipe of acid (1890/1983, 22–3). What one should note here is not primarily the chaos that results from James's attempt to provide a unificatory criterion for the mental, but the fact that he sees the limits of applying psychological concepts as a fully empirical matter.

Things are even clearer when James moves to a discussion of method, in the seventh chapter of the *Principles*, the first section of which reassures that "Psychology Is a Natural Science." "To the psychologist—James tells us in a recurrent phrase[8]—the minds he studies are *objects*, in a world of other objects" (1890/1983, 183). That the method of investigating the mind which he discusses first is introspection does not affect the status of the mind as object, since introspection presupposes an objective point of view. Suppose a psychologist compares a color and how he himself perceives it in adverse conditions:

> In making this critical judgment, the psychologist stands as much outside of the perception which he criticises as he does of the color. Both are his objects.
>
> (1890/1983, 184)

Introspection, then, works well alongside the two other methods James discusses—experimentation and comparison. It is especially experimentation, understood with reference to the German experimental school, which marks a watershed in the development of psychology. The systematic "*siege*" (emphasis in the original) of the mind that issues from this method will conclude, the author expects, with "her overthrow" (1890/1983, 192). Prophetic words. Psychology as a natural science, the thought continues, has already stepped, with Wundt & Co., in its "microscopic" age. Whatever conceptual instability results from the use of introspection will be restored empirically. James even indulges in a bit of *Völkerpsychologie*:

> [P]sychology is passing into a less simple phase. Within a few years what one may call a microscopic psychology has arisen in Germany, carried on by experimental methods, asking of course every moment for introspective data, but eliminating their uncertainty by operating on a large scale and taking statistical means. This method taxes patience to the utmost, and could hardly have arisen in a country whose natives could be *bored*.
>
> (1890/1983, 191–2—emphasis in the original)

Let us now move to the second direction I mentioned, that of delimitation from "metaphysics." James is emphatic on this issue, too. In the *Preface*, for example, we are told that "metaphysics […] spoils two good things when she injects herself into a natural science" (1890/1983, 6). It would count as metaphysical to require an explanation for the genesis of thoughts. It is metaphysical to ask why thoughts express knowledge. It is metaphysical to wonder how the psychologist gets to know what he knows. Even if, as we saw, the realm of mental life studied by psychology is somewhat vague, what falls on the side of metaphysics is certainly not a legitimate object of enquiry for psychology. (Consequently, one might add, it does not belong to mental life.) "About such *ultimate* puzzles—we are told in the context of discussing the method of introspection—[the psychologist] in the main need trouble himself no more than the geometer, the chemist, or the botanist do, who make precisely the same assumptions as he" (1890/1983, 184—emphasis in the original). To fit the pedigree James projects for it,

> psychology when she has ascertained the empirical correlation of the various sorts of thought or feeling with definite conditions of the brain, can go no farther—can go no farther, that is, as a, natural science. If she goes farther she becomes metaphysical.
>
> (1890/1983, 6)

There is little doubt that, despite obvious differences of style, aims, and temperament, when it comes to securing a safe foundation for psychology, James is in accord with Mill about the two complementary ideas discussed above: the study of the mind needs to be conceived on naturalistic lines, even if one starts off with the somewhat undisciplined vulgar psychological concepts;

nonempirical troubles these concepts might pose can, and are to be quarantined within "metaphysics."

Two years after the publication of the *Principles*, a reviewer, George Trumbull Ladd, suggested that James's natural science is only "so-called" (Ladd 1892). To this, James replied in the next (second) number of the *Philosophical Review* (James 1892a). This exchange is a fascinating document, both very much a thing of its time, and uncannily reminiscent of some current discussions. As such, it is perhaps one of the best illustrations of the persistent currents in psychology we explore here, and an exemplary piece of evidence for the claim that conceptual problems come with the territory of psychology, that they survive changes of mores and perspectives, and that they cannot be solved by decree. Ladd questions James on precisely the two points discussed above:

> What, then, does Professor James understand psychology to be; and how does he propose to give to his own psychological opinions the character of a science? The answer to this twofold inquiry will introduce another closely connected: What does he conceive to be the relation between metaphysics and psychology as a "natural science"?
>
> (1892, 27)

On both accounts, Ladd finds the *Principles* lacking. Requiring psychology to be, if at all a natural science, one of the correlations between "thoughts and feelings" on the one hand, and of brain processes on the other, pushes the whole enterprise into obscurity. Moreover, James not only fails to save psychology from "metaphysics," he is often busy doing precisely the latter.

Ladd's reasons for rejecting James's insistence on correlating mental goings-on with neural processes are a mixed story. A young-science narrative overlaps with more interesting conceptual worries. This time, the young science is not psychology itself—which Ladd sees on comparatively *firmer* soil—but brain *physiology*.[9] If in terms of roughly locating, à la Broca, various "faculties"—such as speech or vision—in areas of the brain there has been some success, when it comes to processes in the brain that might correspond to trains of thought, one is in the dark:

> How greatly disappointed we are, therefore, when an advocate of the new "natural science" of psychology restricts all legitimate explanation, by his very conception of such science, to one class of conditions only,—and these by far the most obscure and unattainable of all.
>
> (Ladd 1892, 28)

And a bit later:

> The "thoughts and feelings" we do both know and know about, in a truly scientific way. We can describe them, as Professor James frequently does in such brilliant and interesting fashion. Moreover, we can explain them, by reference to their elements and conditions as existing in other antecedent and concomitant thoughts and feelings. But of their conditions, as existing in the shape of antecedent or concomitant brain-processes, we have no knowledge worthy of being called science. [...] If cerebral psychology is the only scientific psychology, then there is no science of psychology.
>
> (1892, 33–4)

Ladd leaves it open that brain physiology could one day advance to the point at which a "cerebral psychology" becomes possible (1892, 33). But this is a rhetorical gesture; even in that optimist scenario, correlative explanations referring to brain processes would not exhaust the field of psychology. Indeed, "cerebral psychology" is the diagnosis Ladd has for what is essentially *flawed* in James's conception. Suspicion of a conceptual kind is clearly present in this verdict. It is already visible in the first part of the previous quote, where "thoughts and feelings" are seen as explainable in their own terms.[10] And it is even more striking elsewhere in the review. For example, we are told that:

> [A]s to the localization of any of the "higher" forms or factors of thoughts and feelings, we are almost totally in the dark. Nor should we know what to do with *such* centres, if we could succeed in getting any clear trace of their existence.
>
> (1892, 35—emphasis in the original)

James's schematics are, at best, indications of *where*, of location, they say nothing about what is supposed to go on at the putative locations, and in what sense that something corresponds to thoughts. Still he insists on the idea of correspondence as the one which confers scientific character to psychology:

> When, then, Professor James maintains that his oral or schematic descriptions of the brain-processes, which correspond "in a blank unmediated way" to thoughts and feelings, "show what a deep congruity there is between mental processes and mechanical processes of *some* kind"; I must beg his pardon and flatly contradict him. They show nothing of the sort; they *show* nothing of any sort. They assume some sort of unknown congruity; they also serve to impress the uninitiated

reader with the feeling that he is being shown something. [...] [T]he assumption
of the congruity is in no wise dependent upon the advance of science.

                                        (Ladd 1892, 37–8—emphasis in the original)

Fortunately, Ladd grants, James rarely tries to be true to his own declarative
commitments; when he is doing psychology proper (i.e., not the "cerebral" kind
which he preaches), even if he is all over the place, he is generally admirable.
Even when James is not doing psychology proper, however, he is again going
against his own recommendations and engaging in "metaphysics"—indeed,
he is "too metaphysical" (1892, 29) to be scientific. A metaphysics of the mind
is replaced with a metaphysics of the brain, even though the former lies "no
deeper" and is "no more 'cantankerously' or dangerously metaphysical" (1892,
30). More specifically, it is the fact that in James one sees "no end of doubtful
metaphysics of physics" (1892, 52) which compromises his attempt to ground
psychology as a natural science. There is, according to Ladd, a perverse reversal
not only in James's attempt but in this *kind* of effort:

> [H]e does precisely what all who adopt the same conception find themselves
> compelled to do; he becomes metaphysical. He postulates some of those
> abhorred "deeper-lying entities"; and then he puts them through a course of
> conjectural processes in order to explain other (conscious) processes which are
> not conjectural, but are indubitably known to exist. (1892, 33)

The last note, which has already surfaced in some of the previous excerpts, should
be kept in mind; it amounts to clearly rejecting the idea of there being an acute
need to ground, by philosophical *fiat*, psychology. This field, "amply entitled
to be called a science; and even—if you please—'a natural science'" (1892, 50),
is at least in part already familiar—in front of us. Its dissimilarity from physics
or chemistry is not to be mistaken for youthful erraticism; it is genuine, but
not thereby a threat to its scientific status, unless seen through a philosophical
("metaphysical") lens. Even this needs further qualification. As we have seen
above, Ladd is half-prepared to open a door for a psychology that capitalizes
on future progress in brain science. The point remains that even such a future
(to Ladd, perhaps contemporary to us) psychology would not exhaust the field.
It would at best be one kind of psychology alongside those already familiar. It
is a philosophy of psychology which pushes James—and which tempts some of
our own contemporaries—to expect a big explanatory crunch, a collapse of the
plurality of psychology into one explanatory nutshell. As we sample some more

of the chromatic aberration inherited from this choice of lens, we will return to this basic observation.

An accomplished academic himself, Ladd is also, and admittedly, a spiritual man. He may write with an agenda, but it does not seem to this reader that his agenda compromises the points he makes, or the fact that, in this review at least, he achieves something of durable relevance. In James's reply, on the other hand, one sees a different kind of durability; what persists is a clear-cut version of the twin framework explored here: psychology is like physics in its infancy, contemplating a horizon of great discoveries; conceptual worries are detachable—they are to be dealt with in the appendix to the actual science.

James's *Plea* begins on a conciliatory tone, with the usual first move of excusing the predictable embarrassments of a young science. The title of a section of the *Principles* and repeated similar assertions notwithstanding, James denies that he ever

> claimed, for instance, as Professor Ladd seems to think I claim, that psychology as it stands today, is a natural science, or in an exact way a science at all. Psychology, indeed, is today hardly more than what physics was before Galileo, what chemistry was before Lavoisier. It is a mass of phenomenal description, gossip, and myth, including, however, real material enough to justify one in the hope that with judgment and good-will on the part of those interested, its study may be so organized even now as to become worthy of the name of natural science at no very distant day.
>
> (1892a, 146)

The question, then, is how to cover the distance between myth and natural science, as one already succeeded in doing in moving from alchemy to chemistry, and, within the latter, from phlogiston to oxygen. As with a number of contemporary theorists, the idea that this is a distance between points which might not be distributed in a single plane is never taken seriously. In a very telling remark, James justifies his optimism in the *Principles* by suggesting that "treating Psychology *like* a natural science [...] help[s] her to become one" (1892a, 146—emphasis in the original). He does not seem to recognize that this is nothing else than the metaphysical commitment Ladd was criticizing. It is ideology, not science, that works with this kind of performatives, substituting an understanding of the world with its alteration. Here, as elsewhere, one cannot stop admiring, in James, a talent for giving revealing and memorable expression to consequential blunders.

Criticism is also ignored when James moves on to discuss the status of psychology as a "special science" that carves a "mere fragment of truth," just as physics does (1892a, 147).[11] This fragment is legitimate naturalistic territory once "further" worries are cast out. It does not matter if these further worries concern the contentious interpretation of the fundamental concepts the science is done with. To be a science, psychology needs to "renounce ultimate solutions" (1892a, 147). The questions, if not the solutions, are to be kindly "rescued" from the hands of psychologists and "abandoned" to the philosophers (1892a, 149–50). Labor must be distributed, and not only in the benign sense that philosophical concern about psychological concepts should not count as psychology, but in the stronger one that this concern is *inconsequential* for doing psychology. What the "problem" of the existence of an external world is for the physicist, the "problem" of the nature and epistemic status of mental states is for the psychologist. Both take scientifically *harmless* things for granted.

The rhetoric is again symptomatic when James defends himself against Ladd's accusation that he invokes a (yet) nonexistent science of brain processes corresponding to mental phenomena. Without calling it that, James observes correctly the ambiguity in Ladd's criticism. One has to be clear if one's rejection of "cerebralism" is "in principle and entirely" (1892a, 153), or dependent on a contextual—and thus correctable—lack of knowledge about the brain. For James, the former is absurd. He already sees a wealth of evidence against it in, for example, known brain physiology and lesion studies.[12] Not that the experiments are the only discriminating element. James writes, after all, a *Plea*, something directed by definition at the future. Current results aside, what one gets once psychology, in Ladd's words, is "abbreviated" so as to aim for mind-brain correlations is, James tells us, a *program*:

> Not that today we *have* a "science" of the correlation of mental states with brain-states; but that the ascertainment of the laws of such correlation forms the *program* of a science well limited and defined.
>
> (1892a, 151—emphasis in the original)[13]

What matters here is not the choice of words (which simply documents the platitude that psychology is inherently susceptible to manifestoes), but the refusal to answer the more serious part of Ladd's attack. The difficulty which Ladd had tried to voice about the very idea of correlating one kind of familiar things, thoughts, with brain processes is perhaps deliberately misconstrued by James. Where Ladd had been very close to saying that psychology is *not in need* of a program, the *Plea* advised that for "cerebralism" to move forward, all that was needed conceptually was the clearing of "metaphysical entanglements" (James 1892a, 153). But what Ladd had said, on lines we might retrospectively recognize as Wittgensteinian, was that "cerebralism" was itself such an entanglement, one which programmatically forced the psychologist to "explain" the less by the more obscure. The reproach was that James himself was guilty of injecting metaphysics into psychology spoiling both. The misunderstanding of this criticism is clearly echoing in James's concluding lines, where, as a good pragmatist, he presents the matter in terms of temperament and practical value:

> Nevertheless, if the hard alternative were to arise of a choice between 'theories' and "facts" in psychology, between a merely rational and a merely practical science of the mind, I do not see how any man could hesitate in his decision. The kind of psychology which could cure a case of melancholy, or charm a chronic insane delusion away, ought certainly to be preferred to the most seraphic insight into the nature of the soul. And that is the sort of psychology which the men who care little or nothing for ultimate rationality, the biologists, nerve-doctors, and psychical researchers, namely, are surely tending, whether we help them or not, to bring about.
>
> (1892a, 153)

That this sort of psychology—separated from rationality—would ipso facto cease to be psychology as he himself practices it in the *Principles* does not seem to bother James. Neither does the fact that it would have little means to even *talk* about "melancholy"[14] or "insane delusion" (not to mention everyday thought and feeling), though it might indeed cure their symptoms, as it were, under categorically different descriptions. That aside, no one was—as no one is today—trying to steal psychology from James's "practical man" (1892a, 149). The quarrel had been all along with the practical man's *philosophy*.

It is, predictably, James himself who provides, in the *Principles*, a possible fitting summary of his efforts and of the irresistible philosophical temptations they embody. Talking about the status of introspection as a method of investigation and, specifically, about the treatises of a certain Professor Brain, James says that in them

> we have probably the last word of what this method taken mainly by itself can do—the last monument of the youth of our science, still untechnical and generally intelligible, like the Chemistry of Lavoisier, or Anatomy before the microscope was used.
>
> (1890/1983, 191)

The monument, however, is not one which can be finished, just as the youth of this particular science, under this particular understanding, is perpetual. The works would continue nonetheless in the next century of psychology.

IV

Writing in 1916 about the benefits psychiatry would collect if it replaced the "outgrown" vocabulary of psychology with "biological and behavioristic concepts" (1916, 597), John B. Watson refers with admiration to Freud, the truth of whose work he confesses to teach simply by dropping the "crude vitalistic and psychological terminology" (1916, 590),[15] and to William James. Whatever Freud discovered was to be translated in "habit systems" (1916, 590–2) talk. As for James, his presence is explained by his ability to provide suggestive pictures, including one which, Watson claims, facilitates the grasping of behavioristic newspeak by the naïf:

> To my students in psychology I usually introduce the habit terminology somewhat as follows:
>
> Long before Freud's doctrine saw the light of day William James gave the key to what I believe to be the true explanation of the wish. Thirty years ago he wrote: " … I am often confronted by the necessity of standing by one of my selves and relinquishing the rest. […] Such different characteristics may conceivably at the outset of life be alike *possible* to a man. But to make any one of them actual, the rest must more or less be suppressed."
>
> (1916, 590—emphasis in the original)

The irony is that Watson extracts his pedagogical example from the chapter on the self of the abridged version of the *Principles*, published in 1892 under the title *Psychology: The Briefer Course* (James 1892/2001—the quote is from chapter 3, p. 53). A text very much imbibed by the psychology Watson had denounced in his famous manifesto (1913/1994). There is then a further irony—what Freud might have considered a succession of *Fehlleistungen* (slips, *actes manqués*). In the original, "one of my selves" was rather "one of my empirical selves." And where James wrote, in the last quoted sentence, "different characters," in the sense of different *selves*,[16] Watson writes "characteristics." Not even James could be turned on his head without a bit of violence. Watson was about to claim that habit formation is the root of "mental" illness (a dog could be *taught* neurasthenia); therefore, habit modification *via* conditioning should be the key to treatment. Deformed character had always been a puzzle; deformed habit—or characteristic—was a problem.

This anecdote proves little, but it indicates, by the distinction just mentioned—(philosophical) puzzle vs. (empirical) problem—that something of the spirit of Mill's logic of discovery and of James's natural scientific psychology survives in this brave new context. The allergy to puzzles about psychological concepts and, as we will see, the idea that ways to isolate problems from puzzles are readily available to the psychologist are still at work. Indeed, the behaviorist schools of psychology[17] provide some of the best examples of the two commitments we are following throughout the samples discussed here. The unapologetic assertion of these commitments has placed this current of thought in the situation of being the illustration of choice when there is talk of ideology in psychology. Its frankness has made it vulnerable to caricature, which is undeserved, given that, at its best, behaviorism manifested an unmatched lucidity about the nature of its methodological program as philosophical program.

Just two decades after the debate between James and Ladd, Watson's "Psychology as the Behaviorist Views It" (1913/1994) suggests that that kind of debate is without object. Psychology as a putative science of conscious mental states is bankrupt. It has failed to isolate an object of study; it has no methods worthy of the name; it has no principled manner of dealing with divergent results. The diagnosis could not be clearer. Psychology

> has failed signally, I believe, during the fifty-odd years of its existence as an experimental discipline to make its place in the world as an undisputed natural science. Psychology, as it is generally thought of, has something esoteric in its methods.
>
> (1913/1994, 249)

What has led psychology astray was its attempt to define its field by chasing evasive criteria for consciousness, so as to keep itself separate from physiology. Its dependency on introspection has made it "otherwise" (1913/1994, 249) relative to all respectable scientific enterprises. As the behaviorist views it, then, both object and method must go: "[i]t would be better to give up the province altogether" (249) and "never use the terms consciousness, mental states, mind, content, introspectively verifiable, imagery, and the like" (250). In terms of method, psychology is to become "a purely objective, experimental branch of natural science which needs introspection as little as do the sciences of chemistry and physics" (253). Experiments, equally feasible in men as in rats, are to be described "in terms of stimulus and response, in terms of habit formation, habit integrations and the like" (250). Studying the "savages" of Australia, birds or amoebas is different only in terms of complexity; methodologically "I should have followed the same general line of attack" (251). And if this line of attack is followed, it "will remove the barrier from psychology which exists between it and the other sciences" (253).

Watson's revolution, for all its puritanism, conserves the delimitation from philosophical puzzles and the idea that the situation of psychology is to be explained, at least in part, by its being a young science. The former is intrinsic to the radical rejection of a psychology of consciousness.

> The time seems to have come when psychology must discard all reference to consciousness; when it need no longer delude itself into thinking that it is making mental states the object of observation. We have become so enmeshed in speculative questions concerning the elements of mind, the nature of conscious content (for example, imageless thought, attitudes, and Bewusstseinslage, etc.) that I, as an experimental student, feel that something is wrong with our premises and the types of problems which develop from them. There is no longer any guarantee that we all mean the same thing when we use the terms now current in psychology.
>
> (1913/1994, 249)

Speculative concerns are seen as degenerating into problems that are unsolvable by scientific means not as a matter of accident, but as a matter of principle. The very idea of separating the psychological from the physiological—James's search for usable distinctions in dismembered frogs—is bluntly disqualified. The recommended cure is so uncompromising because Watson does not believe there is any chance of success in an effort to gradually regiment—or make more precise—regular psychological concepts. These concepts are not unusable simply because imprecise, but essentially because they carry a philosophical load that cannot be cleaned off as a thin layer of rust might be. They must be quarantined, as infectious pathogens:

> Those time-honored relics of philosophical speculation need trouble the student of behavior as little as they trouble the student of physics. The consideration of the mind-body problem affects neither the type of problem selected nor the formulation of the solution of that problem. I can state my position here no better than by saying that I should like to bring my students up in the same

ignorance of such hypotheses as one finds among the students of other branches of science.

(1913/1994, 250)

If removing the barrier amounts to changing the subject of discussion, so be it. If, however, psychology will insist to be, well, *psychological*, its traditional heritage will continue to derail its efforts to become a science. The same questions will be debated "two hundred years from now" (1913/1994, 250); the spiral will go on. Natural psychology, if one pushes things to their logical conclusion, must be satisfied with becoming *non*psychological psychology. But Watson assures us, in the very last lines of his paper, that not much will be lost. There will be a "residue of problems" (253), surely, but even that will be gradually recovered as behaviorist psychology matures.

The narrative of puberty, in Watson's version, plays its role at this junction. "In psychology—he notes in the tone of a scholarly Saint-Just—we are still in that stage of development where we feel that we must select our material." The situation the behaviorist aims to improve is "similar to that which existed in biology in Darwin's time" (249). The way out is fortunately visible, and there are already areas of psychology that have done better than others.[18] It makes full sense that Watson nominates among the latter, for example, accounts of psychopathology or the "psychology of tests." Moreover, Watson—who had a past in animal research, and was later engaged in work with small children— would also nominate these as solid subjects. In these areas, one was at the largest possible distance from those regions where behaviorism had to confess the temporary feebleness of youth. The weaker regions are what one may expect. Notably, what an otherwise confident Watson admits is that his method cannot handle *thought*:[19]

> The situation is somewhat different when we come to a study of the more complex forms of behavior, such as imagination, judgment, reasoning, and conception. At present the only statements we have of them are in content terms. [...] We should meet the situation squarely and say that we are not able to carry forward investigations along all of these lines by the behavior methods which are in use at the present time. [...] As our methods become better developed it will be possible to undertake investigations of more and more complex forms of behavior. Problems which are now laid aside will again become imperative, but they can be viewed as they arise from a new angle and in more concrete settings.
>
> (1913/1994, 252)

One is reminded of James's "men who care little or nothing for ultimate rationality" (1892a, 153), but with a significant alteration. Watson has no time for gentlemanly division of labor. Whatever is worthy of the name "problem" the scientist should be able to solve. What is not is best ignored. It is not that psychology as natural science moves forward by *exporting* some of its difficulties to philosophy, allowing the latter to complement it. Psychologists are to deal with—solve or dissolve—what problems may come their way. "Metaphysics" is simply a pejorative term for what gets dissolved or rejected. What this means— though this is to push Watson in directions he does not cover explicitly—is that behaviorism as psychology carries with it *its own* philosophy of psychology, of which it makes open use.

This is the element I called "lucidity" above. The psychologist enters in a dispute that is fundamentally one belonging to the philosophy of science and proposes to adjudicate it *as such*. I used Watson's landmark text to suggest that rudiments of this characteristic modus operandi can already be detected in this early manifesto. Certainly, it would have been easier to remind the reader of the clear-cut formulations given years later by Skinner. The first part of *Verbal Behavior* (Skinner 1957, 1–12), for example, retains the qualities of a textbook illustration. But Skinner is best used to look at what comes *after* behaviorism. Watson was challenging an idea of what counts as science; Skinner would become the defender of one. That being said, it is Skinner, summarizing the lessons of behaviorism after another of psychology's "fifty-odd years" circles (Titchener 1914, 5), who gives perhaps the clearest expression to the idea that the psychologist resists philosophy by doing philosophy:

> Behaviorism, with an accent on the last syllable, is not the scientific study of behavior but a philosophy of science concerned with the subject matter and methods of psychology. If psychology is a science of mental life—of the mind, of conscious experience—then it must develop and defend a special methodology, which it has not yet done successfully. If it is, on the other hand, a science of the behavior of organisms, human or otherwise, then it is part of biology, a natural science for which tested and highly successful methods are available. The basic issue is not the nature of the stuff of which the world is made or whether it is made of one stuff or two but rather the dimensions of the things studied by psychology and the methods relevant to them.
>
> (Skinner 1963, 951)

What makes a difference here is that the behaviorist does not claim that his way of doing psychology follows, as it were, naturally or by default; it follows rather from an explicit philosophical *choice*. Now, *Skinner's* may be a defensible or a defeasible option, but this *kind* of choice is one psychology must live with. Being faced with it is a source of serious instability, since one is presented with simultaneously legitimate but incompatible attractors: pay attention to the wisdom of ancestral practices; pay attention to successful natural sciences; work with the inherited concepts that have defined the discipline and its problems; reject accusations of stagnation by showing technical, jargonized prowess. These are not issues that can be bypassed. It matters to insist on this aspect, since, in our story, it is precisely this instability which leads to the peculiar scenery by which one recognizes the margins of psychology.

Responding in 1914 to Watson's attack, Edward Titchener, an introspectionist educated under Wundt, observed how psychology was indeed pulled in contradictory directions. But if the behaviorist was not to be just another biologist, then he had to remember that words had *meanings*, and that thoughts *expressed* facts. If he did, then "behaviorism is correlated with a psychology, with some sort of psychology in the usual sense" (Titchener 1914, 16). "Correlation" suggests that Titchner thought a synthesis was possible. He tells us that one was already talking of "psychobiology" (1914, 15–17); the behaviorist and the introspectionist could *both* be psychologists in their own ways.[20] Of that, Watson seemed oblivious. His attempt to abandon traditional psychology and start anew was guilty on two counts: the approach was "unhistorical"—old news, ignoring, for example, that it was imitating Comte—and, fundamentally, "logical[ly] irrelevan[t] to psychology as psychology is ordinary understood" (Titchener 1914, 4). The latter accusation amounts to a rejection in principle of the choice of explanatory tools made by behaviorists. Where Ladd warned James about the dangers of "cerebralization," Titchener warns that, as the behaviorist views it, psychology might go out of sight. Long before the behaviorist came to the scene, he claimed, psychologists had already been "painfully careful to set their house in logical order." For that, fifty years were nothing, especially when "habits of speech are inveterate, and common sense is extraordinarily tenacious of life" (1914, 2). The behaviorist, however, was not ignorant of either those efforts or their venerability. What Skinner[21] manages to express far better than Watson is that what Titchener called "logical irrelevance" was precisely the means to finally set the house in logical order.

V

Behaviorism as a philosophy of psychology did not arise in a vacuum. What assisted its growth to such confident and self-aware expressions as those found in Skinner was its indebtedness to the general philosophy of science emanating primarily from interwar Vienna. The latter, its merits or faults in other areas aside, came at a price that was noticed not only in humanistic studies narrowly conceived but also in psychology. In the same year Skinner was presenting at Harvard, as the *William James Lectures*, what will become a decade later *Verbal Behavior*, Wolfgang Köhler published a revised edition of his book *Gestalt Psychology* in which he both identified behaviorism as (a misguided) epistemology[22] and made a critical case against its idea of psychology as natural science. The book also offered, in its second chapter, a typical illustration of the psychology as young science motive.

Köhler attacked behaviorism not because it aimed at imitating physics, but because it was a poor imitator. Behaviorists were methodologically overzealous since they miscomprehended the historical and philosophical foundations of mature natural sciences.

> If we wish to imitate the physical sciences, we must not imitate them in their highly developed contemporary form. Rather, we must imitate them in their historical youth, when their state of development was comparable to our own at the present time. Otherwise we should behave like boys who try to copy the imposing manners of full-grown men without understanding their *raison d'être,* also without seeing that intermediate phases of development cannot be skipped.
>
> (Köhler 1947/1992, 42)

The remedy was to return to a "healthy naïveté" (1947/1992, 31), which took experience seriously without succumbing to introspectionism, and which allowed for a less meager diet of functional concepts (53–4). *Gestalt psychology* was, Köhler claimed, such an alternative. Unlike introspectionists, Gestalt psychologists were not aiming at some sort of special access to the depths of experience: "Only simple statements about experience, the kind of statements which all observers of people, of animals, of instruments, and so forth, are wont to make, will be used for our enterprise" (57). This was only the starting point, however, as the eventual aim was to arrive at an account that correlated facts of experience and facts about the brain.[23]

Proceeding in such a way promised to block the undue skepticism of the behaviorists *without* compromising the ideal of fashioning psychology as a proper natural science. Assuming that experience is informative and that it is more or less adequately captured by regular psychological concepts was in any case unavoidable.[24] The very problems one wanted to study were framed in such terms; there was little to do with "the curves alone" (Köhler 1947/1992, 39), one had to be able to *read* them, and this meant relying on the conceptual apparatus the behaviorist rejected.

This otherwise correct observation must be seen in the larger framework of Köhler's criticism of behaviorism. Fundamentally, he claimed that, as in the other sciences, the relevant conceptual framework would gradually *evolve* in the direction of increased objectivity; initial concepts would be adjusted as one proceeded. Surely, the behaviorist was wrong to insist that ordinary reports of experience are *unusable*; but he was not wrong in his generic allegiance to imitating mature science and his hunger for progress. Characteristically, Köhler sees nothing philosophically problematic in this picture of asymptotic refinement; even when he rejects behaviorist excesses, the *need* for such an evolution is not thereby questioned.

With Köhler, we arrive, at least in terms of timeframe, in the vicinity of the cognitive revolution. Even if this is the landing point I have been aiming at, I will not discuss in detail, at this stage, examples of cognitive psychologists who express commitments similar to those we have seen at work in the samples collected above. This is not because such examples are scarce, but because the following chapters discuss cognitive psychological theories which share this general background. Before moving on, however, it will help to have before us, in compact form, a few illustrations of the story of progress in cognitivist clothes. Let us focus on the issue of explanation.

VI

The *locus classicus*, if any, for such a discussion must be David Marr's *Vision* (1982). Even if the book dealt with visual perception, Marr's remarks on how to go about investigating "complex information-processing systems" (1982, 19ff.) were not restricted to vision. Taking note of the bankruptcy of previous attempts to deal with perception—Gestalt, for example, had "dissolved into a fog of subjectivism" (8)—Marr proposed to conceive of vision in a novel way—to see it as an information-processing task. Once this was done, a range of productive questions became available. For example, one could ask:

> [N]europhysiology and psychophysics have as their business to *describe* the behavior of cells or of subjects but not to *explain* such behavior. What are the visual areas of the cerebral cortex actually doing? What are the problems

in doing it that need explaining, and at what level of description should such explanations be sought?

(Marr 1982, 15—emphasis in the original)

Early in his book, Marr proposed a general answer to the crucial last question mentioned above. He distinguished three levels of explanation which, when put together, promised to constitute a complete account of an information-processing device. In the order of abstraction (top-down), these were: (i) a computational theory characterizing the system in abstract terms, as "a mapping from one kind of information to another" (Marr 1982, 24); (ii) a specification of implementation in terms of algorithm and representation; and (iii) the identification of the physical system realizing or carrying that implementation. The levels were seen as "coupled," but only "loosely" (25)—enough so for some explanatory accounts to work fine with a subset of the levels. The critical level, given the information-processing perspective chosen by the author, was nonetheless the first (27). *The question to ask was*, as per above, "What is this device doing?" where the answer was not *primarily*, for example, "It is going through a <while> routine," or "It is switching on this circuit," but something like: "It is *adding* these values," "It is *comparing* these objects," or "It is *rotating* this shape."

Since this model was a take on psychological explanation as such, it was in no way limited to perception. If one conceived of vision as an information-processing task, then why not regard thinking, remembering, inferring, wanting, intending, fearing, and so in much the same way? For many cognitive scientists, there seemed to be no principled reason to resist the adoption of Marr's model. The psychologist as reverse-programmer could, in using it, capture earlier intuitions and ask new, sharper questions. To give an example from psychopathology, one could now investigate properly the distinction between functional (no obvious brain damage) and organic (detectable brain damage) psychosis. Computers could suffer from software errors, too—and the levels of functioning/explanation were, after all, only "loosely coupled." Generally speaking, "functional" could be substituted with "computational," as the (functional) language of psychology could be seen as an approximation of a computational theory.

If one does not assume the antecedent plausibility of some version of machine functionalism, then this approach does not begin to be a model for psychological explanation. This is not to deny the obvious merits of Marr's approach.[25] It is to observe that without what he calls "the right prejudices" (1982, 6) there is no reason or pressure to accept that ordinary psychological concepts capture, even vaguely, computational operations or functions governing the transformation of data arrays. To believe that they do counts merely as a symptom of embracing the computer as monopolistic metaphor of mind and of progress in its study.

An example of the transition from Marr's remarkable (and tragic[26]) effort to deal with vision—of which speculating on psychological explanation had been an instrument—to more philosophically ambitious programs is John Morton's volume (2004) on modeling developmental disorders—a book which does not deal primarily with the disorders, but with how to understand them. Morton, too, distinguishes between explanatory levels à la Marr. Two are obvious—behavior and brain processes can be observed, but it is hard to *correlate* them, at least in humans (2004, 20). This means that an intermediary level of explanation is needed, which is not observable and which does not introduce an independent ontology. This is cognition.

At the level of cognition, one captures what is not describable in the language of biology, brain functions that are in some sense "higher"—things like perception, memory, or language. Even if these are (problematically) designated as *brain* functions, the psychologist is after specifying their architecture in *computational* terms. When Morton rightly observes that "[t]he language of function is the language of psychology" (2004, 21), he really means "the language of computation."

So how does explanation proceed? One settles on the "invariants in behavior" (30) and then proposes bits of software[27] capable of producing those invariants. In general, the pattern of explanation runs as follows: "*C* enables *B* where *C* is a cognitive mechanism and *B* is a pattern of behaviour"; in the case of disorders: "a problem with *C* causes a problem with *B*" (32). An autistic child, for example, may lack "mentalizing skills" *because* a certain computational device is missing or malfunctioning, while for a blind child it may be harder to acquire those skills *due* to reduced input for that device (47–49). The resulting hypotheses can be adjudicated, even if "the rules for postulating cognitive entities are neither clear nor agreed" (23). The important gain, Morton claims echoing Marr, is that one arrives at a novel way of thinking about *explananda*. But, as with Marr, this is precisely the problem. We have not been given good reasons to think that psychological concepts designate either higher brain function or objects in the programming sense[28] of the word. To elaborate as if this was settled is perhaps no fog of subjectivism, but it is fog nonetheless.

The hopes of Mill and James that natural science will dissolve the philosophical worries haunting psychology also have counterparts in more recent cognitive psychology. To refer to a benchmark example, Susan Carey describes the goal of her volume on *The Origin of Concepts* as "to demonstrate that the disciplines of cognitive science now have the empirical and theoretical tools to turn age-old philosophical dilemmas into relatively straightforward scientific problems" (2009, 4). The book, impressive as it is, demonstrates no such thing, even if it does present a sophisticated theory of concepts. Carey *relies* on a truly problematic two-factor (causal history + conceptual role) theory of content. She assumes the problem of how bits of brain or bits of software carry *meaning* solved or in any case *solvable*. This is not a trivial assumption.

In the final chapter of the volume, after presenting her theory, Carey confronts the issue of philosophical skepticism about the foundational choices of her project (she discusses Putnam and Kripke on the one hand, Fodor on the other). Her defense, however, is informed by the antecedent commitment to a two-factor theory of content. If, for example, one insists on "external" social and causal chains as determinants of reference, then the psychologist can declare reference and "wide" content not especially *interesting* and be happy to focus on the more exciting phenomena related to "narrow" content (i.e., content-in-the-head): inference, categorization, language comprehension, and so on (Carey 2009, 503ff). This kind of reply misses the point, however, since the disagreement about meaning remains moot. At issue, even if one does not go further than Putnam and Kripke, is whether there *is* any such thing as content-in-the-head. Perhaps it should be obvious that there is, but it remains the case that in Carey's theory this is something assumed, not proven.

For a final example, consider not a particular psychologist, but what is possibly by now a whole niche of developmental psychology, built on the so-called violation of expectation experimental paradigm. An expression of surprise which children share with adults is looking longer at something unexpected. Infants can also have age-specific behaviors, such as modifying their rhythm of sucking. The violation of expectation method takes advantage of the ability to quantify such behaviors—for example, looking times measured with eye trackers[29]—and especially of the fact that such procedures do not depend on language. They are thus readily usable with preverbal children, and they have been prominent in recent years in many developmental studies.

The kind of questions which this paradigm is thought to provide access to does indeed violate lay expectations. By comparing what children—often very young—seem to expect or fail to expect respectively, researchers can try to reconstruct putative expectation-generating mechanisms. Given that we are within cognitive psychological theorizing, these mechanisms are typically described as varieties of inference. So, for example, of 10-month-olds one can now ask if they estimate the value of a goal relative to the effort an agent is willing to make to reach that goal: "Do infants use the cost that an agent expends to attain a goal state in order to infer the value of that goal state for the agent?" (Liu et al. 2017, 1038). The structures that support such inferences are part of an "intuitive" psychology, so one should perhaps refrain from asking what "inference" is supposed to mean here. As we have seen with older examples, such concepts are supposed to take new meaning, as part of an apparatus of discovery.

The focus here should be on the questions asked, not on the method itself, which has resulted in fascinating experiments and is a genuine innovation in the field. Essentially, the cognitive models proposed in the wake of this innovation suggest the possibility of extending the application of concepts such as *belief*, *intention*, *goal*, *reason*, or *understanding* beyond the rudiments of linguistic and social competence. The relevance of this maneuver for a discussion of what I termed "margins" should be clear, but this is a point to which I will return.[30]

Outsider worries aside, the explanatory weight placed on the violation of expectation paradigm has resulted not only in an avalanche of studies but also in confusion. An important thread in this literature started with the idea that one can test for understanding beliefs—that is, *false* beliefs—at preverbal ages. Traditionally, the threshold of understanding that others may believe something falsely had been set at around 4 years of age, and the standard "false belief test" or "task" involved *asking* children how other agents (originally dolls) would act given what these agents did or did not witness (Baron-Cohen, Leslie, and Frith 1985). But with what Scott and Baillargeon have called "nontraditional tasks" (2017)—nonverbal tests, simplified but presumably still indicative of belief attribution—the age limit was pushed to around 15 months and even less (see e.g. Onishi and Baillargeon 2005, Baillargeon, Scott, and He 2010).

The replicability of the experimental results that led to such conclusions has been questioned by other developmental psychologists (e.g., Dörrenberg, Rakoczy, and Liszkowski 2018), but suppose replicability was not a problem. One would still be faced with the difficulty of making sense of the results. Not a trivial task, as what has happened in this respect is probably worse than what Tyler Burge diagnosed as "overinterpretation" (2018; see also Jacob 2020 for criticism). To think that the "mentalistic" interpretations that are suggested fail because of rather extreme evidential underdetermination is to miss the sheer strangeness of their starting assumptions, or to think they are not an unsurmountable issue. The mistake has already been made if one accepts that belief-attribution can be a *candidate* interpretation.

The way out, it seems to me, is not to suggest more frugal interpretations on Occamian grounds, but to observe that when we bracket our familiarity with

15-month-olds and with more or less typical contexts of belief attribution we simultaneously give up any hope of clarifying what we may mean by "belief." It does not help to insist that *in some reduced sense* an infant can still conceive of epistemic states *as such*. We do not know how to properly reduce the sense. The variations of the initial studies seem to attest that what takes place is in fact a kind of conceptual liquefaction. Take, for example, the cases in which infants seem to attribute false beliefs to *objects*, for example, to a toy crane (Burnside, Severdija, and Poulin-Dubois 2020). It is close to self-refuting, I think, that this is thought to open even more problems, such as explaining how infants manage to overcome a hypothesized animistic stage. It should not be part of deference to science to remind ourselves that *we know* that 15-month-olds can be as animistic as pigeons can be superstitious.

VII

We are still very much contemporary with, at a minimum, the spirit of Mill's general outline for studying the mind, and with its commitments, which we saw reverberating in the sample collected above. The scope and methods of psychology have shifted often enough, but here is an ideal that refuses to mutate. This spirit of conquest is manifest in the transition from quarantining conceptual difficulties to declaring them solvable with empirical means[31]—the latter a trait not accidentally shared by behaviorism and cognitivism. It is at this point, from a philosophical perspective at least, that the story of progress reaches its climax.

As with other narratives of advancement characteristic of the modern world, this one too has generated opposition. The very persistence of the modern spirit in psychology invited stubborn, and sometime vehement, attempts to exorcise it. The philosophies of science that have lobbied the assimilation of psychology to the natural sciences have been met with resistance emanating from a number of corners. Some of the dissenters have cared little for the narrow understanding of the term "science" inherent in the "naturalization" of psychology; some, on the contrary, have thought that much depended on rejecting this restrictive conception and enlarging the scope of "science" so as to situate psychological study closer to research in the humanities or the humanistic social sciences (seen as legitimate, though separate, epistemic efforts). Some critics have come from within psychology or the social sciences, others from philosophy or the larger areas of the humanities. Most of their ideas have by now no impact on how psychological research is done.

The examples discussed above should, however, remind us that criticism at least in the form of conceptual vigilance is in good order, so perhaps its older versions, contemporary with the various turning points in the history of psychology, are worth reconsidering. I think that, as it often happens, it is primarily historical evidence that, by now, exposes the ideal of an uncompromising "naturalization" of the many things called "psychology" as hollow. The same historical record, however, is that which, upon reflection, should also block the idealization of this hollowness. Criticism has seldom shown moderation. The two lessons are complementary.

More often than not, when the preoccupation of psychology with imitating the natural sciences like physics or biology is documented as a persistent source of conceptual instability, this is done to suggest that that way only havoc lies. At the same time, most critics will reject the suspicion that thereby they move dangerously close to a version of anti-scientism. But qualifications aside, the consequence of such attacks tends to be a *global* skepticism about psychology as a scientific effort performed as empirical science habitually is. This kind of skepticism should be resisted.

We have seen enough of psychology as a young science to know that sobriety would be in order. But a radically skeptical judgment, too, would be without object, fetishizing anachronisms, and subject to ironies parallel to those provoked by the relentless optimism of some psychologists. There is no need for another general judgment—positive or negative—about the prospects of a scientific psychology. Psychology is done and has been done according to the scientific mores of its times, and any reasonable analysis needs to start from this fact. That being said, this is not an attempt to find a middle ground vacated once two opposing positions have been dismantled. The aim rather is to locate and describe a family of cases in which optimism and skepticism move in different dimensions.

The background for what follows continues to be the plurality of psychology—a reminder of those analogies that keep coming up in this region: psychology as diverse and opportunistic as medicine or anthropology, psychology as complex and fluctuating as meteorology or (natural) history. Given this background, I propose to confront the ideal documented above—that of a discipline ever expanding by discovery—and suggest that it has limited application, not that it is nonsensical. Its limits, I will argue, can be seen if one observes that for some subjects, notably those marginal relative to the paradigm of mature and socially competent individuals, a way of doing psychology begins to fail *as* others quite likely begin to work. One can find areas where the positivistic ideal has a place;

one can thereby see areas where it is unproductive. This is, of course, very far from an exhaustive cartography.

All this is not to say that, generally speaking, naturalistic optimism on the one hand, and skepticism on the other, suffer from an equal lack of lucidity. It is in fact hard to resist skepticism while noting that it has a point when it exposes, in Wittgenstein's words, the "confusion and barrenness of psychology" (1953/2009, 243—II, § 371). Resisting global skepticism will be a mixed story with more than a few loose ends. The way to illustrate the cluttered horizon ahead of us is perhaps to return to Ladd's observations on James. James does his best psychology, Ladd notes, when he is *untrue* to his philosophy of psychology. It is safe to assume that this still happens in many cases. Declarations that philosophical commitments are taken seriously should not always be taken seriously. It is best if one only focuses on those areas where criticism is of ideology as opposed to science—and is also of plausible consequence. The areas where the regular, explanatory psychological concepts become unstable constitute such an example, since here it will matter if it is solely ideology, as opposed to legitimate standards of application, that forces said psychological concepts into use.

The direction we follow from this point on, then, is roughly this: the commitment to fashion psychology after the natural sciences which the skeptic resists will *not* always count as ideology. As in many other fields, we start, as Köhler suggested, with a pre-theoretic localization of some questions as psychological. Some, justifying the older optimism of the behaviorist, or the more recent and inherited one of cognitivists, will really be responsive to good old natural scientific treatment. Some will not. But it is not as if the half-truth of the hardnosed natural psychologist is the missing half for the half-truth of the skeptic. The fragments probably do not belong together—but they are of value nonetheless. In many cases this incompatibility will not make much of a difference. Psychologists will probably learn more and more about thoughts and feelings, about motivations and decisions. The dispute about the status of the findings, their repercussions, or the best vocabulary to express them—that is, the weak points where the incompatibility breaks the ice—is likely to remain unsolved, but relatively benign. Things are arguably different when it is not so clear whether, or in what sense, the subjects of research think, intend, have reasons, or decide. When it is not clear *either* that they do not. This marginal territory matters not because it has general lessons to teach psychology, but precisely because it is not at all obvious that it has.

Perhaps a shift of terminology will help to set the stage in brighter light. If we are to look at the margins, then it is crucial not to render their geography as resulting in the familiar problems of the possibility of an *un*translatable language, of there being mind and rationality we *could* not comprehend as such, of stepping *outside* the galaxy of recognizable forms of human life. Here we talk about regions that border our language and our "form of life" *from within*. In the following we look therefore at ways to resist their explanatory assimilation or leveling without thereby conceiving of them as purely alien.

3

Enter the Skeptics

I

One skeptical tradition can be traced, in more than one way, to Mill. In 1883, Wilhelm Dilthey published what was intended to be the first volume of an ampler project, *Einleitung in die Geisteswissenschaften*, or the *Introduction to the Human Sciences*.[1] The book was never finished—Dilthey was known, after all, as "the man of first volumes" (Makkreel and Rodi 1989a, 3)—but its first part, followed by a series of essays, became an influential reference in arguments for resisting the assimilation of the study of mind to the methods of the natural sciences.

The concept of *Geisteswissenschaften*, which Dilthey brought to the forefront of this debate, has a somewhat ironic history. It had been introduced by the historian Johann Gustav Droysen in the early 1840s (Makkreel 1975/1992, 36), but it became common reference only after 1849, when Mill's *Logic* was translated into German. It was then used as an equivalent for Mill's "moral sciences." It is in this context that Dilthey recruits the term for a rather different enterprise, recognizing the uneasy character of the choice:

> I shall follow those thinkers who refer to this second half of the *globus intellectualis* by the term *Geisteswissenschaften*. In the first place, this designation is one that has become customary and generally understood, due especially to the extensive circulation of the German translation of John Stuart Mill's *System of Logic*.
>
> (Dilthey 1989, 57)[2]

Dilthey's concept has a larger extension than Mill's and is embedded in a struggle against Mill's envisioned uniformity of science. The "human sciences," for Dilthey, were the humanities but also the social sciences, psychology as well as esthetics.[3] Fundamentally, they were *not* sciences of nature, and, unlike in Mill's outline, they were not even *like* the former. Dilthey's overall goal was to arrive

at a principled framework within which the *Geisteswissenschaften* would enjoy a
"relative independence" (Dilthey 1989, 69) in terms of scope and method. This
was autonomy to be won in the face of the escalating prestige of the natural
sciences and of their philosophical avant-garde. Dilthey was reacting to what he
saw not only as an assault on, but essentially as a *disfiguration* of a viable field of
study. He was aiming for a way to avoid the "civilizing" zeal of Comte and Mill,
which misconstrued both method and object in the study of mind and culture,
without swerving into unanchored relativism:

> The answers given to these questions by Comte and the positivists and by J. S.
> Mill and the empiricists seemed to me to truncate and mutilate [*verstümmeln*]
> historical reality in order to assimilate [*anzupassen*] it to the concepts and
> methods of the natural sciences. The reaction against their approach [...] seemed
> to me to sacrifice the legitimate independence of the particular sciences, the
> fruitful power of their empirical methods, and the certainty of their foundation
> to a subjective and sentimental mood which seeks nostalgically to recall by
> means of science a mental satisfaction that has been lost forever.
>
> (Dilthey 1989, 49–50)[4]

Dilthey's attempt to resist the assimilation (*anpassen* = to level, to accommodate) and
mutilation (*verstümmeln* = to mutilate, to maim) of the human studies developed
in stages and, at each point, consisted of both critical and constructive elements.
He was more hesitant with the latter, but eventually they led him in the direction
of hermeneutics. The critical aspects of his view matter more in the context of our
discussion. A few of the constructive points related to the problematic intersection
of *Natur* and *Geist* will also help, in that they will reveal the view of the margins of
psychology recommended here as, in a sense, Diltheyan.

    Let us explore these elements by starting with an issue which, if taking
advantage of retrospection, might seem derisory. Why should a debate about
the human studies matter for *psychology*? This was not a problem for Mill, since
he argued for the unity of science, so the fact that psychology was placed under
moral sciences made no difference for its status. But, to paraphrase James's
sensible man, if it came to a choice, as it seemingly does with Dilthey, why would
anyone think that psychology should rather go with history and esthetics than
with chemistry and biology? The question is somewhat misleading and cannot
be answered in one move.

    Even if his perspective fluctuates from the project of the *Einleitung* to his
later writings, a relative constant in Dilthey is the primacy and reality of what is
given in experience.[5] This is the starting point for *all* scientific enterprises—"All

science is experiential" (Dilthey 1989, 50)[6]—and there is no going behind, as it were, the seeing eye. The success of the natural sciences has not been based on *that*, but on abstracting certain elements from experience, notably teleology or purposiveness. This does not threaten natural sciences as such, but neither does it manage to do away with the pressing reality of purposiveness[7] as given in the nexus—*Zusammenhang*—or totality of psychic life. This totality or connectedness is not something *arrived at* by amassing of evidence, discovery of causality, or speculative/hypothetical generalization. It is already given as such as a basic fact of conscious life (in typical, mature human beings), and what needs to be done is not synthesis, but description and analysis of experience. It is at this level that the *Geisteswissenschaften* receive their foundation, and this task is to be handled by a descriptive psychology. So not only is psychology a part of the human studies, but it *grounds* them by giving an empirical—not empiricist— and descriptive account of experience.

> Psychology can be a foundational human science only if it stays within the limits of a descriptive discipline that establishes facts and uniformities among facts. It must clearly distinguish itself from explanative psychology, which strives to derive the whole human, cultural world by means of certain assumptions. [...] [It] is the first and most fundamental of the particular human sciences. [...] Because of psychology's place in the system of the human sciences, it is a descriptive science [...] and must be distinguished from an explanative science, which by being hypothetical, attempts to derive the facts of human life from simple assumptions.
>
> (Dilthey 1989, 84)[8]

This is not to say, however, that descriptive psychology is the only psychology there is. Dilthey does not reject completely explanative psychology, but, at least at times, relegates it to a role of patching grey areas where the hypothetical approach is the only means of investigation available. Makkreel and Rodi (1989a, 15) argue that in the *Einleitung* explanative psychology is pictured as *dependent* on the foundational descriptive enterprise. Later, notably in the *Ideen* (see below) their divorce would become sharper. This may be so, but things seem already reasonably clear.

Psychology plays a *double* role, of which the descriptive one is fundamental. Its hypothetical-explanatory branch is not to be eliminated, but its application is secondary and much more localized. It is in this secondary role that psychology seems to touch on the realm of natural science. If Comte and Mill thought that bad metaphysics blocks the assimilation of psychology to the realm of the natural sciences, Dilthey thinks that bad metaphysics underlies all attempts to assimilate psychology. The single-minded struggle of psychology to establish itself as a natural science—and nothing else—in the nineteenth century was very much a trait of the post-Cartesian intellectual world:

> The metaphysics of the spirit (rational psychology) was then connected to the mechanistic conception of nature and corpuscular philosophy when they gained dominance. But every attempt to formulate a tenable notion of the mind-body relation on the basis of this theory of substances and by means of this new conception of nature was a failure.
>
> (Dilthey 1989, 59–60)[9]

But it is not only this particular conjunction that erodes psychology from the inside. This *kind* of effort is misplaced. Dilthey diagnoses it as being symptomatic of a certain cultural context, which is a correct but overoptimistic verdict in that it misses the fact that one is faced with a recurrent tendency which has by now taken many shapes and has adapted itself to a number of jargons. The project of the *Einleitung* is not by accident presented in words that have not lost their sharpness:

> I will attempt to show that the search for a universally recognized metaphysics was conditioned by a state of the sciences that we have left behind us, and consequently that any metaphysical grounding of the human sciences is a thing of the past.
>
> (Dilthey 1989, 51–2)[10]

It is also not by accident, perhaps, that such a project remained unfinished. About a decade after the *Einleitung*, however, Dilthey would publish another important work which would place his view of psychology in a clearer framework. *Ideen über eine beschreibende und zergliedernde Psychologie* ("Ideas Concerning a Descriptive and Analytic Psychology"), published in 1894, built on the central themes I have already mentioned introducing at the same time some important nuances. As in the *Einleitung*, Dilthey is critical of explanatory psychology and its metaphysical aura, he resists a psychology that works primarily by introducing and testing hypothetical constructs, and he rejects the analogy between the methods of psychology, seen as fundamentally descriptive and starting from an experienced whole, and those of the natural sciences. Let us focus on a few nuances.

A prominent change of accent is the central role played by the distinction between explanation and understanding, which works in parallel with that between *Natur-* and *Geisteswissenschaften*: "Die Natur erklären wir, das Seelenleben verstehen wir" (Dilthey 1894/1990, 143); "We explain nature, we understand psychic life."[11] The distinction is not new, but here it becomes (and from here on will remain) crucial for the methodology of human studies. Already in the *Einleitung* Dilthey was writing within a tradition which some trace back to Vico's *verum factum* (Hacker 2001b, von Wright 2007). A more relevant character of this tradition is, however, a historian we have already met, Droysen. Writing about method in historical studies, Droysen describes three, not two, continents, on the *globus intellectualis*:

> According to the objects and nature of human thought, there can be three scientific methods: the speculative (philosophical or theological), the physical, and the historical. Their essence is: to discern, to explain, and to understand. This is reflected in the traditional catalog of the sciences: logic, physics, and ethics. These are not three paths leading to one end, but the three sides of a prism by which the human eye, unable to withstand the brightness of the eternal light, reconstructs it from its color reflections.
>
> (Droysen 1882, 11)[12]

Dilthey was making use of ideas already in place, surely, but this needs to be seen in a context in which the division between *erklären* and *verstehen* becomes especially relevant for psychology. We are so situated that the psychological concepts used to illuminate our existence are not to be seen as theoretical posits but as inherently geared onto a nexus—a system of connections—which is "concretely lived" (*erlebt*) (Dilthey 1977, 35, 1894/1990, 152). It is this localization, this familiarity which is not simply empathetic or subjective, but acquired by humans as social and cultural beings, which underlies understanding. Only when psychology remains in this familiar territory, immune to the insecurities inherent in the merely hypothetical, can it play its foundational role for the rest of the human studies.

Another important nuance is in the relief of Dilthey's criticism of explanative psychology,[13] especially when it comes to pinpointing how hypothetical constructs fail to make contact with what he takes to be the immediate psychological reality of a coherent and lived whole. The dramatic consequence of the proliferation of hypotheses rotating, as displaced gears, in thin air, is that there is no clear view as to what might *decide* among them. The only comparable case is, revealingly, metaphysics:

> The general struggles which go on there are no less violent than those in the metaphysical field. One sees absolutely nothing, so far as that is concerned, which can decide the issue of the struggle. To be sure, explanatory psychology consoles itself by thinking of the time when the situation of physics and chemistry did not seem any better [...] [T]he irresolvability of the metaphysical problem concerning the relations of the spiritual with the corporeal world prevents reaching an exact and sure knowledge of causes in this domain. No one can thus say whether this struggle of hypotheses will ever come to an end in explanatory psychology, not when it will occur. When we seek to establish complete causal knowledge, we therefore find ourselves transported by a kind of spell into a maze of hypotheses with which one can in no sense hope to confront psychical states of affairs.
>
> (Dilthey 1977, 26)[14]

The very choice of vocabulary is striking here, and somewhat tamed in the English translation. What is missing is not the current solvability of an issue, but a conception of what could *count as* the issue being settled. The metaphors are visual (*Horizont, Nebel, Aussicht*). What is missing is a horizon; it has been lost—Wittgenstein *avant la lettre*—in a hypnotizing fog of hypotheses.

A final aspect, and probably the one which matters most in this context, is also one anticipated in the *Einleitung*. The study of human life takes place in the context of its being conditioned by nature, and Dilthey is not after denying obvious facts, like the dependency of mental life on the activity of the nervous system, even if he sees human beings as a realm within a realm.[15] Psychology is in a peculiar situation because at the limit of its founding role as a descriptive enterprise, it touches on the territory of the natural sciences. Things are not settled at the border between *Geist* and *Natur*, but the two obviously intersect. One can study the intersection by taking the perspective of the natural scientist. One is thus free to observe influences or conduct experiments that establish the impact of, say, physical conditions on the psychological. It is in this context that Dilthey remarks that the "extended observation of developmental and pathological states" (1883/1990, 15)[16] could contribute to clarifying how the mental is conditioned by the physical. The immature and the abnormal invite a perspective which otherwise stands clearly *outside* the realm of psychology. Just a few pages later, Dilthey mentions two so-called transition-points (*Übergangsstellen*) (1989, 70, 1883/1990, 18) between human studies and natural sciences, where the disciplines "intermingle" (*vermischen*).[17] One of them is the point at which "nature influences the development of the mind" (Dilthey 1989, 70).[18] This does not have to be read in a developmental key (acculturation takes a wider sense), but it does include that perspective.

Things are clearer in the *Ideen*, though this is not in any sense a key topic of that work. There we find a formulation that is very close in spirit to the present study:

> At the frontiers of nature and of mental life, experimentation and quantitative determination have been shown, for the formation of hypotheses, to be as useful as in the study of nature. One can establish nothing of this in the central regions of psychology.
>
> (Dilthey 1977, 28)[19]

It is only when the nexus of mature mental life is *not* in place that "constructive" psychology—the examination which starts from pieces which fail to cohere—gains grip. *Verstehen* goes with the nexus, and it falters where it does. This leaves intact the areas where psychology acts as a descriptive foundation for the human studies without thereby declaring the margins nonpsychological. The independence of the "central regions" of psychology comes with a dilution of sovereignty at the margins.

> This [descriptive] psychology has for its object what one *regularly* finds in the nexus of *adult* psychic life. It describes this nexus of the inner life of a *typical* man.
>
> (Dilthey 1977, 35—emphasis added)[20]

This is not to be seen as a price which could have been lower or higher, a kind of institutional dispute or a case of specialization. It is already clear enough in Dilthey—and it will become clearer in the following—that the reference to the usual mental life of typical, mature persons is a matter of meaning, of how some of the key psychological concepts are grounded and work. In the terms I have used previously, it sets a measure of things.

One does not have to think that Dilthey's larger project is revivable to grasp the importance of the discontinuity he observes between "borderlands" and the focal area where psychological concepts have all the clarity that they *can* have. Is this clarity a matter of anything like Diltheyan lived experience? Unfashionable as it may seem, I do not think that this is as trivially disposable as we have the habit of thinking these days. But in any case taking a stance on the matter is not crucial in this context, and there are alternatives, some of which I will gesture toward shortly. What matters here is that in this light it is a mistake to claim that anything further is to be established about our core psychological vocabulary by pushing it into the hypothetical structures which one is forced to use at the margins. It is also a mistake to think that it has only been temporarily difficult to grasp psychologically the character of these regions.

II

Dilthey eventually abandoned the project of a descriptive psychology able to play a foundational role for the human studies—social sciences here included—because of growing suspicion about the adequacy of an account based on lived experience.[21] He was led toward a hermeneutical approach and a focus on history; if his earlier view of psychology influenced Husserl (Biemel 1968, xvi–xvii), at this point he was himself influenced by Husserl's turn-of-the-century *Logical Investigations*, and his theory of understanding history would further leave a mark on Gadamer's writings. Dilthey's defense of the autonomy of the *Geisteswissenschaften* acted as one important part of a larger confluence that would solidify in one of the major traditions in social scientific research. Max Weber notably contributed to this by developing the methodological aspects of the notion of understanding (*Verstehen*), which he considered characteristic for this kind of study. After all, sociology, too, had been haunted by positivistic ghosts, starting with the classical works of Comte or Durkheim. The extensions would reach, *via* Weberian methodology, the monumental *Psychopathology* of Jaspers, in which the limits of *verstehende Psychologie* would circumscribe "the sublime object of psychiatry" (Woods 2011), schizophrenic psychosis—or more precisely "delusion proper" (*echte Wahnidee*) in Jaspersian terminology (Jaspers 1997, 106–7, 1913/1973, 89–90).

It is perhaps no accident that the tradition Dilthey helped consolidate emerged from reflection on the nature and status of historical knowledge,[22] and that it has often returned to this initial anchor. It is not only that the cultural context in which this tradition developed was one in which interpretation of others—and especially of *past* or different others—became important; the deeper force at work here seems to have been a fascination with the notion of human beings as the only animals with a history, a representation of human nature as, at least in part, historical—continuously rebuilt on the treasured remains of its past, on culture and traditions, on language and myth. For psychology, already ambiguously and uncomfortably sat in the forum of the human studies, the turn to history and historicity has always meant an erosion of its relevance and territorial claims, built as they were on natural scientific ideals. There is an inherent tension here. As in Dilthey's case, the more marked the emphasis on history, the more fragile the position of psychology. Depending on how one sees the latter, this can be taken either as a sign of its not belonging in the first place in the architecture of the human studies conceived as an autonomous enterprise, or as a legitimate curbing of its scientist pretensions. Neither is *strictly* speaking true, and, as was already suggested, this is not a fork one should break, since it makes little sense to succumb to psychology's drive to become one unitary thing, to choose roads once and for all.

Writing a few decades after the work of the "lonely and neglected genius Dilthey" (1992, 171), Robin George Collingwood offers a striking example of a radical decision about the balance of power just mentioned. In a number of writings[23] that, for the most part, have been left unfinished because of his untimely death, and were published posthumously, Collinwood claimed that the true science of mind was history. Psychology was to be returned to its "original" (pre-eighteen century) position of dealing with instincts, sensations, feelings and the like (Collingwood 1999, 82, 84); not with thought, in any case, which was *the* subject matter of historical research. Let us explore a few of the fundamental steps that led Collingwood to this startling conclusion.

There is, to begin with, a vehement rejection of positivistic naturalism as applied to the study of history and to the human studies generally. Collingwood's diagnosis is formulated in unambiguous terms. The traditional disciplines or sciences of man like logic, ethics, and aesthetics have been usurped[24] by what promised to be a scientific study of human nature modeled after the natural sciences. As a matter of principle, this was not a promise that could—or can—be kept, because it resulted from confusion about what mind, thought, and action are. The issue, however, was not simply the misunderstanding and misuse of the concepts paradigmatically associated with the mind. The damaging impact of positivism occurred as part of a "fight for intellectual dominance" (Collingwood 1999, 80). The metamorphosis[25] of psychology into a putative study of thought was a symptom both of misguided science and of folly in the *politics* of science. The latter emphasis is not one we will explicitly follow in this context, but the reader should keep it in mind.

With positivism, Collingwood also rejects the usual "young science" defense used by psychologists to justify the state of their discipline. He will advance, as we will see shortly, a rather different explanation for this state of affairs. In an essay dated 1935, we are told that:

> It is vain to ask for time, on the plea that the science is yet in its infancy; the question is whether, in attempting to support the traditional conception of human nature, it is not wholly on the wrong lines. One thing is, I think, clear: that the progress which psychology is making at the present time is altogether independent of any such conception, and is leading further and further away from it.
>
> (Collingwood 1935/1999, 196)

And in the *Idea of History* that:

> [T]he representatives of psychology, would say that the science of these thinkers[26] was not sufficiently scientific: psychology was still in its infancy. But if we ask these same men to produce here and now the practical results for which those early students hoped, they excuse themselves by saying that psychology is still in its infancy. Here I think they wrong themselves and their own science. Claiming for it a sphere which it cannot effectively occupy, they belittle the work it has done and is doing in its proper field.
>
> (Collingwood 1992, 208)

Note that there are two overlapping threads in these formulations. One is that psychology is "wholly on the wrong lines," that it aims for something it is not equipped to achieve; but—and this is the second aspect—progress is not denied. The fact that psychology systematically misplaces itself does not mean that it has no place at all. That it has is shown by the fact that there has been progress— in those areas it can "effectively occupy"—even if this is done *against* its self-conception.[27] The reason psychology fails is that it tries to apply the methods of natural science in a context where, in a sense, there is nothing to apply them to. Mind strictly speaking—our rational nature—is not a proper *object* of natural scientific investigation, but a subject of history. The reason for which psychology does not fail completely is that there are peripheral regions of the mind like feeling or instinct (our animal nature or mind's proximal environment) that are to be studied with scientific means.

According to Collingwood, the study of nature and the study of mind bifurcate because natural events are phenomena that can be explained by placing them in lawful regularities—they only have an "outside," if the paradox is allowed, constituted by whatever "can be described in terms of bodies and their movements" (Collingwood 1992, 213)—whereas (human) actions also have an "inside" that must be grasped if one is to make sense of them. The inside of an action is a thought. Collingwood mostly refers to actions as "expressing" thoughts, but sometimes he switches to a causal vocabulary. The latter introduces a series of largely verbal difficulties, which, however, will not be discussed here. The contrast Collingwood wants to draw is otherwise clear enough. Science works from mere perception of, as it were, flat events. The task of history, on the other hand, is the understanding of human actions, and this is done by recovering the thoughts they express or have expressed.

> The historian [...] is investigating not mere events (where by a mere event I mean one which has only an outside and no inside) but actions, and an action is the unity of the outside and inside of an event. He is interested in the crossing of the Rubicon only in its relation to Republican law, and in the spilling of Caesar's blood only in its relation to a constitutional conflict. His work may begin by discovering the outside of an event, but it can never end there; he must always remember that the event was an action, and that his main task is to think himself into this action, to discern the thought of its agent. [...] To the scientist, nature is always and merely a "phenomenon", not in the sense of being defective in reality, but in the sense of being a spectacle presented to his intelligent observation; whereas the events of history are never mere phenomena, never mere spectacles for contemplation, but things which the historian looks, not at, but through, to discern the thought within them. [...] For history, the object to be discovered is not the mere event, but the thought expressed in it. To discover that thought is already to understand it. After the historian has ascertained the facts, there is no further process of inquiring into their causes. When he knows what happened, he already knows why it happened.
>
> (Collingwood 1992, 213–14)

In doing this, history proceeds not like geology or paleontology, sciences that reconstruct a dead-and-buried past. History faces a past that continues to impact the present—which is alive in it (Collingwood 1992, 225). The historian, if successful, uncovers not the extraordinary, but the familiar, in the form of thought informing actions. His method for understanding the actions of his ancestors or contemporaries—or even his own non-concomitant actions— is *re-enacting* or rethinking the relevant thoughts. Collingwood is obviously close in this respect to Dilthey's descriptive psychology and to *Verstehen* social science. His notion of history[28] is, to say the least, generous, covering areas not traditionally associated with the study of historical events.[29] It is in this light that his skepticism not only about psychology, but also about the social sciences, should be seen. It is a skepticism emerging both from a choice about the concepts of history, historical method, or historical understanding, and from what seems to be a misunderstanding of proposals similar in substance to Collingwood's. For example, he tends to be critical of both Dilthey[30] and social scientific research, claiming that the specter of positivism still haunts Dilthey's views or a science like anthropology.[31]

Neither this exegetical issue, nor the setting up of proper limits of the concept of history, need trouble us in this context. Collingwood's view of history is relevant here only because it is at the same time a view about psychology. This is so, first, in the sense that Collingwood sees his project as a study of mind, and whatever psychology might be it should have an interest in *that*. Second, situating thought and action in the domain of historical understanding results in a very restrictive mapping of the territory left to psychology—a field that is conceived according to its own self-image as an ordinary natural science. The latter aspect is of more interest, but it is best to start with the former, specifically, with a return to the method of historical understanding: re-enactment.

The task of the historian, Collingwood suggests, is one of discernment. History's domain is *Res Gestae*, human deeds (Collingwood 1999, 40–1). These have circumstances: they happen in a certain era, say, or in certain geographical space, or in a specific climate; they happen to people with certain dispositions and temperaments. All these elements might help the historian in his effort, but his task is not thereby one of arranging circumstances. Ultimately, what matters is the thought expressed in an action. "All history is the history of thought" seems to be Collingwood's favorite slogan. "At bottom—he claims—[the historian] is concerned with thoughts alone" (Collingwood 1992, 217). It is the thought that the historian must discern in the actions of men by taking it in, making it a part of his own mental metabolism.

Re-enactment has complexities and hesitations parallels to those associated with *Verstehen*. It should not, for example, be read as empathy, since emotion is something Collingwood is happy to leave to psychology. But, as Collingwood's examples show, it is neither a mere reconstruction of isolated practical reasoning. Thinking happens as part of larger (even public) assemblages, and it is to be recovered as such. Collingwood is again close to Wittgenstein when he talks of a "historical understanding, whose function is to understand the flux of events as they actually happen, seeing them in their actual *connexion* with one another" (Collingwood 1935/1999, 189—emphasis added).

History, to summarize, reconstructs the narrative of reason in action; all else is incidental and circumstantial, a matter of the actors having a scene to perform on. Given this image, the question immediately arises as to the possibility of writing a history of *un*reasonable actions. How is one to re-enact the thoughts of prophets and tyrants, of witch-hunters and mass-murderers? Are these *expressive* failures, that is, failures to *act* according to thoughts that are there, or are they failures to *think*, that is, the results of the inability to form thoughts in the first place? Could there be a history of *un*reason? Can the two possibilities be always distinguished?

Collingwood has no satisfactory answer to this difficulty (which is, of course, not particularly his). He does not want to deny the obvious: that history must be, if anything, the history not only of human triumph but—and perhaps especially—of human madness and stupidity. Accordingly, one attempt to answer this problem is a version of charity: it is a measure of the qualities and limits of the historian how far he can push the limits of his understanding; these limits speak, mostly, about *himself*:

> [W]henever [the historian] finds certain historical matters unintelligible, he has discovered a limitation of his own mind; he has discovered that there are certain ways in which he is not, or no longer, or not yet, able to think. Certain historians, sometimes whole generations of historians, find in certain periods of history nothing intelligible, and call them dark ages; but such phrases tell us nothing about those ages themselves, though they tell us a great deal about the persons who use them, namely that they are unable to re-think the thoughts which were fundamental to their life. [...] It is the historian himself who stands at the bar of judgement, and there reveals his own mind in its strength and weakness, its virtues and its vices.
>
> (Collingwood 1992, 218–19)

As far as it goes, this is a plausible reply. It points in the direction of reasonable doubt and is reminiscent of what Wittgenstein says about Frazer (see below) and of Quine's recommendations for the radical translator. But this move cannot solve the matter in principle. Might not the historian take as an example of practical reason what was an explosion of passion? Might not there be truly alien cultures? Why is there not a history of animals? The issue is not one of probability, but of possibility—of intelligibility and its domain.

A more solid attempt to limit, in principle, as it were, the possibility of unreasonable action is Hegelian in spirit. In the *Idea of History*, for example,

Collingwood comments approvingly on Hegel's notion of the *cunning of reason*: "If it is said that human thought is often or generally far from reasonable, Hegel will reply that this is an error which comes of failing to apprehend the historical situation in which a given piece of thinking is done" (Collingwood 1992, 116). The fault is again the historian's—he proves unable to reconstruct the circumstances of thought. In many cases of apparent unreason, moreover, what the historian should find is indeed *expressive* failure. People often are unable to reach their aims. Their deeds accordingly may seem, in some sense, degenerate or irrational. But many of these actions that may strike the historian as unintelligible are simply failed *attempts*, unsuccessful efforts at reaching aims that were reasonable in their context.

Dray and van der Dussen observe correctly that this too suffers from the problem mentioned above. Collingwood needs to say something about the distinction "between an absence of reasons and the presence of bad ones" (Dray and van der Dussen 1999, xxxv), and simply insisting on the second aspect cannot exorcize the first. The mistake, they note, is "to claim re-enactive understanding of actions which were irrational in the sense not just of being badly informed, but of being confused or illogical; for such actions would express no valid argument to be re-enacted" (1999, xxxvi).

Collingwood is aware of this resistant difficulty, and this awareness leads to a certain oscillation between the limits of the historian and the limits of *history*. It is symptomatic that the perceived threat of unreasonable—and therefore unintelligible—action is dealt with by stipulation:

> *Res Gestae* are not the actions, in the widest sense of that word, which are done by animals of the species called human; they are actions in another sense of the same word, equally familiar but *narrower*, actions done by reasonable agents in pursuit of ends determined by their reason. These include [...] acts done by an unreasonable agent in pursuit of ends [...] determined by his unreason; for what is *meant* by unreason, in a context of this kind, is not the absence of reasons, but the presence of bad ones; and a bad reason is still a reason.
>
> (Collingwood 1999, 46–7—emphasis added)

A related move—also significantly at odds with the idea of attributing limits to the historian—is to make thought a matter of *degree* and correlate it with historicity. Human societies are not essentially different from animal ones, though they are obviously not on the same level either. One should keep in mind that human beings have a pre-history, and "[t]he historicity of very primitive societies is not easily distinguishable from the merely instinctive life of societies in which rationality is at *vanishing-point*" (Collingwood 1992, 227—emphasis added). Here again we have a limit that qualifies history, not the historian. Intelligibility carries its own conditions of breakdown that become visible as it touches on the "merely instinctive life" not only of individuals, but of whole societies. The image is similar to that suggested by Dilthey's transition points.

One nuance is especially important in this attempt to tame the problem of understanding the unreasonable. Historical knowledge can go as far as thoughts go, as far as reason does not approach its vanishing-point. But history and mind do not *condition* each other; they are two faces of the same development. This seems a gesture in the direction of the *public nature of thought*, an aspect that is clearly visible when Collingwood describes thought as gradually becoming "more frequent and more essential to the life of society," and as constituting a "historic inheritance" (1992, 227).[32] With this view of thought as an aspect of a certain kind of public life should come an implicit recognition of the incapacity of history conceived à la Collingwood to *fully* assimilate pre-history. This recognition is perhaps what one should see in the role assigned in this scheme of things to psychology. There is a wider sense of action and mind than history can cover; history, built on re-enactment, misses the peripheries. Enter psychology, as the lesser complement of history.

Collingwood is especially dismissive of the claims of psychology to investigate human nature and human reason with the means perfected in the sciences of nature.[33] One aspect of his criticism, as per above, focuses on the idea that history is the proper study of mind. Another one is that psychology has used illegitimately the prestige of natural science to displace the traditional "criteriological" sciences—for example, logic, which conceived of studying thought in terms of its being *true*, or ethics, which studied actions in terms of their being *good* or right. Yet another aspect is a more constructive suggestion: let psychology occupy the territory left after history has reached the frontiers of its sovereignty. Psychological theorizing should not extend to reason, thought, and action, but is free to explore sensation, feeling, instinct, or appetite—in one word, the *psyche*.[34] This third thread of criticism is more relevant in this context.

For Collingwood, this conception amounts to a work of *restoration*—psychology is returned to its pre-Enlightenment position (Collingwood 1999, 82, 1935/1999, 176, 1948, 112ff). A marginal role relative to that it has desired, but one in which, Collingwood claims, the progress psychology has made can be seen in an adequate light. There are two main directions in which Collingwood considers that psychology has turned out to be illuminating. One was already mentioned and could be designated generically as the "study of feeling" (Collingwood 1948, 116). In this position, psychology studies the "proximate environment in which our reason lives"—"sensation as distinct from thought, feelings as distinct from conceptions, appetite as distinct from will" (Collingwood 1992, 231). The other has psychology enter the scene when the self-understanding that is characteristic of reason breaks down, that is, in cases of flagrant irrationality and *mental illness*. Psychology, in this role, supplements the work of the historian confronted with the utterly bizarre.

The second compliment paid to psychology is especially interesting. As Ryle, Collingwood seems to have seen in psychodynamic theories a great promise of progress in psychology.[35] He compares it with the revolution taking place in physics at the beginning of the twentieth century—both supposed examples of the collapse of the Enlightenment conception of science. As Watson, Collingwood notes that this psychology is successful due to its focus on psychopathology, which, we might suppose, keeps it anchored in the sphere of the *psyche*, and safe from extravagant temptation:

> [A] new psychology has arisen based on the idea of a single stream of psychical energy developing through a type of process peculiar to itself; and, directed as it primarily is to coping with the problems of mental disease, this new psychology seems a providential gift to a world whose only trouble is that it has lost its nerve and sense of direction.
>
> (Collingwood 1935/1999, 176)

The reading of this as arguing for the reorientation of psychology away from the domain of understanding and reason, from applying natural scientific methodology to thought, is supported by the fact that we are reminded of the merits of psychodynamic theories precisely in the context in which Collingwood claims that psychology has nothing to say about human nature. If there is such a notion, it is historical, not psychological: "Modern psychology is thus, on its more progressive side, a witness against the conception of human nature, and for the conception of human history, as fundamental to the study of man" (Collingwood 1935/1999, 196). Psychology progresses *against* its ideal of being a science of human nature, and it progresses in dealing with human beings who are recognizably *un*natural: beyond history, outside the public arena of thought. If psychology remains nonetheless a study of mind, it is not of mind in the "narrow"—and more relevant—sense in which history studies it:

> In realizing its own rationality, mind also realizes the presence in itself of elements that are not rational. They are not body; they are mind, but not rational

mind or thought. To use an old distinction, they are psyche or soul as distinct from spirit. These irrational elements are the subject-matter of psychology.

(Collingwood 1992, 231)

Collingwood shares what we may call the Rylean outlook: psychology can only tell us why we are deceived. His notion of history has obvious similarities with Dilthey's descriptive psychology. He faces analogous problems with the notion of understanding, and remains unable to settle the issue of understanding coming to an end, of there being a limit to it or perhaps a transition between it and something else: the irrational, the instinctive, the illogical. Psychology, whose natural scientific ambitions are perhaps hypostasized by Collingwood, is conceived as a modest speculum, adequate at best for these dark and marginal regions.

While, in the attempt to provide a clean field for psychology, James wanted to abandon "metaphysical" questions to philosophers, and Watson simply dismissed such worries altogether, Collingwood claims that this kind of maneuver, intended to open up a space for a science of human nature, denatures the study of mind, relocating it in a fictional bubble. To psychologize the mind is to "dementalize" it.[36]

The defense of the autonomy of the human studies is, as we already see with Dilthey and Collingwood, a dispute in which the role and nature of psychology come into focus. This clash of intellectual traditions cannot, of course, be reduced to a quarrel about psychology. It is important nonetheless that the rise of psychology as a discipline informed by the Cartesian and then the positivistic ideal of unified science is seen from early on as a particularly pressing issue for the humanities. The examples of Dilthey and Collingwood attest that this happens before the solidification of the hermeneutic school of philosophy, and before the considerable impact of Wittgenstein's later philosophy on the social sciences. Critical tools, inherited from the interpretive tradition of the humanistic studies, were available and they were used to challenge the self-image of psychology. They were also used constructively, in the attempt to specify a legitimate role for psychology, either as partly within the *Geisteswissenschaften* (Dilthey), or tentatively limited to a natural-scientific enterprise dealing with the animal aspects of human beings (Collingwood). Both examples point to the crucial role of the philosophy of history and of its problematic in this debate. Indeed, one can observe a certain dialectic linking history and psychology: the contextualization and attention to difference of the first counteracting the generalizations and abstractions of the second. These lessons remain valuable.

III

A typical retrospective look set in this early-twenty-first-century intellectual climate will perhaps have little patience with, or use for, the historicist tradition and its focus on reconstructing locally the significance of human action. What should *that* teach us about current psychology? There is a bit of irony here, because in reflecting on our own ways we may find ourselves questioning not only the reasons we have for preferring other ideas, but the "spirit of the times"—our times, that is. We would be, in the case, in the vicinity of a trope that historicists such as Ranke thought indispensable for at least historical explanation (Beiser 2011, 280). Similarly, the *ex cathedra* dismissal of psychology by Collingwood may very well look as a dusty example of hubris and nothing more. I have already signaled that, philosophical haughtiness aside, there is an important insight in the division of labor he applies to explaining mind and its peripheries. For the final part of this chapter, it is worth discussing briefly the contours psychological explanation took in the eyes of philosophers of history motivated by other "prejudices."

Postwar philosophers of history, like Patrick Gardiner, still felt it was important to clarify what makes historical knowledge scientifically respectable. In doing that, Gardiner provided an answer to the attempt by Hempel & Co. to assimilate the explanation of historical events to the law-based model of explanation in the natural sciences. Gardiner's take on the matter is rather prudent—he does not want to inflate the explanatory unicity of history. In a sense, what the historian is doing is rather ordinary, something that we all do, which is explaining the actions of others by "fitting a particular action within a certain pattern"—"the pattern of [...] normal behavior" (Gardiner 1952/1978, 124–5). Sure, the historian is far more careful with reconstructing the pattern from the evidence than one tends to be in everyday circumstances. But the procedure has nothing esoteric about it, if we look at how the relevant concepts do their work. The influence of Ryle should be recognizable.

Part of Gardiner's moderation in replying to the positivist enthusiasms of that era involved his explicit rejection of Collingwood's flirtation with the idea that the historian enjoys special access to the "inside" of past actions—to the thoughts of others, that is—via re-enactment. There is no need for special access, since all that can be done is to construct and adjudicate hypotheses about others using familiar experiences as a "guide" (Gardiner 1952/1978, 129). This does not generate unusual problems with attributing, say, particular reasons or intentions to people in the past, since we already know the criteria for applying such concepts. Rylean anti-mysterianism preserves, in Gardiner, even its ironical bent. It would be chasing ghosts to imagine that "historians are in possession of an additional power of knowing which allows them to 'penetrate into' the minds of the subjects of their study and take, as it were, psychological X-ray photographs" (1952/1978, 128).

This hardnosed attitude regarding the potential difficulties generated by the psychological dimension of historical explanation has its cost. We have seen how Collingwood reflected on the challenge of explaining unreasonable actions: let *the historian* think again, there is method in madness. This is arguably part of the larger problem of dealing with the *extra*ordinary. Now, history, which has had a long affair with the idea that it is ultimately the story of Great Men, cannot avoid navigating this distance between the mundane and the exceptional. Here Gardiner's otherwise healthy allergy to "mystery" becomes somewhat shallow:

> It may be objected that very often, in the case of the historian, for example, understanding is assessed in terms of a capacity to account for action by extraordinary persons in unfamiliar situations. [...] And what happens when we read the case-books of neurotic behaviour provided by a psychologist? Why do we so often feel that the analyses given are 'right', although the behaviour and emotions recorded are frequently of a kind remote from our own experience?
>
> (1952/1978, 131–2)

This being the 1950s, instead of "psychologist" read, for example, "Freud."[37] What to make of the fact that a psychoanalytical case narrative strikes one as plausible? Retrospectively, we know that that eerie feeling of plausibility eventually exploded in intellectual bankruptcy. (We also know that narratives of this kind have lost none of their popular appeal.) In any case, Gardiner seems to think that explanation can get off the ground if there is "some likeness—even if this is remote" (1952/1978, 132). Clearly, he has the historian's work in mind, but we can redirect the question to the psychologist. If we do, I think the initial reasonability of "some likeness" begins to dissolve. The emphasis must fall, eventually, on it being "remote."

Writing a few years later, William Dray attempts a selective rehabilitation of Collingwood's insights. Dray is more confident that attributing reasons for acting to an agent is a distinct kind of explanation. He stresses, that is, discontinuity where Gardiner was more prone to present a view of overlapping threads. When she explains a past action, the historian attributes a "calculation" to the agent performing that action—

> the one the agent would have gone through if he had had time, if he had not seen what to do in a flash, if he had been called upon to account for what he did after the event, &c.
>
> (Dray 1957, 123)

This is part of what it means to treat an action as "purposive." Note that the person doing the action has no better recourse if in a position to clarify to herself or others what she did. Our reasons may sometimes be transparent to ourselves only in retrospect. And if we do look at them, we at the same time weight them as good or bad reasons. Dray is, I think, spot on when he insists on this normative dimension of reason-giving. It is not a detachable feature, but intrinsic to the enterprise:

> The goal of such explanation is to show that what was done was the thing to have done for the reasons given, rather than merely the thing that is done on such occasions, perhaps in accordance with certain laws […] the infinitive 'to do' here functions as a value term. I wish to claim therefore that there is an element of *appraisal* of what was done in such explanations.
>
> (1957, 124)

It is not, of course, that people always act with good reasons. But as the more recent literature on charity as criterial for interpretation has shown, there is not that much room for attributing terrible reasons for action to others. Something must generally count as a good reason for an action in the eyes of the person performing that action to count as a reason at all. It is not in dispute that that person can be wrong. Empathy à la Collingwood allows the historian to understand that to an agent, in her particular circumstances, what turned out to be poor reasons had at that earlier time taken rosier nuances and as such led to action.

What matters in our context is that this normative focus contributes to restricting the area where such explanations have a point. Dray, too, confronts the problem of explaining unreasonable deeds, but sets it in a larger framework, because opaque behavior may not be the only instance in which reason-giving falls outside its proper domain of application. He seems politely critical when he points to the difference between what a historian would do and the case of psychoanalysts who extend "the presumption of rationality" to submerged motives because they find it "therapeutically useful" (1957, 137). Even if one cannot set a clear-cut limit to using this kind of explanations, it should at least be clear that they are not universal. They are in fact bordered by other kinds of explanations, arranged, as it were, concentrically:

> [I]t is nevertheless necessary to recognize the fact that there will be particular cases in which we find it impossible to rationalize what was done, so that if an explanation is to be given at all, it will have to be of another kind. To say *a priori* that all actions must have a rationale, no matter how hard to discover, is just a dogma [...]. In the ordinary course of affairs, rational and non-rational explanations of actions are alternatives—and alternatives sought in a certain order. We give reasons if we can, and turn to empirical laws if we must.
>
> (1957, 138)

Without sharing Dray's aims, I think this latter point is crucial. The explanatory default is generated by our familiarity with concepts that are normatively colored. It is their range, however loosely determined, that also decides how far this central area extends. It does not extend indefinitely. If we now switch perspectives and look from a distance, arguably the order is still there, but "the ordinary course of affairs" is not, so we should expect to experience that order in reverse. Our first contact should be with natural scientific alternatives to reason-giving.

As we have seen, philosophers of history often seem to think that these alternatives are in fact what psychology delivers. But to the extent that the language of psychology is itself an extension of familiar, that is, normative, notions (what would it mean to have beliefs without being in a position to question their reasonability, etc.), this may be wishful thinking. In this light, one is still left with the question of how to begin to talk about the margins, if not in the language of function in which psychology is at home.

4

Wittgenstein and the Limits of the Exotic

I

In an essay written in 1939 (1999—chapter 3), Collingwood includes a brief sequel to *Gulliver's Travels*. The reader is invited on a side path modeled on Swift's Laputa—Lagado story, where he meets a "sect of philosophers," voluntarily deaf and intent on translating the talk of music of their very musical fellow citizens in terms based on measuring and weighting. The philosophers are so determined, since they believe that nothing can be known except in such terms. This is how they proceed in order to learn about music:

> They take musicians, and seat them upon certain thrones, having a great many callipers and measuring-tapes arranged upon a kind of scaffolding above them, and weighing machines below. Then they cause others to play music. While this is going on, they note with the utmost exactitude every change in the size, shape, position, or weight of each bodily part in those who are seated upon the thrones, and print all these notes in their *Transactions*, together with the conclusions to which they lead. And although their Science of Music is still in its infancy, having been practised only for some seventy years, and with all the newest improvements in the thrones for no more than twenty-three, they have good hopes of bringing it to perfection in time.
>
> (Collingwood 1999, 89–90)

This is, of course, a ridicule of psychology. But one could force another reading of the situation—a naïve interpretation that ignores the polemical aims of both Collingwood and Swift. Imagine facing this curious practice as a field anthropologist. You are to describe what the native philosophers are doing. Are their experiments and publications about *music* in any recognizable sense?[1] Are they really getting at something else? Are they playing, being childish, or perhaps crazy? Are they simply opaque from your perspective? Do you need to become deaf and weight musicians for a while to see the point of all that?

The intended theme in this case was skepticism about psychology, but we can turn the situation in such a way as to illuminate it as *psychologically* problematic: what are these people thinking—are they thinking at all? With such questions we return to the hesitations—inherent in the defense of the autonomy of human studies—about the limits of understanding, and the role of psychology vis-à-vis these limits. Locating psychology and endowing it with a territory seems to depend on settling in some sense the issues raised by notions like *Verstehen* or re-enactment (and related ones, such as empathy, *Einfühlung*, and so on). This should also contribute to answering the question of what happens as understanding falters. Is there anything to illuminate beyond it—and if yes, what should be one's source of light?

What is needed is a clarification of the notion of limit, and in this respect the previous discussion does not go far enough. A number of alternatives suggest themselves at this point. One way to go is to follow the *geisteswissenschaftlich* tradition in the direction of hermeneutics. More sophisticated accounts of interpretation and its contextual and historical dependencies could illuminate the difficulty at hand. This is not a path I follow here. One reason is the unfortunate ignorance of yours truly. Another reason is that I suspect it would take us *away* from the relevant limit cases, which bring into question the very *possibility* of a hermeneutical approach. It would also take us away from a close engagement with naturalistic psychology and social science—to go with hermeneutics seems, in a sense, already to judge in favor of skepticism about psychology.

A distinct manner of proceeding is to reconsider the problematic confronted by the humanist tradition by placing the spotlight over the very concepts that constitute this problematic. Why is it that we seem to face a problem of *reconciling* psychological concepts—otherwise familiar elements of thought and talk—with a certain view of the world in which natural science plays a decisive role? Are psychological concepts pressured outside their traditional roles and destabilized as they touch upon the "natural" because they belong to a separate domain conceived as a section of reality which science fails to cover? In other words, is the psychological (and generally "culture") an *enclave* which, from the scientific point of view, remains a blank area on the map of a world otherwise conquered and colonized by science? A temporary enclave, as such enclaves are, as light and magnetism used to be, and as "dark matter" and "dark energy" are nowadays? Or is it perhaps that territorial metaphors are misleading in this respect, and a symptom of persistent dualistic predispositions? What if one saw

Dilthey's transition points (*Übergangsstellen*) not as border checkpoints, but as a switching between lenses? Some people wear two kinds of glasses, depending on what they are doing (e.g., reading versus driving). But if psychological concepts do not in some sense map (onto) a *realm*—say, the "inner" or Dilthey's empire within an empire—then what are they doing? This is indeed the question that one should be asking, since the clash discussed here is, at its heart, one about the nature of these concepts.

At this point too, one faces a number of options. The one that I propose to follow is to turn to Wittgenstein and try to use his observations about psychological concepts and psychology, especially those about psychological difference. Multiple threads in Wittgenstein's philosophy are relevant to in this view, and it will not be possible to follow them all. The focus will be on a set of remarks that deal with the idea of a *limit of understanding*. Without further qualification, this label covers in fact a number of separate ideas. Two will be discussed in this context.

The first is what I have already referred to as "anthropological difference." One could be faced with communities and cultures one has a hard time making sense of. This is the stuff of anthropological sci-fi (e.g., Clarke 2012, Sagan 2016), and also of journalistic reports of enduring fascination (e.g., Raffaele 2006). In historical terms, early cultural anthropology often expressed its failure to comprehend the exotic by dehumanizing it, considering the "native" less as an object of interpretation as one of hypostatization (Civilize him! Exterminate him! Revere him!). Perhaps the perfect dramatization of this way of seeing was the "human zoo"—an extension in the late nineteenth and early twentieth centuries of the older cabinets of curiosities.[2] In such ethnographical theaters, people (including children) brought from the colonies were required to perform their difference for the entertainment and education of metropolitan audiences (Blanchard, Boëtsch, and Snoep 2011). The semantic family centered on the notion of "savage"—beast or *bon sauvage*—suggests precisely this failure of comprehension; it provides names for a limit, since being savage is remaining outside the conceptual scheme that provides for mutual intelligibility and compromise among the "civilized" peoples. Conceptualized in such terms, it becomes doubtful whether the savage speaks and reasons in the sense that "we" do.

There are a number of threads in Wittgenstein's work that dispute this kind of view, and he discusses both actual and hypothetical examples in which the degree of (initial) incomprehension varies. His criticism of Frazer is perhaps his most substantive engagement with the idea of whole human communities being prisoner to silly empirical or inferential mistakes. This set of remarks, placed in context, will serve here as contrast for challenges to understanding which, unlike the anthropological ones, may prove extremely resistant.

The second sense in which understanding reaches a limit is psychological, and this concerns us more. The relevant cases here are those that do not allow for a natural or habitual application of psychological concepts. One notorious example is a certain Mr. Ballard, a deaf-mute who convinced James that he had sophisticated—for example, theological and metaphysical—thoughts before he had any kind of language. Wittgenstein disputes this claim in the *Philosophical Investigations* (1953/2009, §342), not necessarily as false, but as a case in which concepts such as *remembering* and *thinking* are destabilized to the point that one cannot tell either that they apply or that they do not. Cases such as Ballard's are not representative of whole cultures or functioning communities, and they do not count as instances of "logically alien thought" (see below), though the frontier is not always impermeable. They happen *closer* to home and raise a problem precisely because of their rather familiar queerness. What we are after in following Wittgenstein's remarks about such cases is an understanding of what destabilizes psychological concepts in marginal cases, and of whether this thinning of sense can be compensated by regimentation, essentially by a concept-introducing psychology.

Besides these two threads of thought there is a third one that must be mentioned, even if it invites a rather different problematic and, as such, it will not be discussed in the following. It is best to deal with it now, so as to avoid later confusions. The idea of there being a limit to understanding, in this reading, refers to a difficulty that is inherited by Wittgenstein from Kant and especially from Frege. This is the notion of there being thought that cannot be comprehended as a matter of *principle*, because it faults logic. What is confronted here is not the merely exotic, but difference in another, maximally radical sense. The question is about the possibility of *illogical* thought. Could there be people that can be said to think illogically? Could we perhaps in some sense guess, apprehend, or get some extra-logical grasp of what they are up to, so that to become convinced that they *think*? Could we compare their mentalities to ours? Kant and Frege, in different ways, rejected this possibility as a contradiction in terms: logic is not incidental to thought; it conditions thought in the sense of specifying where the concept of thought applies. To think *means* to think logically. To "think" otherwise is, in Frege's word, "madness" (*Verrücktheit*) (Frege 1964, 14, 1893, xvi)—that is, we could only have an illusion of making sense of what strikes us as illogical.

Wittgenstein was not satisfied with Frege's take on the matter, but he too resisted divorcing thought from logic. The divorce would mean the dissolution of the very framework which allows for something to count as thought. The persistent problem here is that the expressible/interpretable *seems* to have a larger scope than the logical. Is there a logical limit to thought then, one that *traverses* the expressible? No, but it matters how one rejects that proposition—how one interprets, for example, Wittgenstein's ladder metaphor in the *Tractatus*: has he managed to express ("whistle") something which stands beyond logic? This— the idea of expressively transgressing logic—is an important issue in its own right, and one which has been intensely debated,[3] but it is not the same as the problem investigated here. We look at attempts to account for actual, recurrent *psychological* difference; the possibility of authentic *logical* deviance is not unrelated to this concern, but it remains a separate issue which, to keep things manageable, will not be discussed in this context. The logical alien indicates, admittedly, a pressing difficulty, but it remains just one of a *number* of partially overlapping (therefore partly relevant) paths which cannot be explored here.

Another example, to open a brief parenthesis, is the kind of abysmal *moral* deviance Isaiah Berlin was prepared to regard as insanity.[4] What if individuals who otherwise seem functional flout moral norms[5]—to an incomprehensible degree? This has obvious connections with the endless discussion on what used to be the psychiatric diagnosis of "moral insanity" (Hanganu-Bresch 2019), traces of which survive in current conceptions about the nature of psychopathy.[6] A medical-causal explanatory toolbox clashes here with a more familiar ethical-normative repertoire. I leave this puzzle aside.

The margins of psychology that will be explored here—the infant and the madman—are not core preoccupations of Wittgenstein. He is, however, interested in the learning of language and in how people gradually become at home in certain forms of life; he is also preoccupied with instances of irrationality, and, at points, fearful of madness. The role of such remarks should not be overstated, but they will provide a useful context for the discussion. Context which otherwise will be based more on the general views about psychological concepts and psychology which are at work in Wittgenstein's later philosophy.

Before we move on, it should be said that the angle on the psychologically marginal provided by Wittgenstein should be seen as related, but not continuous to that characteristic in the defenses of the autonomy of humanistic studies. From that perspective, we have looked mostly at the early struggles with the idea of culture bordering nature, of understanding touching on explanation, of reason touching on irrationality, of history and psychology oscillating over, and trying to seal, in their separate ways, a number of tectonic rifts. We move now to questioning the nature of the fault lines. What if one tried to pour cement in a gap without depth?

This is not to say that one can expect a succession of steps in which Wittgenstein solves the problems left unanswered by the *Verstehen* tradition. This is not the place to evaluate the relation between Wittgenstein's philosophy, especially the later one, and the humanist tradition. But a few basic things can be said. Wittgenstein was not directly interested in the specific problems raised by humanistic anti-positivism, although there are intersections, notably those determined by the centrality of language, by the role of culture and history, and by a certain skepticism about the usefulness of applying the scientific method to illuminate the life of thinking, talking and convention-loving beings such as us (Hacker 2001b, von Wright 2007).

If it makes little sense to see Wittgenstein as a part of the *geisteswissenschaftlich* tradition, the effort to resist the equation of serious study to natural scientific methodology—of drawing a principled limit to what science has to say about us—is shared. One *can* see him as providing clarifications of some difficulties faced in the defense of the autonomy of the human studies, though not perhaps to those difficulties as conceived from within that tradition. In this sense, the uneven preoccupation that informs the reactions to positivism at the end of the nineteenth and the beginning of the twentieth centuries gets a much clear expression—it culminates, as it were—in Wittgenstein. This is what Hacker seems to suggest when he diagnoses and contrasts the hesitations about the notion of understanding in the *Geisteswissenschaften* to the view of language, meaning, and action provided by Wittgenstein. On the one hand,

> The terms in which such thinkers [those in the tradition that descends from Vico to Dilthey and Weber] and their followers attempted inchoately to articulate the character of the form of knowledge and understanding that they thought distinctive of hermeneutics, "fantasia", "inner understanding", *Einfühlung*, "acts of divination", "empathetic understanding" (and, in the twentieth century, "reenactment" (Collingwood)), were obscure and their attempts to explain them were philosophically unilluminating.
>
> (Hacker 2001b, 54)

On the other, there is the way out of the obscurity suggested by Wittgenstein. His philosophy opens a perspective in which what matters is not so much the notion of *method*, as the activity of understanding that becomes possible once the relevant concepts—thought, meaning, intention, understanding itself, and so on—are seen in their interdependencies within specific forms of life. Understanding then appears not as a technical achievement, but primarily as a regular, though often difficult, fact of human life.

The diagnostic component of the above seems somewhat rushed. There is nothing rudimentary about the thinkers Hacker mentions, some of whom we have met in this book, too. It seems more likely that certain kinds of solutions were not available from the standpoints they were committed to. Perhaps this has to do with the fact that their efforts were mainly constructive—that a *counterpart* to scientific methodology was their aim and, as such, the result was often a kind of parallelism (where explanative psychology does *that*, descriptive psychology will do *this*). They took seriously ideas that Wittgenstein opposes in a rather different way, not by balancing them with an equal weight, but by evaporating their mass, by deflating their urgency. It is best not to see Wittgenstein as solving so much as dissolving the problems faced by someone like Dilthey. That this contributes to making understanding less mysterious goes without question.

II

Wittgenstein uses often throughout his later work examples in which one is to contemplate hypothetical communities or "tribes" that are dissimilar in various ways and degrees from "us." Some such scenarios demand that the reader consider radical deviance:

> What would a society all of deaf people look like? Or a society of "mental defectives"? An *important question*! What, that is, would a society be like, that never played a lot of our ordinary language-games?
>   [Cf. Z 371] (Wittgenstein 1990a, 169e—§957)[7]

Some others depart from "home" in a more gradual fashion. In the remarks collected in the two volumes of *Last Writings on the Philosophy of Psychology*, for example, Wittgenstein repeatedly invokes the case of a tribe that deals with lying in unfamiliar ways. They treat it as perversion and even madness:

> Could one imagine that people view lying as a kind of insanity. They say "But it isn't true, so how can you say it then?!" They would have no appreciation for lying. "But he won't say that he is feeling pain if he isn't!—If he says it anyway,

then he's crazy." Now one tries to get them to understand the temptation to lie, but they say: "Yes, it would certainly be pleasant if he believed—, but it isn't *true!*"—They do not so much condemn lying as they sense it as something absurd and repulsive. As if one of us began walking on all fours.

(Wittgenstein 1999, 20)

Such hypothetical cases do not necessarily imply differences in nature (i.e., biological or psychological) between people we are familiar with and these beings. For example, the members of a tribe may have biological traits that made it especially hard for them to pretend, and *this* leads to a convention that marginalizes pretense in their culture. But the convention or habit may appear in the absence of any such traits or dispositions, just as people speak different languages not because they inherit in their genes a preference for the sound of, say, French as opposed to Chinese.

In proposing such examples, Wittgenstein is not interested in doing fictional anthropology. The point of them (most of them anyway) is to clarify *familiar* ("our") concepts that may appear as problematic when subjected to philosophical reflection. Moreover, the hypothetical deviations are supposed to contribute to a general picture of how concepts are "infused" with meaning by being embedded in various practices. By considering people who act and think in ways that are increasingly distant from the familiar, one is presumably mapping the behavior of one's own concepts. Successive modifications can transform a recognizable form of life into one which becomes increasingly opaque. At home, we recognize what people mean, aim at, think, or feel in what they do, and we treat them accordingly based on this recognition. When what people do becomes less and less similar to what we are able to recognize as characteristic, for example, aiming at something or having a certain feeling, we are less and less in the position to apply the relevant concepts to their behavior. Changing the ways people act— modifying forms of life—*eventually* results in destabilizing whole arrays of concepts that are endemic to those forms of life.

When practices vary, what gets displaced is not an ideal, and the meaningful application of concepts does not depend on ideal conditions. Before concepts become uprooted or destabilized, the procedure of imagining variations and deviations from the familiar can point in the direction of noting the familiar in the apparently bizarre. This is to say that differences often illustrate unproblematic extensions and projections of regular concepts. Not every difference amounts to what Wittgenstein calls "limiting case" (*Grenzfall*) (Wittgenstein 1953/2009—§§ 385, 420).

To think otherwise has led to one of the characteristic mistakes of early anthropology, as I have pointed out earlier. In the idea of the "primitive" a series of prototypical images overlap: natural, subhuman, barbaric, infantile, impulsive, credulous, stupid (Winch 1964). It is noteworthy that this happened to some extent even when in case was not some exotic culture, but the roots of Europe's own.[8] First at the beginning of the 1930s, and then later on (after 1936, probably in the late 1940s [Wittgenstein 1993, 115]), Wittgenstein attacked this stance as manifested in Frazer's *Golden Bough*. His remarks on the matter are of interest because they point to the faults of regarding a whole culture as childish or mad, and especially because they serve as contrast to the cases in which such psychological qualifications *have* a place.

The remarks on Frazer are interesting also because a number of Wittgenstein's themes and preoccupation intersect here. As in other occasions, there is a personal engagement with the idea of viewing human life exclusively through scientific lenses. There are also similarities with what Wittgenstein writes elsewhere about religion and generally about spiritual life, and with his notes about art and aesthetics. Of course, as Hacker advises in his polemic with Cioffi (Hacker 2001a, 75, see also Cioffi 1998), since this is a fragmentary and unpolished text, it was never meant to withstand significant interpretive pressure. But that there are debates about it attests that this set of remarks is substantive enough to drive some lessons home.

A last aspect that reveals these remarks as especially interesting is their subject matter. Wittgenstein meditates on the genetic explanations suggested by Frazer for bizarre rituals—the succession of the priest-kings of Nemi or the Beltane fire festivals. It is noteworthy that what made the ritual murdering of the priest-king studied in the *Golden Bough* striking—and demanding of explanation—was that it seemed without precedent *in its own times*.[9] The ceremonial seemed barbarous even when one tried to adopt standards fitting classical antiquity. The fact that this ritual stood alone in its native environment makes it a particularly suitable matter of reflection in our context. Its isolation invited, as it were, digging under the appearance, and tracing the origins and motivations of the ritual in such a way as to render it transparent—an instance of which is what Frazer did. But all this excavation, Wittgenstein would claim, does not collapse the initial discomforting appearance. If one is after *that*, then one does better staying at the surface.

Frazer begins the *Golden Bough* with a reference to the ethereal quality of Turner's 1834 homonymous painting. He then sketches in no less Romantic terms the terrifying rite of succession that governed the tenure of the sacerdotal office of "king of the sacred forest" at Nemi:

> WHO does not know Turner's picture of the Golden Bough? The scene, suffused with the golden glow of imagination in which the divine mind of Turner steeped and transfigured even the fairest natural landscape, is a dream-like vision of the little woodland lake of Nemi—"Diana's Mirror," as it was called by the ancients. No one who has seen that calm water, lapped in a green hollow of the Alban hills, can ever forget it. [...] Diana herself might still linger by this lonely shore, still haunt these woodlands wild.
>
>   In antiquity this sylvan landscape was the scene of a strange and recurring tragedy. [...] In this sacred grove there grew a certain tree round which at any time of the day, and probably far into the night, a grim figure might be seen to prowl. In his hand he carried a drawn sword, and he kept peering warily about him as if at every instant he expected to be set upon by an enemy. He was a priest and a murderer; and the man for whom he looked was sooner or later to murder him and hold the priesthood in his stead. Such was the rule of the sanctuary. A candidate for the priesthood could only succeed to office by slaying the priest, and having slain him, he retained office till he was himself slain by a stronger or a craftier.
>
> (Frazer 1890/2009, 12–13)

What could have led a group of people in a society that we otherwise recognize as orderly and "civilized" to act in such a manner and, moreover, to regard their practice as belonging to the category of the sacred? To answer this question, Frazer engaged into a monumental effort of documenting similar practices in various ("primitive") cultures. The project was to gradually put together an image from bits and pieces recovered from a diversity of sources. The murderous ritual at Nemi made little sense as it stood, but if one could show that it *descended*[10] from "motives [that] have operated widely, perhaps universally, in human society" (Frazer 1890/2009, 15), then it would ipso facto be explained, and its significance unearthed.

    Wittgenstein expressed his doubts about such a project. It will not matter here whether Wittgenstein is correct in his criticisms *of Frazer*.[11] What does matter is the rejection of infantilizing the people engaged in such rituals as being disconcertingly unable to overcome error. If that were the case, a whole culture could be suspected of something akin to malignant irrationality. Resisting this comes up repeatedly in the remarks on Frazer:

> Frazer's account of the magical and religious views of mankind is unsatisfactory: it makes these views look like *errors*. [...]

The very idea of wanting to explain a practice—for example, the killing of the priest-king—seems wrong to me. All that Frazer does is to make them plausible to people who think as he does. It is very remarkable that in the final analysis all these practices are presented as, so to speak, pieces of stupidity. But it will never be plausible to say that mankind does all that out of sheer stupidity.

(Wittgenstein 1993, 119)[12]

A bit later, in the context of distinguishing between the effects of false opinion and certain human actions that Wittgenstein calls "ritualistic," we are told that it would be silly to think that a mistaken "physics" is what grounds rituals (1993, 128–9). After all, Wittgenstein notes, the same person deemed "savage" is *not* a prisoner of false physics when it comes to building his hut or preparing his weapons (124–5). So how is one to think that this individual is blinded by stupidity when it comes to issues of life and death? "Frazer would be capable of believing that a savage dies because of an error" (131).[13] This kind of stance that comes close to regard the "savage" (note that the individual acts as proxy for his culture here) as out of his senses (*wahnsinnig*) is qualified by Wittgenstein as itself devoid of sense (*unsinnig*):

The nonsense here is that Frazer represents these people as if they had a completely false (even insane) idea of the course of nature, whereas they only possess a peculiar interpretation of the phenomena. That is, if they were to write it down, their knowledge of nature would not differ *fundamentally* from ours. Only their *magic* is different.

(Wittgenstein 1993, 141)[14]

Absurd and brutal as they may be, the human deeds that trouble us express something recognizable—that is precisely *why* they trouble us in the first place. These people are not alien or mysterious, but closer to us than we may like to think. A terrifying ceremony like the combat and killing taking places in Diana's grove wears its character on its sleeve. It is not the origins of the ritual, but what it is transparently about—human sacrifice—that upsets us. These stories are sinister because they produce echoes that resonate in us. Paraded in order to mark the separation between us and the "savage," they instead reveal an unspeakable continuity. It is a measure of the interpreter's own limited horizon that he defuses the darkest aspects of these actions by presenting them as blunders. Wittgenstein is not far from other critics of Victorian anthropology.

The main thrust of Wittgenstein's remarks on Frazer takes, however, a specific coloring, since it goes against the idea that explanation (in terms of origins) is what should *settle* cases like the Nemi ritual. The alternative to explanation that is suggested by Wittgenstein is description[15] and especially "perspicuous representation" (*übersichtliche Darstellung*) (1993, 132–3) or the seeing of connections. The point of presenting this example here deviates, however, from the original effort of suggesting a better approach. One could perhaps agree with Cioffi that explanation, including the genetic kind, *is* needed, and that the important dispute revolves around what one understands by "settling" the bizarreness of tales like that of the murderous priest-kings of old (Cioffi 1998, 81–2, 105–6). But that Wittgenstein does or does not, in this context, succumb to a kind of obscurantism in rejecting all explanation does not affect a separate lesson of these remarks. The lesson is that the cost of attributing massive irrationality to what is unmistakably a *culture* very rapidly escalates, making the attribution itself more irrational[16] than whatever it is supposed to explain.

The discussion of Frazer distributes a specific emphasis on this point, since one deals with a community which acts in a manner which seems the very opposite of the reasonable. The ritual they practice, moreover, is exceptional in their own circumstances, its origins or original significance probably lost to the practitioners. But, for Wittgenstein, not even *all* these elements put together can show that the participants are blind to what they are doing, that they do not *express* a vision of life, but exhibit perverse barbarity.

This is not the place to discuss Wittgenstein's claim that "primitive" behavior is not essentially a matter of opinion (1993, 122–3) or having reasons (138–9) for what one does, though it is surely interesting that he considers the connection between "us" and "them" as operating at the more elementary level of instinct and "instinct-actions" (137). This suggests that, at least in one dimension, the transparency of the ritual is not one of reason attribution. Whatever one may think of *that*, the critical force of the remarks on Frazer survives. At this level, Wittgenstein's aim is to erode the plausibility of the conception which accounts for "barbarous" actions in terms of *erroneous* opinion and *dubious* reasons. The relevant practices are not of the kind one asks reasons for; if one insists on that, nothing illuminating will be said—or it *may* happen that nothing helpful is said.[17] But this does not mean that things are done blindly and some of the participants end up dead by mistake. The practice *plays a role* in that community, and its role is recognizable, since we have, as Wittgenstein says, a "magic" of our own (for example, we tame, in our own ways, similar fears).

To say that a practice is ungrounded in (false) belief is not, in this context, to make it opaque or "childlike" (*kindliche*) (Wittgenstein 1993, 140–1). It is to say, rather, that eventual false belief and bad reason are incidental to the practice; righting the opinions of the participants may very well leave the practice intact. Its meaning (and its effect on us) emanates from its character, from the fact that it does play a role in the life of a human community—that its very savagery makes it a functional element of a functioning culture. This is what most troubles us. And this is a crucial aspect of the example, one which relates it to a typical concern in the philosophy of history and the social sciences. There is an enormous anterior plausibility to the fact that a functioning human community, even at its most seemingly bizarre, does *not* indulge in random acts.[18] Cultures arrive at various manners of dealing with and expressing the facts of human life. Some such avenues of expression turn out to be dreadful. But they are dreadful because we recognize them, when honest, as our own possibilities. This is to say that, for all their distance and difference relative to our perspective, *psychologically* (for all we know), the priest-kings of Nemi or the people participating in the human sacrifices that survive in the form of the Beltane fire festivals are *unexceptional* human beings. They do not represent a margin of psychology—and if anthropology ever takes us to one, it will be by accident.

If an obscure killing taking place in Roman Italy may seem too faint of an example to convince us of this important lesson, consider the genocides of the past century. Hacker mentions in his comment on Wittgenstein's remarks on the *Golden Bough* Golding's *Lord of the Flies* (Hacker 2001a, 77). Those children, one may say, turn into monsters; but this is a way of saying that they arrive at a terrible way of *losing* their childhood. They are neither childlike nor mad. And neither were the calculating butchers of the concentrations camps or of the Gulag. Writing the fictitious autobiography of an SS officer, Jonathan Littell begins with this plea, which is worth keeping in mind:

> Oh my human brothers, let me tell you how it happened. I am not your brother, you'll retort, and I don't want to know. And it certainly is true that this is a bleak story, but an edifying one too, a real morality play, I assure you. You might find it a bit long—a lot of things happened, after all—but perhaps you're not in too much of a hurry; with a little luck you'll have some time to spare. And also, this concerns you: you'll see that this concerns you.
>
> (Littell 2009)[19]

Insisting that the exotic practices of foreign or past cultures may pose difficulties for understanding without, however, bringing it to a halt raises the question of what, if anything, could produce such an effect. Is one to think that, no matter how a community of human beings acts, one should be able to make sense of their behavior? As suggested above, this question has a lot to do with the *decision* of qualifying a group of people as a *community*, and their actions as embedded in a *culture*. That is to say that the very idea of a functional assembly carries with it an assumption of intelligibility that is extremely hard to dispute.

Admittedly, one could insist that the possibility of community which would be *dys*functional in a sense which would allow the secession of intelligibility from culture cannot, from where we stand, be excluded. *Could* there not be human *thought* that would remain opaque to us *in principle*, and not, for example, as a matter of Victorian hypocrisy or fragmentary evidence? Insisting on his question, unlike the case of considering actual bizarre communities, switches gears away from the psychological; it points in the direction of the already mentioned issue of logically alien thought. Our goal, however, is to turn not away from, but closer to psychology.

III

In discussing Wittgenstein's remarks on Frazer, I emphasized that the cost of blurring the distinction between observed anthropological difference and its putative psychological causes is usually exorbitant. But I also observed that there is little sense in conceiving this demarcation as impermeable or clear-cut. Our aim should not be seen as one of determining the array of psychological profiles that are compatible with the existence of a working human community, specifically with what we recognize as culture. The perspective was the opposite: given that we recognize a set of practices as cultural, as expressive of the life of a community, the amount of instability in applying standard psychological concepts, or the amount of opacity attributed to the practitioners is thereby limited. Perhaps this would be better expressed in saying that there is little space left for psychological *speculation* once the action of individuals is seen as embedded in a culture that provides for its significance.

This limitation happens as matter of principle, since categorizing something as a cultural practice carries with it presuppositions about the motivations, reasoning, and reasonableness of the agents involved in the practice. It makes no sense to suggest that a group of people engage in, for example, a religious practice (one which plays a role analogous to some of our own religious practices) while claiming that these people neither feel nor think more or less like we do, that we are in the dark about them, that they may just be very stupid, mechanical, childish, or mad. This is not a matter of discovery or of the fact that we cannot be wrong in applying certain concepts, but of being clear about what a decision to apply these concepts involves. If we find it unreasonable to deny that the life of a group of people amounts to culture, then it is also unreasonable to deny that they fall within the range of our psychological concepts.

The point can be stressed in this way: to qualify a difference as anthropological or cultural is thereby to *exclude* serious psychological difference. This is surely too strong, and at most of expository use. But it suggests a perspective in which the anthropological loses critical mass at a separate stage—*earlier*—relative to the psychological.

We now gradually turn to the area where the psychological *is* detached from culture, where the characteristically human life and the application of psychological concepts come close to coming apart. Wittgenstein discusses such examples in a number of places, and we will make use of his remarks, notably of those he made on a case described by James, that of a deaf-mute who claimed to remember having had sophisticated thoughts before he learned language. Let us begin, however, with a stream of ideas in which there is a *tension* between diagnosing a gap as anthropological and considering it psychological. Perhaps if one looked at more ambiguous cases than the one described by Frazer, his view, if not his case study, could after all be justified. Perhaps the contrast we aim at illustrating is not a contrast at all, but a line drawn arbitrarily across a spectrum. We leave central Italy behind and travel to the eastern Mediterranean and back in time to the beginnings of the Greek world. If, metaphorically, the mind was invented there, perhaps the kernel of truth in this metaphor could be uncovered at the same location.

We know that the first Greeks built a sophisticated civilization and fought the battles of the *Iliad*. Europe often wanted to see in this dawn its own; Achilles and Hector have been assimilated to its pantheon. But, as with Frazer raising doubts about the significance of more recent Roman happenings, one can wonder whether we have not missed the strangeness of Homer's world because of our familiarity with Plato's. How did the early Greeks think *before* they invented the mind (*nous*), when most of the categories which their classical descendants definitively put on the map were not in place? Were they merely speaking a somewhat different and more primitive tongue? Have we simply lost too much of their world to even imagine it? Are the remains that are still with us in stone and in hexameter remains not only of a distant way of life, but also of minds different from our own? Finally, are these, in such a context, different questions?

Writing in the mid-1940s, Bruno Snell invites the reader to give up the comfort of false familiarity:

> The Iliad and the Odyssey, which stand at the source of the Greek tradition, speak to us with a strong emotional appeal; and as a result we are quick to forget how radically the experience of Homer differs from our own.
>
> (1953, v)[20]

According to Snell, what the great epic poems open to us is a landscape undergoing a tectonic transformation. The early Greeks do not arrive, like Columbus, to a continent already there, waiting to be put on some monarch's map. They stand at the beginning of a long process that would result in a truly novel way of seeing people. This is what Snell means by the *discovery* (*Entdeckung*) of the mind:

> They did not, by means of a mental equipment already at their disposal, merely map out new subjects for discussion, such as the sciences and philosophy. They discovered the human mind.
>
> (1953, v)[21]

Before this process arrives at its classical results, one can indeed get glimpses of a world very different from ours. Homer is about as far as we can see, and his distance means that his world is also the strangest.[22] It is crucial to note how Snell reads this difference. His driving question is on the lines of "what did these people know about themselves." And the answer is set in terms of a conceptual repertoire as illustrated by the use of language in the oldest remaining testimonies—the epic poems. The evidence being considered is given by what, at origins, were orally transmitted chants in which strata of language agglutinated. Snell tries to reconstruct from the language of Homer— one significantly different from classical Greek—a manner of thought which, in a sense, predates thought.[23] He is not so much speculating about the psychology of the first Greeks as laying out the view at work in their concepts of mental processes, action determination, and so on. It is informative, however, how difficult it is to find a way between psychology and worldview that avoids ambiguities:

> If, therefore, in the chapters to follow we shall venture to say that Homer's men had as yet no knowledge of the intellect, or of the soul, or therefore of many other things, we do not thereby mean that his characters were not capable of joy,

or reflection, and so forth. We merely want to stress that they did not conceive of these matters as actions of the intellect or the soul; and it is in this sense that they did not know the two. [...] Of course there was 'something' which occupied the place later conceded to the intellect, or the soul; but to ascribe the latter to the Greeks without qualification would make us guilty of confusion and lack of precision. For the existence of the intellect and the soul are dependent upon man's awareness of himself.

(Snell 1953, viii)[24]

Snell insists on this being conceptual deviance, and he documents it in numerous circumstances—from the multitude of verbs related to seeing, to the absence of nouns designating body (*demas* does not approximate the later use of *soma*) or mind (*psyche* and *thymos* are not used as *nous* would be), to the impact of the substantivization allowed by what would become the definite article.[25]

The difficulty here is that of keeping apart concepts from what they are concepts of. No, the Greeks do not discover a preexisting continent, but "of course there was something there." What? *They* thought of themselves differently; can *we* think of them in our own terms? Do we have a choice? Is "they thought" the past tense of "we think"? Snell sometimes seems to hesitate, but he is clearly inclining *against* making these ancestors of ours into aliens. Both the hesitation and the inclination seem natural.

Just a few years after Snell, R. B. Onians published a book similar in spirit to Snell's *Entdeckung*: *The Origins of European Thought* (1951/2000). Onians, too, contrasts the Homeric world with the familiar clarity of the classical era:

When in the fifth century the clear day shines, it is through a different atmosphere and upon a different world. It is to Homer, above all, that we must look for hints of the earlier beliefs. [...] The perfection of his art and the rationalism of his race must not blind us to the strangeness of his world.

(1951/2000, 2)

Like Snell, Onians focuses on the language of Homer to illustrate this strangeness. And he tries to work with a similar set of oppositions. The early Greeks were not a different kind of animal; they *just* had a different mindset. After listing a number of examples in which Homer's heroes act in horrific ways Onians writes:

The difference lies not so much in their nature as in the ideas and ideals by which they lived. It is not difficult to produce a parallel to many of these features, to one here and another there, in the subsequent history of Europe; but such barbarism of action, whether survival or recrudescence, is almost invariably accompanied by barbarism of thought, by crude superstitions and fallacies.

(1951/2000, 7–8)

This reaction is, recognizably, close to Frazer's. One can but shudder at the facility with which blood is spilt or at the matter-of-fact way in which people let themselves be pushed around by the blind whims of the gods. One shudders and one takes this to indicate a *gap* that has to be bridged somehow. The very expression "barbarism of thought" is a sign of struggling with the evidence. Onians tries to find a path in a fragment of a language by now displaced, and it is as if this was a solitary monument left behind to testify about what, to us, is unspeakable.

What Snell and Onians, philologists specializing in classical languages, struggled to avoid—the idea that the conceptual rift between current Western civilization and older cultures is indicative of a "natural" displacement—was explicitly embraced in the 1970s by another eccentric, the psychologist Julian Jaynes. In *The Origin of Consciousness in the Breakdown of the Bicameral Mind* (1976/2000), Jaynes put forward the idea that in the *Iliad* and in the remains of other early civilizations one could see evidence of a different human psychology—one antedating conscious mind. Homer's language poses difficulties of translations because it is a window to a world in which humans still lack inner spotlights. Snell's progression of understanding—a somewhat Hegelian view of the mind coming into its own—is recast by Jaynes as a psychological hypothesis. In a tone similar to that of the philologists, Jaynes asks: "What is mind in the Iliad?" (1976/2000, 69). But he also asks: "[W]hat is the psychology of the Iliadic hero?" (73), and his answer has a very different sound:

The picture then is one of strangeness and heartlessness and emptiness. We cannot approach these heroes by inventing mind-spaces behind their fierce eyes as we do with each other. Iliadic man did not have subjectivity as do we; he had no awareness of his awareness of the world, no internal mind-space to introspect upon. In distinction to our own subjective conscious minds, we can call the mentality of the Myceneans a bicameral mind. Volition, planning, initiative is organized with no consciousness whatever and then "told" to the individual in his familiar language, sometimes with the visual aura of a familiar friend or authority figure or "god", or sometimes as a voice alone. The individual obeyed these hallucinated voices because he could not "see" what to do by himself.

(Jaynes 1976/2000, 75)

Jaynes's bicameral mind hypothesis interprets the gods of old as action-controlling hallucinations not dissimilar in nature from the putative voices heard by Jeanne d'Arc.[26] This "preposterous" (Jaynes 1976/2000, 84) idea never made it to the mainstream of psychology, and it is evident that the critical part[27] of Jaynes's book is stronger than its speculative effort. But the latter remains not only a fascinating piece of guesswork, but, seen from our context, also a particularly clear example of psychologizing an anthropological discontinuity. The struggle of Snell and Onians takes a doubtful turn in Jaynes; a problem explicitly set as—and, one assumes, inspired by—difficult translation becomes an attempt to explain the origins of consciousness. This happens even if the evidence considered is more or less the same, and even if Jaynes is not blind to the fact that what he deals with is *cultural* change. The instability of translating at a distance becomes the fragility of subtracting from familiar experience its very familiarity. These are two different pressures on the imagination: the first demands us to imagine something that is *difficult* to envision; the second wants us to imagine *differently* without being able to specify what this difference consists in.[28]

In criticizing anthropomorphizing psychology, Jaynes describes how one may look at a worm that is cut in half. Does it "writhe in agony"? No, we are told. "Most people will identify" with it, but this will be *their* agony, not the worm's (1976/2000, 6). Later on, Jaynes notes, in a similar critical tone, that

> [s]omehow we still wish to identify with Achilles. We still feel that there must, there absolutely *must* be something he feels inside.
>
> (1976/2000, 84)

This is true, but Jaynes misidentifies the source of this absolute must. There is *so much* that we share with Achilles and his world, despite our many differences. That he feels comes up as certain against this background. We are told what he does, we unearth the stones he walked on, we sail the same seas. This is why his story, strange as it may be, moves us. To think of him, with Jaynes, as a "noble automaton" (1976/2000, 75) is not repulsive, as cutting a worm may be, but a nonstarter. Snell remains the more lucid guide to our—and his own—difficulty:

> At bottom, of course, we must be convinced that despite these complications the strange thoughts are intelligible to us, and that there is a vital meaning in what we have delimited, although we may not be able to define its precise significance

in our own words. We need not be unduly sceptical, particularly when the foreign material is Greek.

(1953, vii)[29]

The three examples we have briefly considered could be dismissed as intellectual curiosities. They are here, however, not because of their eccentricity, but because they illustrate the genuine difficulty of confronting forms of life different from those familiar to us. Psychological concepts play a role in these contexts, since we *are* trying to understand what the king-priests of Nemi or the Greek warriors who took Troy thought and felt, why they acted as they did. It would be hard for us to even conceive of the problem without appeal to such concepts. But once these notions become part of one's effort at intelligibility, one runs the risk of seeing the difficulty, the wound needing suture, as itself psychological. The mistake in this is to fail to observe that "psychological" bifurcates in the two cases. On the one hand, in noting that we deal with psychological concepts, one indicates that, pre-theoretically, these concepts cover a certain part of the life of a human being: thinking, feeling, suffering, remembering, pretending, and so on. One can call this part of human existence the life of the mind, if one does not forget that these notions do not function as theoretical constructs in a model of a private entity called "mind," but as crucial elements of a public (inter-individual) interpretive framework. This is why—and this is the sense in which—Snell and Onians find themselves speculating about the mind of the early Greeks when they struggle to make sense of (translate) their language.

On the other hand, to say that the gap seen in anthropological discontinuities is psychological in nature is to suggest that what is needed is a theory of mind, a functional diagram of individuals specifying their reasoning, emotive, or mnemonic capacities. This is a different subject from the one just mentioned. In Jaynes's words, the issue, thus conceived, is relegated from the philologist or historian to the examination of "psychohistorical scientists" (1976/2000, 76). Now, it is not that the two enterprises could not work in parallel. Perhaps the scientist could tell from the skulls of Achilles's warriors that they had tendencies unheard of nowadays. This could help one understand what happened under the walls of Troy. What the "psychohistorical" enterprise cannot do is *take over* the problem of intelligibility; this problem is historical, not psychohistorical. Neither Homer's verse nor Achilles's skull could *ever* show that Homer or Achilles had no soul. We look at their deeds and see it. That their agony is ours counts for, not against, its being genuine.

IV

The step that takes us to the psychological side of the contrast we are considering is dissolving the circumstances that usually support interpretation by placing the actions of individuals in the public matrix of sense-making. We have considered practices that, from our perspective, seem bizarre. Now we aim at finding situations in which bizarreness is not a matter of practice, ritual, or culture—cases in which, instead of synchronizing social behavior, bizarreness erodes it, amounting to *faux pas* or *contretemps*. Isolated individuals who raise serious problems of interpretation in their own social environment pose such a challenge; they, unlike whole cultures, can fall through the net of concepts that makes us intelligible to each other. For such a story, we return to William James.

In the ninth chapter of the *Principles*, entitled "The Stream of Thought," James contrasts thinking in words with thinking in "tactile and visual images" (1890/1983). James is ready to concede that linguistic thought is "handiest" in most cases,[30] but he sees no principled difficulty in picturing the contrast as one between more or less inter-translatable media. One can think in words *or* in images, as one can ask a question in English or in Chinese. To support this claim, James appeals to the recollections of one Mr. Ballard, from whom he quotes extensively:

[A] deaf and dumb man can weave his tactile and visual images into a system of thought quite as effective and rational as that of a word-user. *The question whether thought is possible without language* has been a favorite topic of discussion among philosophers. Some interesting reminiscences of his childhood by Mr. Ballard, a deaf-mute instructor in the National College at Washington, show it to be perfectly possible. [...]

"In consequence of the loss of my hearing in infancy, I was debarred from enjoying the advantages which children in the full possession of their senses derive from the exercises of the common primary school, from the every-day talk of their school-fellows and playmates, and from the conversation of their parents and other grown-up persons. I could convey my thoughts and feelings to my parents and brothers by natural signs or pantomime, and I could understand what they said to me by the same medium; our intercourse being, however, confined to the daily routine of home affairs and hardly going beyond the circle of my own observation [...] I began to ask myself the question: *How came the world into being?* When this question occurred to my mind, I set myself to thinking it over a long time. My curiosity was awakened as to what was the origin of human life in its first appearance upon the earth, and of vegetable life as well, and also the cause of the existence of the earth, sun, moon, and stars. [...] The source from which the universe came was the question about which my mind revolved in a vain struggle to grasp it, or rather to fight the way up to attain to a satisfactory answer. When I had occupied myself with this subject a considerable time, I perceived that it was a matter much greater than my mind could comprehend; and I remember well that I became so appalled at its mystery and so bewildered at my inability to grapple with it that I laid the subject aside and out of my mind, glad to escape being, as it were, drawn into a vortex of inextricable confusion. [...] I remember that my mother once told me about a being up above, pointing her finger towards the sky and with a solemn look on her countenance. I do not recall the circumstance which led to this communication."

(James 1890/1983)

Two years after the publications of the *Principles*, James would come back to this topic, trying to support his case by adding to the story of Melville Ballard the recollections of another educated deaf-mute person, Theophilus H. d'Estrella, "instructor in drawing [...] at the California Institution for the Deaf and Dumb, and the Blind" (1892b, 614). In correspondence, d'Estrella wrote to James as follows:

Hitherto till this time [~ 5 years of age, when d'Estrella's mother died] I had but a little, if ever possible, of instinctive language. I could hardly make intelligible signs; but my mother might understand my gestures, that is, such as were moved by feelings for what I should either wish or deny. For example, the idea of food was aroused in my mind by the feeling of hunger. This simply constitutes the Logic of Feeling; bear in mind that it is different from the Logic of Signs. I could neither think nor reason at all, yet I could recognize the persons either with delight or with dislike. Still, nearly all the human emotions were absent, and even the faculty of conscience was wanting. [...] But no sooner had I been left in charge of my guardian than the knowledge of good and evil was opened to me slowly but surely. [...] Not only could I think in pictures, but almost spontaneously I was also able to learn how to think and reason. My mental condition was favorably elaborated and properly reduced to the Logic of Signs. How were the essential signs acquired? My mother must have known my wants beforehand, without any forced attempt on my part. But my guardian was a stranger to me, and could not understand my desires. It was necessary that she or I would seek something rational or conventional to make us understand each other.

(1892b, 617–18)

And a bit later:

> Mr. Wilkinson, when he was my teacher, used to make me write about what I did before I came to school. It helped me much thus to repeat the memory. Ever since my recollections have been the same, though the words have changed now and then to get better style and more definite meanings in language. It shows that I thought in pictures and signs before I came to school. The pictures were not exact in details, but were general. They were momentary and fleeting in my mind's eye. The signs were not extensive but somewhat conventional after the Mexican fashion not at all like the symbols of the deaf and dumb language.
>
> (622)

James saw in both these cases evidence for thought in the absence of language. Sure, d'Estrella and Ballard mention expressing themselves by using signs. But it is also true that both examples—the second less than the first—are deeply ambiguous[31] in what they describe as spontaneous signing. Is one to regard Ballard's "natural signs and pantomime" or d'Estrella's minimal "instinctive language" as instances of sign *language*? At least d'Estrella seems to explicitly deny this reading, when he refers to his *later* evolution toward "the Logic of Signs." This does not make the recollections less ambiguous, but one can accept that perhaps James is not stretching *too* much the original reports when he reads them as claiming thought without language. About d'Estrella, for example, James says that, unlike his conventional signing, "his cosmological and ethical reflections were the outbirth of his *solitary* thought" (1892b, 623—emphasis added). It is reasonably clear that James tries to *isolate* what he takes to be a genuine, though perhaps ephemeral, phenomenon that is to be described in typical psychological vocabulary (these people think, reflect, believe and wonder as naturally as they fear and desire). Notably, the accuracy of their reports as instances of *remembering* is not questioned, and this despite d'Estrella's telling remark that the meaning of his memories became "more definite" once he could use words. That the uncritical acceptance of such autobiographical reports as authentic recollections is dubious would be stressed by Wittgenstein in the context of his attack on the privatization of thought.

James is one of the characters that appear frequently—with and without explicit mentioning—in Wittgenstein's remarks. The only other psychologist confronted by Wittgenstein so often is Köhler.[32] James's comments on Ballard make for one of the more interesting examples discussed in the *Philosophical Investigations*.[33]

After sampling Ballard's memories of his pre-linguistic metaphysical thoughts and briefly describing James's interpretation thereof, Wittgenstein asks:

> Are you sure—one would like to ask—that this is the correct translation of your wordless thoughts into words? And why does this question—which otherwise seems not to exist—arise here? Do I want to say that the writer's memory deceives him?—I don't even know if I'd say *that*. These recollections are a strange memory phenomenon—and I don't know what conclusions one can draw from them about the narrator's past!
>
> (1953/2009, § 342)[34]

Ballard's autobiographical report is strange (*seltsam*) because one has difficulties finding a place for it in the familiar framework of remembering and describing one's thoughts—or so Wittgenstein claims. The report is *extra*ordinary in this specific sense. James, however, presented it as an unproblematic case of remembering, since he wanted Ballard to confirm his theory of thinking. James, as illustrated above, believed that thinking can take place in images, that it can then be rendered into words, and that it must happen at an earlier stage than its expression, the latter being merely a vehicle for an already existing content. Wittgenstein would be critical of all these views. Fundamentally, it was his skepticism about the separation of thought from the *possibility* of its expression that made the Ballard case relevant material for this part of the *Investigations*. While the concept of thinking is not the main focus in our context, it is necessary to note the role the concept plays in the attack on James.

If, at least at the early stages of his signing, Ballard *could* not have expressed his metaphysical thoughts,[35] then the question is not whether he perhaps was thinking of *something else* at the time, or whether he *mis*remembers *what* he then thought. The question rather is whether he was capable of *thinking* any such things, and whether he *remembers* what he presents to James—and what James accepts—as authentic memories. It is the larger aim of this section of the *Investigations* (§§ 316–362) to reject the conception of thinking as a process happening in the private or "ethereal" sphere of the mind, and only incidentally expressed by means of a public language. This is the theme—a recurrent one in Wittgenstein—in which the discussion of Ballard's autobiographical notes is embedded.

To the extent that Wittgenstein's criticism holds, the answer to the question regarding thinking must be in the negative: it is doubtful that Ballard was capable of thinking the thoughts he mentions. There might have been (psychological) happenings that inclined Ballard to later describe things the way he did. The criticism does not erode *this* possibility, but the manner in which Ballard and James describe the situation. Wittgenstein's diagnosis, that is, comes not as an observation about what went through Ballard's mind and what did not, but about the proper manner of *characterizing* his past predicament.

It is important to note that the concepts of *thinking* and *remembering* do not occupy symmetrical positions in this discussion. The larger target is, as mentioned, thinking, but the immediate concern is with what may be called the "evidential status" of Ballard's recollections. If one imagines oneself confronted with the young, pre-verbal (probably pre-linguistic) Ballard, then, given his expressive poverty, one should not attribute to him (nonverbal?) thoughts about the origins of the universe or the divine. But confronted, in the narrative's present, with an educated and linguistically sophisticated Ballard, could one be similarly skeptical about his "memories"? By "now," Ballard is well within our form of life; he can participate as well as anybody in the language games in which people discuss their memories, past thoughts, and so on. So the question about *remembering* seems to ask for a different treatment. It presents us with a puzzle, and it is precisely the fact that the question is slippery which makes it interesting in the present context. Let us try to explain why Ballard's self-portrait as a young man is hard to keep in focus.

One can assume that Ballard is honest—convinced that he is aiming at articulating genuine memories; all kinds of things could have led him to the conviction he voices. None of this is at issue. The point is that, recognizing that his testimony—and its phrasing—cannot be easily ignored (indeed, the default would be to accept what someone tells us he remembers), we cannot overlook our separate conviction that a pre-linguistic Ballard *could* not have thought what he claims to remember having thought. This is the puzzle. The application of the concept of *remembering* is caught here between two sources of pressure: (i) people are normally authoritative when it comes to their memories—the standard is to accept their testimonies; (ii) the thoughts one can remember are those one could have expressed (even if one did not). This second constraint issues from Wittgenstein's view that expression and thought hang together; expressible thoughts (a pleonasm) are *all* the thoughts one could entertain.

In ordinary circumstances, these forces are aligned, but here they pull in opposite directions. In Wittgenstein's terms, the concept of *remembering* is uprooted from the usual range of language games that grounds its meaning. This is why in Ballard's case it is more appropriate to be circumspect about the very application of the concept of *remembering* than to insist on this being a case of *faulty* remembering. One is at a loss when one tries to interpret Ballard's autobiographical notes because familiar words ("thinking," "remembering") are forced into unfamiliar uses, and their meaning, thus unanchored, fails to carry over. We do not manage to assimilate Ballard's claims to any array of connections, analogies, or comparisons solid enough to carry their weight. They float freely and this is why one does not know what to say about them.

In his exegesis of this passage (1993, 365–7),[36] Hacker notes the importance of the fact that Wittgenstein asks whether Ballard provides a "correct translation" (*richtige Übersetzung*) of his pre-verbal thoughts. The question is rhetorical, formulated in these terms not because Wittgenstein accepts that what happens when thought is expressed is *translation* from an inner representation—say, a sentence in Mentalese—to a public language—say, a sentence in English. Indeed, in these paragraphs of the *Investigations*, as in other occasions, Wittgenstein clearly rejects this view of thought and expression. In a regular context, Hacker observes, the question would be "senseless" (1993, 366); for a person expressing his thoughts, there is no gap between expression and thought in which error could intervene, derailing expression from what it is an expression of. This happens not because we are very good at expressing ourselves, but because the concepts of *thought* and that of *expression of thought* function as a "grammatical" tandem.

That the question seems to invite itself in the case of Ballard does not indicate that it begins to make sense in this exceptional scenario. The issue of translation appears as a *symptom* of what was called above "destabilizing" of the grounds of applying certain concepts. One is "tempted" (*versucht*) to take the question seriously (Wittgenstein 1953/2009, §288); one "would be inclined" to answer it (*möchte antworten*) (1953/2009, §348). Hacker compares the paragraph on Ballard (§342) with an earlier paragraph, §288, which appears in the context of discussing sensations. The reaction of "not knowing what to say" that is induced by the bizarre character of Ballard's recollections (§342, §348) is explained by reference to this paragraph, *mutatis mutandis*, as issuing from a serious erosion of the context of using certain expressions. What if someone claimed that he understood the word "pain," but then confessed *not being sure* whether what he experienced at that moment was pain?

> [W]e'd merely shake our heads and have to regard his words as a strange reaction which we can't make anything of. (It would be rather as if we heard someone say seriously, "I distinctly remember that sometime before I was born I believed ... ")

That expression of doubt has no place in the language-game; but if expressions of sensation—human behaviour—are excluded, it looks as if I might then legitimately begin to doubt. My temptation to say that one might take a sensation for something other than what it is arises from this: if I assume the abrogation of the normal language-game with the expression of a sensation, I need a criterion of identity for the sensation; and then the possibility of error also exists.

(Wittgenstein 1953/2009, §288)[37]

Here, too, confronted with a strange reaction (*seltsame Reaktion*), one should not assume that the case can be decided in terms of applying regular concepts (that hypothetical person either feels or does not feel pain, either knows or does not know what "pain" means). It is noteworthy that Wittgenstein compares this deviant use of "pain" with being confronted with an individual claiming to remember having beliefs in utero. Such a suggestion could be seen as the extreme version of Ballard's autobiography. The idea of intrauterine belief is so utterly unanchored from even the most liberal meaningful application of the concept of *belief* (what can a fetus *do*?) that it destabilizes in the same move both the characterization of this situation as one of *believing* and as one of *remembering*. The critical observation here is that if recognizable expressions of sensation/thought are not available, the language game in which the relevant concepts are embedded is "abrogated" (*abgeschafft*), and the application of those concepts is thereby excluded or at least seriously undermined. The perspective opened by this "abrogation" or undoing is as of a conceptual state of exception.

It should now be clear why Ballard could be seen as an instance of the psychologically marginal. Even if one leaves the "widely ramified" (Wittgenstein 1998, §110) concept of *thinking* aside, since it may enlarge the scope of the discussion beyond the manageable,[38] the concept of *remembering* is a *bona fide* psychological notion, if anything is. This concept has a considerable range of uses, but it is nonetheless dependent on publicly recognized—paradigmatic—contexts of application. A case like Ballard's does *not* flatly eliminate all grounds for applying the concept, but instead *destabilizes* or erodes these grounds: one is driven to continue to apply the concept in a situation where it has, at best, fluctuating traction. It is not as if one would commit a mortal sin if one made the effort of taking Ballard at his word. One would instead find oneself wondering *how* to do that, without having a durable solution in sight.

This is not an unheard of situation; ambiguity, vagueness, and contradiction are part of life. We can even imagine scenarios in which accepting Ballard's recollections plays a fruitful role; perhaps it helps him make peace with a traumatic childhood. But James wants something else, and more, from this case. He presents it as *evidence* for a theory of thinking; he takes Ballard's testimony as an informative—indeed *decisive*—case of remembering having thought such and such. The ambiguity is not lived with, but ignored, brushed under the carpet. So the case is given a misleading presentation. To put it bluntly, speculation about a curiosity comes to decide on the lens through which one sees paradigmatic, unambiguous situations. This makes James's account symptomatic of a kind of theorizing in psychology that insists on illuminating the typical by placing the spotlight anywhere else. This is why James is *worth* criticizing: because of the weight he places on an example that could not work as a sample, a case too fragile to even support itself.

One way to contextualize Wittgenstein's brief discussion of James's Ballard would be to situate it in the framework of the philosophy of psychology which is scattered in the *Investigations* and in most of Wittgenstein's later work. This would be perhaps advisable if this essay was about Wittgenstein, but, in the current context, it is more than needed. The point of inviting Ballard in was to illustrate a difference which is of importance for our aims, that between interpretative challenges or gaps which are best seen as "anthropological," bridgeable within one's conceptual repertoire, and those which are properly speaking "psychological," that is, which raise doubts about the very applicability of one's interpretive apparatus. To make this point, it is not necessary to embrace Wittgenstein's views about psychology. All that is needed is his perspective on how concepts, psychological concepts here included, acquire meaning. Fundamentally, this is the view that meaning is a public affair, an accomplishment in the shared life of a community of human beings, belonging with its historical achievements and practiced culture, and less with the intracranial happenings of individual members.

This is already a commitment that some will regard as dubious, and the best that can be done here is to present it transparently. A substantial defense of this view is beyond the scope of this book, and if this is seen as too much of a cost, so be it. I take it that this commitment is *minimal* in the following sense: it does not force a bet on any particular *theory* of concepts; it is rather a critical stance that blocks the recurrent temptation to privatize concepts—and consequently language and thinking. Moreover, as just mentioned, this is not automatically a commitment to what Rorty has called, following Strawson, the "Wittgensteinian hostility to the mental" (1980, 232),[39] and certainly not to what Meredith Williams has described as "Wittgenstein's nihilistic moral for psychology" (1999, 244).[40]

To read Wittgenstein's unmistakable skepticism about certain claims and strands of psychology, for example his ongoing engagement with people like Köhler or James, as a global and radical rejection of the possibility of psychology might or might not be adequate exegesis. Without an ideologically regimented idea of science,[41] or of what a scientific psychology should look like, it seems strange to claim that the *possibility* of scientific psychology is threatened by Wittgenstein's remarks. Hacker, for example, has often insisted that this is not the case: "It would be mistaken to suppose that Wittgenstein was setting his face against experimental psychology or against the investigation of whatever forms of psychophysical parallelism may be found to obtain" (2000, 114). Be that as it may, it is not an issue that needs to be settled here.

Even if one goes with the not very likely interpretation that Wittgenstein aims at excluding psychology from the scientific enterprise, we are not forced to follow this route here. Yes, the larger aim of this essay is to expose the "confusion and bareness" (*Verwirrung und Öde*) (Wittgenstein 1953/2009—II, §371) of a certain way of doing psychology in non-paradigmatic situations, to illustrate a derailment of the experimental method which "does *something*," but is deployed in a way which does not solve our problems (Wittgenstein 1990a, §1093) in those regions. However, as mentioned, all we need commit ourselves to in this effort is a general perspective on (psychological) concepts. Concepts live in the games people play; despite their flexibility, they are not freely transplantable organs.

At least one more aspect of Wittgenstein's philosophy of psychology must be mentioned in the same spirit (it need not be decided here). This is the question of whether psychology is to be conceived as a concept-*introducing* discipline. This is especially relevant for marginal regions, where, one might say, since regular concepts falter, they can always be extended by stipulation or supplemented with technical jargon. Wittgenstein wrote against equating regular psychological concepts with technical terms. For example, in the context of introducing a sketch for a typology of psychological concepts, we are told that:

> Psychological concepts are just everyday concepts. They are not concepts newly fashioned by science for its own purpose, as are the concepts of physics and chemistry.
>
> (Wittgenstein 1990b, §62)[42]

In another set of notes, we find the following analogy:

> Can the psychologist teach us what seeing is? He doesn't teach us the use of the word "to see". Is "seeing" a technical term of psychology? Is "dog" a technical

term of zoology? Perhaps the psychologist discovers differences among people that are not noticed in everyday life and show up only under experimental conditions. But blindness is not something that the psychologist discovers.

(Wittgenstein 1999, 52)

The second remark suggests an important nuance. The psychologist *could* discover things we did not know about us. One can only presume that he then could also name them. But by psychological concepts, as things stand, Wittgenstein seems to refer to *regular* (interpretive) concepts. So finally being told what *seeing* (or thinking, intending, feeling pain, etc.) is by the psychologist is out of the question. This latter claim is all we need in the following—it is, after all, the same as the one mentioned above: regular concepts derive their meanings from regular use; (most) psychological concepts are everyday concepts. The theorizing which will be criticized later in this essay is done essentially by hijacking such regular concepts. If a skeptical element is to be kept, it is that which reminds of the requirements of a functional conceptual economy: introduction of novel concepts works because a solid conceptual net is already available, and is therefore limited.

> Sometimes it happens that we later introduce a new concept that is more practical for us.—But that will only happen in very definite and small areas, and it presupposes that most concepts remain unaltered.
>
>   Could a legislator abolish the concept of pain? The basic concepts are interwoven so closely with what is most fundamental in our way of living that they are therefore unassailable.
>
> (Wittgenstein 1999, 43–4)

With some caution, one can assume that this applies to psychology as a scientific enterprise, too. But be that as it may. The bottom line here is that we can live with a conception of psychology which does not exclude that the discipline can be scientific or concept-introducing. It does not matter if this is not Wittgenstein's view.

Imperial Borderlands; McDowell's Reasons

I

To study the mind, as with any complex object, a logic of inquiry would dictate an ascending approach, from the faintest intimations, to the pinnacle of sophisticated culture. Mental stuff is distributed on a gradient, and research moves, as expected, against it. This, at least, is the logic of inquiry recommended around the 1880s by W. L. Lindsay in a two-volume monograph on the psychology of "lower animals." Suppose we leave aside the fact that we have already seen versions of this idea paraded and deflated, and spend more time with this Royal Society fellow who, by now, is only remembered as a footnote to Darwin's *Descent of Man*.[1]

Before publishing his magnum opus, Lindsay extended his observations as physician at the Murray Royal Asylum in Perth to the mental life of animals. In the 1877 paper that Darwin quotes *en passant* as evidence for insanity in animals, Lindsay calmly announced that "[g]enerally, then, it may be stated that insanity in the lower animals is virtually the same as that of man"—in terms of "Symptomatology and Forms," for example (1877, 20). A dog may suffer for rabies, "but ordinary mania and melancholia are also present." In magpies, less meditative animals surely, "the usual form of mental or moral perversion is *kleptomania*" (1877, 27). Nostalgia can be a cause of mental disturbance, as can the "want of leadership"—whatever that may mean in the animal case (1877, 28). We began with the reasonable precept of studying *simpler* instances of mind, and here we are, in the company of anomic pets.

In this particular case, at least, the path should not be surprising. One year earlier, Lindsay had had this to say about Venus's flytraps that close on nonedible targets: "this does not always happen; and, when it does, it is to be attributed to an *error* which the plant not only *discovers*, but *rectifies*" (1876, 519). As in some current hip philosophies, mind had crossed regna. It was to be seen at work in the "purposive action" of plants. Phrased this way, what might have been a usable description of a natural phenomenon becomes an example of making a mess of both what we know and what we don't. This is a path on which we move from what we understand to some extent—say, rapid plant movement and heliotropism, animals in discomfort or traumatized—to conjuring mysteries.

In the fifth chapter (vol. I) of his monograph, Lindsay takes this genealogical perspective on mind from the mistaken but innocuous attributions sketched above to an emblematic dark place. Looking for the "dawn of mind," he compares children and "savage" cultures. This is part of a larger framework in which not only children and people of color[2] but also madmen and criminals are pictured together as feeble-minded. This is the trope of whole cultures as, at best, infantile in its sinister, non-hypothetical embodiment. We return to it to extend the criticism in the previous chapter. More importantly, this is also a reminder of the hazards of discussing limits of understanding—a problem which I will address in the next chapters.

Among the fifty-two traits of merely embryonic psychic life that Lindsay thinks he and other gentlemen of the era had observed in "savages" are some that immediately question the very humanity of the peoples talked about:

> "Among the Soudan negroes there is no family or personal love." [exemplifying trait 12]; "The universality of *infanticide*." "Insensibility to kindness; absence of gratitude." "*Incapacity for education* or instruction, for progress or improvement; including untamability." "Incapacity for *generalisation*." "No idea of *time*." "No *history*;" "The absence of *arts*" "Even the *forms of insanity* in savage and semisavage races resemble those which are commonest among the lower animals."
>
> (1879, 42–5)

It is as if attribution has suddenly swung in the opposite direction, generating a complementary set of mysteries: human beings reduced to killing and sometimes eating their young and old—out of sheer stupidity and malice; without memory, without art, even without language; prostrate except when hungry; emptier than Jaynes' pre-Homeric Greeks. Lindsay misses the point that such "observations" amount to a *reductio* of themselves. He fails to see that he has given up almost all handles, rendering these "races" effectively opaque in the very act of perorating about the rudimentary anatomy of their character. What he thereby makes fully transparent is the enormity of prejudice in *his* culture, its preference for, and

anthropomorphizing of, the "well-bred dog," its predictable dehumanization of
the colonized "natives" and of domestic underclasses:

> If the student will take the trouble of comparing, one by one, the negative
> qualities—intellectual and moral—of savage man, as hereinabove described,
> with the positive qualities of certain other animals—especially the well-bred
> dog—the conclusion arrived at will probably be what appears to me the inevitable
> one—that *psychical superiority* frequently pertains to the 'lower' animal and not
> to man!
>
> (1879, 50)

If this is clearly psychology with eyes wide shut—and fortunately far behind
us—the problem of describing the interval between diluted (or different?) and
full mental life is still with us. The problem is orthogonal, to use the distinction
introduced in the previous chapter, to anthropological difference. Culture means
intelligibility, something thoroughly penetrated by reason when looked at from
the inside. But with psychological difference we face a problem which should
be familiar by now. We have seen, with Wittgenstein, a careful attention given
to the context of applying psychological concepts, and a push-pull strategy to
test their limits—to show that application can dissolve into conceptual illusion.
We now turn to another school of philosophy that has tried to bring order to
our commerce with notions related to thinking by excavating a persistent and
misleading mythology. I conclude the skeptical scrapbook assembled in the last
chapters with a brief visit to Pittsburgh.

II

One foundational drive of analytical philosophy, Robert Brandom has suggested,
was to show that concepts work in a stratified manner, and that there is no way
to decide on their content while ignoring the specific physiognomy of each layer.
There is, for example, an important difference between concepts that merely
label and concepts that genuinely describe; the latter amount to "classification
with *consequences*" (2009a, 123). To describe by applying a concept means to be
able to track at some distance in logical space *what follows* from that decision.
In describing x as a *threat*, one is thereby committed to connect it to things such
as prevention, mitigation, or confrontation. The picture would get considerably
more complicated with a concept like *belief*. Mere labels—which do not require

such tracking—are what one sees in a classification one doesn't know, or perhaps need not know, the significance of. An example may be a differential response to stimuli in some animals. Or one may think of deriving absurd humor from adrift labels, as in this fragment from Bukowski's *Factotum*:

> "Now," he said, "you see these cartons. You put the brake shoes into the cartons. Like this."
> Mr. Henley showed me.
> "We have three types of cartons, each printed differently. One carton is for our 'Super Durable Brake Shoe.' The other is for our 'Super Brake Shoe.' And the third is for our 'Standard Brake Shoe.' The brake shoes are stacked right here."
> But they all look alike to me. How can I tell them apart?
> "You don't. They're all the same." (2006)

Presumably, moving from the level of labels to descriptive concepts "marks a giant step forward in the phylogenetic development of sapience" (Brandom 2009a, 133). With sophisticated devices such as conditionals, which require language and logical operators, sapience reaches even higher ground.

Brandom is asking in this paper how philosophy failed cognitive science. It must be a rhetorical question, because even if philosophers have not done enough to convince scientists to pay attention to insights such as the above, critical ideas have long been in the open, in various forms. Indeed, they have been openly disparaged, as if philosophy as a discipline was the last refuge of irrelevant reactionaries.[3] I have tried to suggest above that this reaction has itself been driven by philosophical prejudice. Be that as it may, what matters here is the substantial claim which underlies Brandom's analysis: to begin talking about the meaning of a concept one needs to have in view an inferential web. Concepts that come to carry explanatory weight, as psychological concepts do, work and are understood in such nets. To think that one can dispense with this inferential neighborhood and still have functional concepts is to entertain a version of what Sellars called "the myth of the given."

Brandom is expressing in a particularly stringent manner what is perhaps the main tenet of the so-called Pittsburgh school of philosophy. Starting with Sellars and continuing in the friendly debates of Brandom and John McDowell, this thread of philosophical literature stressed the linguistic or language-like nature of thought. In this light, concepts such as *belief* are to be analyzed by looking at the role beliefs have in reasoning, and by noting that reasoning is a game played according to norms.[4] As Clifford noted long ago, we hold, and should hold, believers accountable (1877/2021). It should be obvious, even in this low-resolution sketch, that such a view will be at odds if not with the relatively liberal everyday use of psychological concepts, then with their use in scientific psychology. Animals and preverbal children, for example, cannot be said to have the complex orientation to the world captured by the concept of *belief* except, maybe, in a "derivative" and "parasitic" sense (Maher 2012, 33). We talk this way, but it is really just "as if" talk. Concepts are the endowment of "*sapient*, rather than merely *sentient*" beings, as Brandom puts it (2009b, 10).

Rather than focusing on norms of reasoning in the abstract, I think it fits better the discussion in the previous sections to (also) have in view the cultural life of human communities. It also helps to have a more charitable—and realistic— picture of the relation between philosophical analysis and empirical research in psychology. For this, McDowell is a better guide than his companions.

III

It is particularly McDowell's development of the Aristotelian idea that characteristically human life happens in a landscape of our own making—a "second nature"—that is relevant in our context. This extends to taking seriously the fact that human beings are inheritors of traditions and languages, that they treasure them and raise their children in the shadow of the monuments of their culture—"prior embodiment[s] of mindedness" (McDowell 2000, 125). This is a perspective of a more ecumenical rationalism, but rationalism it is nonetheless. In elaborating Sellarsian themes—and, in a larger picture, the Kantian project— McDowell also confronts the difficulties inherent in this kind of approach. The intelligibility that is (second) natural to us is constituted in the process of acquiring the citizenship of the "space of reasons," a process which may be equated with *Bildung*.[5] Mind is not simply something that grows in us, like our bones grow. We—a plural, transgenerational "we"—tend to it. The very word "culture" points to this often tacit, but enormously important, fact about our *becoming* human.[6] The biological substrate is of course there, but it is not the proximate environment of mind. While "beginning as mere animals, human beings mature into being at home in the space of reasons" (McDowell 2000, 184). We should thus set the concepts we use to understand our minds in their proper framework. The problem, as I have suggested, is to square this with a scientific worldview, to resist within reason the ubiquitous talk about naturalizing the mind.

One thing that cannot be given up is the idea that, as *rational* animals, our lives take place in an environment where reason-giving is a permanent possibility.

It is only here that we are able to understand ourselves as the concept-using beings that we are, because concepts powerful enough to get this enterprise off the ground only work within these bounds. We might be "craving for external friction" (McDowell 2000, 11) in order to ground this seemingly unanchored space, but, again, this is what it means to succumb to the mythology Sellars denounced. We cannot, and anyway there is no need to, do better. Naturalization in the sense popularized by evolutionary psychologists misses the point that the fundamental concepts that we use to understand ourselves as having reasons for acting or for holding beliefs already have a natural home. What mature and socially competent members of a culture are able to do when they give, accept, or reject reasons, when they judge them to be passable or pitiable, is the main load-bearing structure of this home. Yes, this structure can support using said concepts at a distance, but it does not allow for relocating them.

What then, should one say, if impressed with this perspective, about cases of limited or incipient rationality that we do witness in animals, children, and mentally ill individuals? One look back at the beginning of this chapter may remind us that there is danger in the very idea of attributing limited rationality. It seems that projecting anything less than the full thing into others tends to result in trouble. It is also obvious that we cannot do without such attributions. The least that can be said is that one should be careful not to replace one misconception (our relation to the world is mysterious!) with another (it must be a miracle that children cross the Rubicon of mind!). It is a point of this book that at the margins we are imperfectly served by our indispensable notions. I do not think that McDowell has a decisive answer to this either, because I do not think that one is in the cards. But what he does suggest is quite subtle.

Contra Brandom, for example, McDowell observes that there is more to our attributions of knowledge to animals and preverbal children than a dispositional account would imply:

> I see no reason to think the knowledge of animals without conceptual capacities is only loosely so called, just because it is not the interesting kind of knowledge that the Sellarsian conception fits. I see no reason to think there is nothing really there but actualizations of responsive dispositions. The implication is that, say, a cat's awareness of the prey it stalks is no more genuinely a case of awareness than is an "awareness" of the presence of moisture shown by iron filings in rusting. This is the kind of thing nobody but a philosopher would suppose. (Descartes, perhaps.) I want no truck with it.
>
> (2002, 104)

Philosophy can fail cognitive science in more than one way, and this is a lucid coming to terms with some of its unfortunate decrees. Brandom's extreme analogy with a piece of iron "classifying" features of its environment by a differential response (rusting or not) is a self-defeating caricature. What McDowell calls the "self-moving lives of animals" is already infused with awareness, just not the one which eventually becomes ours. And we know that; any serious discussion must begin from the fact that we know that animals have complex awareness, and that human children, even when faced with severe adversity or biological misfortune, almost always succeed in acquiring language and in navigating their culture. Accepting all this does not evaporate, however, the difficulty of approaching marginal areas.

This is a problem not because a perspective such as McDowell's *has to* accommodate or settle every ambiguous or marginal case. The pressure, rather, comes from the kind of intelligibility provided by natural sciences, which seeks in the ambiguity of the gray areas an opportunity to level the space of reasons—to naturalize it according to a standard of nature that, against McDowell's dictum, does *not* include second nature (2000, xx). Another important worry stems from ethical concerns about treating ambiguities, by default, as dehumanizing, or as a license to treat other sentient beings as objects. Both reactions are misguided. The point of restrictive topological metaphors, of noting that not everything that is purposive falls in the realm of reasons, is not a prescription on the lines of "when in doubt, refrain from interpretation"; it is to be clear about the practices of understanding that we normally engage in anyway.

To use the example of development, we look at first natural capacities that support, and ultimately allow for, "initiation" in the space of reasons—for example, tracking the perception of others by firstly following their gaze.[7] Such abilities *are* connected with second natural achievements, such as understanding beliefs. Treating children as being able to handle beliefs is not only vindicated as they grow, but it is part of the process that literally transforms them into rational beings. Language proficiency is perhaps the best metric of the descriptive—and not merely pedagogical—adequacy of such attributions.

Early on, however, children are not citizens of the space of reasons; there are no two ways about that. Moreover, some human beings never achieve, or lose, full citizenship. Are we then restricted, in their case, to the expressive resources that we use to explain the natural world? The latter is an especially hard case, because the focus with children is on a maturation *interval*—which is crossed, and in which parents and other caretakers are invested. With what Tumulty has called cases of "diminished rationality," we are in a more problematic region, especially if we follow her suggestion that a consistent McDowell must place the experience of such a person on the same level with that of animals (2008), and that we may moderately resist this view by pointing to contexts of charitable socialization. Given McDowell's refusal to "credit brutes with an inner world" (1998, 311)[8]—even if they are sentient beings, not automata—we face what I take to be inacceptable consequences. But such a literalistic reading, I would argue, is not unavoidable. One way to approach the problem is to use McDowell in a manner somewhat similar to Thornton (2000) or Broome and Bortolotti (2009)—that is, to stress not the narrow reading of rationality, but his anti-reductionism. The great majority of cases of *failing* norms of rationality we should still want to describe in psychological terms, precisely because these will not be the natural scientific explanatory terms of the psychologist. We would do well, that is, to resist defaulting to opacity as far as we can, noting at the same time that our concepts will begin to destabilize as norms of reasoning fade out. These norms wax and wane even in unproblematic contexts, after all; their authority is not an all-or-nothing business. Charitable interpreters build on a preexistent flexibility. Even taking this way, however, because we are still in a rationalist framework, we eventually need to contemplate the possibility of opacity. As we enter the vicinity of its "event horizon" the form our disorientation will take becomes, I suspect, an ethical decision. It will have, or lack, the generosity of embracing, arbitrarily as it were, what one does not understand. One might thus express not one's understanding, but one's character.

To return to the relation between this contemporary version of rationalism and the scientific study of mind, McDowell is well aware that his demanding view of concepts and content implies unpalatable consequences for a certain way of doing psychology. He is careful to avoid what he calls "rampant Platonism"—conceptual abilities seen as otherworldly—but he will not compromise in the face of "bald naturalism"—the view that conceptual abilities *must* be "domesticated" (McDowell 2000, 73), or seen as reducible to the facts that form the subject matter of natural science. McDowell claims that rejecting naturalism thus understood should *not* trouble psychology—or cognitive science generally. Psychology is free to work with a notion of content, as it must, but that notion is not thereby made continuous with the conceptual content that is a trademark product of the space of reasons. In discussing animal perception, for example, McDowell presses this point as follows:

> I do not mean to be objecting to anything in cognitive science. What I do mean
> to be rejecting is a certain philosophical outlook, one that could be expressed

like this, if its proponents would consent to use my terms: delineating the contours of a subjectivity and delineating the contours of a proto-subjectivity are two tasks of much the same kind; they differ only in that they involve two different modes of orientation to the world, and so two different sorts of content.

(2000, 121)

That a mistaken philosophy is at work in this assimilation is an important point (recognizably, an echo of what we have seen earlier), but perhaps McDowell is overly optimistic in expecting that the relevant philosophical outlook is dispensable in cognitive science. In practice at least, as we will see in the next chapters, this perspective goes without question. What one often finds is, in McDowell's own words, a picture of the typical, mature abilities "welling-up to the surface" (2000, 55) of strata that are more or less like them. This produces the familiar result of explanatory leveling—a double injustice: to those powers that are ours as inheritors of a wealth stored in language and tradition on the one hand, and to the genuine difficulty posed to those abilities by ambiguous and marginal situations.

IV

One should not expect such Kantian variations to be decisive as criticisms or corrections of cognitive scientific excesses, at least not in the sense of having an impact on the dominant explanatory discourse in the field. And, as I have suggested, a rationalist point of view will generate its own problems in marginal cases, which are not necessarily easier problems. To vary examples, if one does not enjoy robust control over one's own mind, and is thereby to "be committed to the care of doctors rather than philosophers" (Kant quoted in Thomason 2021), is then one's *personhood* to some extent brought into question (see e.g. Murphy 1972)? It seems dubious that this should depend, at the end of the day, on others' charity in interpretation, even if such practices are thoroughly structured by shared norms. (Perhaps *especially* since they are structured by shared norms— again, see the beginning of the chapter.)

It should not be a surprise that stressing the normativity of meaning also reveals the fragility and limitations of interpretive practices. This does not make the picture of *Bildung* resulting in second natural achievements less illuminating. I remind the reader that we are not after a replacement—the point is not to substitute one grand theory in psychology with another. The point is rather meta-theoretical: to resist the inflation of the conceptual scheme that originates in our self-understanding by assembling a number of sources of skepticism. None of these sources comes without costs, and they are not all compatible. Nonetheless, if read as concomitant symptoms of philosophical discomfort with what is, after all, a philosophical choice, they should erode the ease with which cognitive science treats the margins as more of the same. As Shaftesbury (1708) has taught us, enthusiasm is healthier when curbed.

This is not likely to happen. Psychology has been fighting an uphill battle to establish its respectability as a scientific discipline. A consequence of this effort has been a tendency to concentrate on a single explanatory pattern, modeled on that seemingly at work in established natural sciences. The regular psychological concepts that the science of psychology has imported from common use have suffered various deformations due to this conformist pressure. They have been treated as temporarily acceptable pre-theoretical approximations, well suited for the needs of a young science, or as senseless rubbish to be thrown away together with other myths and prejudices. This approach resulted in explanatory violence done especially in cases which remain inherently ambiguous relative to the paradigm of typical, socially competent human beings. Either such cases have been seen as scaled or refracted images of the paradigm, allowing for unproblematic extensions and projections of explanatory devices, or the marginal situations have been themselves considered particularly informative about the paradigm.

I have suggested that a recent embodiment of this perspective of progress conquering previously gray areas is cognitive science, which tends to interpret psychological concepts as information-theoretic notions applicable to large classes of information-processing machinery. This seems to allow for theory construction that avoids classical philosophical concerns (rationality, conventionality, etc.) about using interpretive concepts with sense in ambiguous scenarios. Thus, even if cognitive psychological theorizing wears the relatively new clothes provided by the metaphor of the computer, at least in its treatment of marginal cases it remains prone to old mistakes.

Here we have considered old answers to these old mistakes, in order to emphasize the conceptual continuity between what we witness today in some regions of psychology and what happened when this science was, if not young, then at least young*er*. Even with this incomplete view toward the roots of our current problems, we should be better situated to confront them not as artifacts of our own intellectual milieu, but as persistent temptations. If developmentalists or psychopathologists may continue to have little time for the *geisteswissenschaftlich* tradition, or for Wittgenstein's numbing doubt—or for the current critics for that matter—philosophy cannot avoid the responsibility of confronting endemic philosophical mistakes, and of reminding itself and others that it has for long secreted both those very errors, and the required cures.

6

Early Childhood as Margin

I

The reader will have noticed that I have often suggested above that living with doubts is the better or more honest option when faced with puzzles of understanding. This is the place for me to live up to this criterion of honesty. I returned to work on this material as our son was entering his second year of life, and I had ample opportunity for questioning my ideas. Was I writing about failing to share a world with an infant as I was unmistakably beginning to share a world with mine? Was I in any sense diminishing not what children could do in the abstract—but what my child was doing right in front of me? At times, thinking of these issues felt like a betrayal, and my worries have not fully evaporated.

I write this as someone who is witnessing in wonder as a 14-month-old discovers the world, himself, and us, his parents. This is not some strange, distant process, but what is at the moment the most familiar and intimate part of my world. This is a world that we create together, even if not symmetrically, and a world I can only describe in familiar terms: wanting, believing, remembering, understanding, and so on. I fail to imagine any other way of meeting each other. Still, I criticize below a type of explanation in developmental psychology that seems to do precisely what I do these days all the time: extend basic interpretive concepts to explain what very young children are up to.

With all my doubts, I think the criticism stands, and for a reason that is rather prosaic. It matters what game one is playing. To my eyes, at least, raising a child means understanding and imagining the budding of a person, projecting an anticipatory and nourishing light onto the merest promises, because even the merest promises in a child are nothing short of extraordinary. A world is thus weaved, and our children naturally take root in it and weave it further. Furthermore, this place is not simply a construction site for a mind, but a landscape filled with the echoes of our deepest biological nature, anchored in touch and timed by heartbeats. It is primarily an affective cocoon.

Does all this *justify* extending to infants a way of thinking about people which is paradigmatic for mature individuals? There is no point in raising this question in the scene I outlined above, or in its larger setting. It is what we do—it is, in a sense, what we are. Only a misunderstanding would equate this predicament with a kind of hypothesis testing. The logic here is not of taking a step back from our behavior and perhaps discovering at some point that we have been mistaken all the time. That simply is not a possibility. We live with ambiguities, and we do not treat them as amenable to further evidence. Such looseness also allows us to enjoy intuitive certitudes, as it happens in scintillating moments of seamless, wordless understanding.

If we now move to the kind of epistemic effort involved in developmental theorizing, the issue of choosing one's explanatory concepts *well* cannot be avoided. In this setting, one is looking, say, for ways of describing potential causal chains leading to developmental milestones, or species-specific adaptations that made humans language learners and interpreters of minds. We are no longer in the region of domestic banalities, but in one of advancing and adjudicating testable theories. The "unnatural nature of science" (Wolpert 1992) should manifest itself here—independently from banality and custom. This is easier claimed than done, I think. Rather than making this point in the abstract, I will try to illustrate it below by way of example.

II

In the attempt to find illuminating analogies, psychology has been compared with many things. Among them, as we have seen, medicine surfaces quite often. Perhaps the analogy holds even in ways it has not been intended to hold. Take, for example, the illustration below (figure 2),[1] a fragment of a medieval medical text. The intention may very well be to represent fetuses in the womb, but to a modern eye the depictions show four human beings of indeterminate age in postures that resemble more gymnastics or ballet than the typical fetal position. They are enclosed in a kind of envelope, but not in a particularly claustrophobic manner. Their body proportions might be those of kindergarten children (except for the smallish heads), but they could also be those of adults if one compares them with contemporary iconography. We might be puzzled, if unable to retrieve a larger context, that such inaccurate depictions made their way even in treaties aimed at imparting knowledge of gynecology.

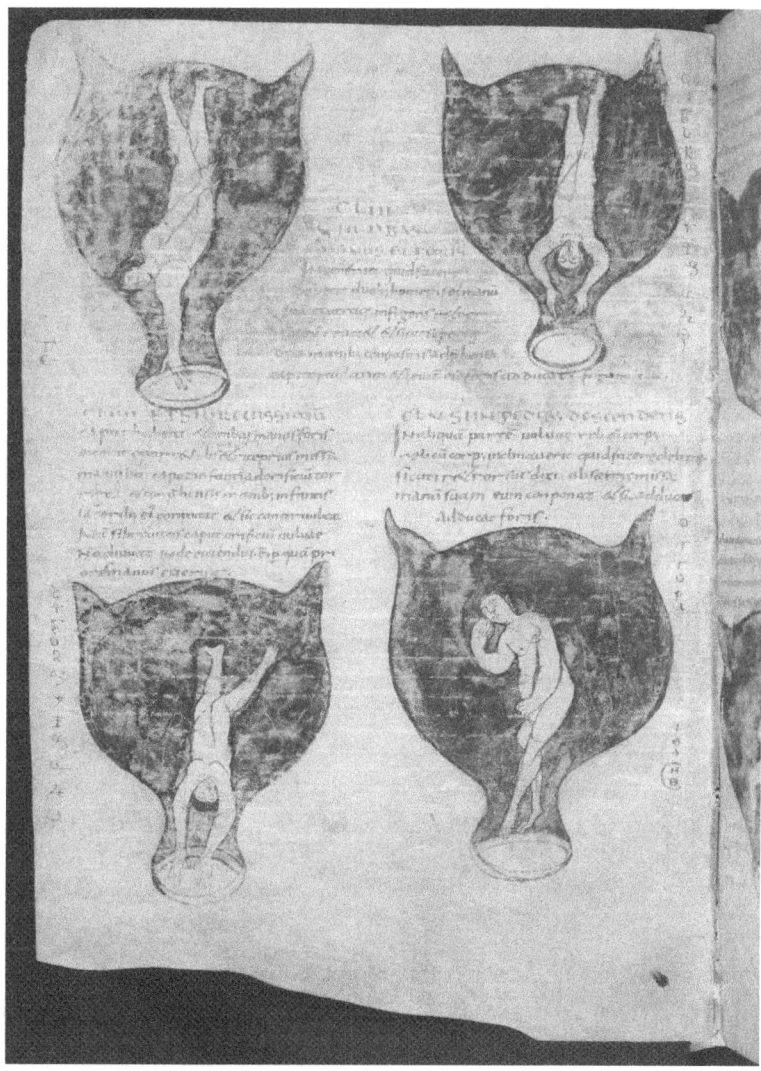

Figure 2 Avianus Vindicianus [Tractatus medicinae]; Gynaecia. Ninth and tenth to eleventh centuries. KBR—Cabinet des manuscrits—Fonds général—Ms. 3701-15, folio 58 © KBR.

Taking a larger view, it is by now a common place that artistic representations of children, at least in Western iconography, manifested for a long time a failure to show them—and perhaps even to see them—in their real proportions. One can hardly avoid to connect such a discussion with the literature on conceptualizing childhood inaugurated by Ariès (1960), pushed to strange territory by the speculations of "psychohistorians" like Lloyd deMause (1975), and qualified by rigorous critics like Linda Pollock (1983). Representations, from this standpoint, could be indicative of the importance of children and of the significance of childhood, accuracy being taken as a proxy for interest or affective investment. I leave it to the reader to explore this connection.

It may be an interesting counterpoint to remark that what seems failure in the representations of children in the distant past might have been to some extent intentional. We may situate it, or see it as an expression of belonging to a tradition, as one can still see these days in the Byzantine religious cannon. Be that as it may, it remains an interesting question why this persisted in the medical context, too, where proportionality presumably mattered. It may be the case that other features, such as relative position or a generic anatomical description, mattered more than proportion. But this is beside the point here. Metaphorically at least, one can relate this defect of vision to a certain reflex of abstracting, as it were, the future adult from a yet undeveloped frame.

The modern discipline of pediatrics has established itself precisely by rejecting this reflex. In her brief history of medicine, Jacalyn Duffin prefaces the chapter on pediatrics with the forceful words one of the specialty's pioneers, Abraham Jacobi, placed in an introductory chapter to a late-nineteenth-century "cyclopaedia" of childhood diseases:

> Pediatrics does not deal with miniature men and women, with reduced doses and the small class of diseases in smaller bodies, but … has its own independent range and horizon, and gives as much to general medicine as it has received from it.
>
> (Jacobi 1889, 2, Duffin 1999, 303)

One may wonder whether in rejecting one kind of illusion—that children are mini-adults—Jacobi does not already leave room for another—that pediatrics has so much to teach general medicine.[2] That this question has a place is one of a number of interesting analogies between pediatrics and developmental psychology. Roughly, developmental theorizing seems subject to parallel pairs of vulnerabilities.

In 1876, Hippolyte Taine published in the *Revue Philosophique de la France et de l'Étranger* a paper in which he documented the way his daughter learned to speak (Taine 1876). The article was in fact a concise diary that covered the child's first two years of life. It was not the first attempt of this kind (Levelt 2013, 94–7), but it would start a revolution (Ingram 1989, 8, Levelt 2013, 98). Taine's article was translated the following year in *Mind* (1877), which motivated Darwin to publish his own study on the subject, based on notes kept "thirty-seven years ago with respect to one of [his] own infants" (Darwin 1877, 285). A whole industry of "baby diaries" followed. David Ingram dates "the period of diary studies" in language acquisition as going from Taine's 1876 article to the establishment of developmental research programs inspired by behaviorist psychology in the mid-1920s (Ingram 1989, 7ff). But this is not to say that this form of study disappeared or did not continue to exert influence—Piaget is perhaps the best known example of its later incarnations.

The diaries were largely impressionistic, focused on detailed description. Some parents were obviously better observers than others (which is why some of the best work of this kind still constitutes a legitimate research corpus). But, as Ingram observes, "[i]t would be unfair, however, to say that these studies were void of theoretical assumptions" (1989, 9). Ingram points out, next, that already in Taine the performance of the child in acquiring language is seen as emanating, in part, from an inner source of order. And Taine was not to remain the exception. "When the question arose—Ingram notes—the most frequent view was that the child brought a great deal of internal linguistic organization to the task" (Ingram 1989, 9). Here is a striking summary from Taine that anticipates to some extent the career of this trope:

> The variety of intonations that it acquires shows in it a superior delicacy of impression and expression. By this delicacy it is capable of general ideas. We only help it to catch them by the suggestion of our words. It attaches to them ideas that we do not expect and spontaneously generalises outside and beyond our *cadres*. At times it invents not only the meaning of the word, but the word itself. Several vocabularies may succeed one another in its mind by the obliteration of old words, replaced by new ones. Many meanings may be given in succession to the same word which remains unchanged. Many of the words invented are natural vocal gestures. In short, it learns a ready-made language as a true musician learns counterpoint or a true poet prosody; it is an original genius adapting itself to a form constructed bit by bit by a succession of original geniuses; if language were wanting, the child would recover it little by little or would discover an equivalent.
>
> (Taine 1877, 257–8)[3]

At the end of this passage, two themes intersect. First, in acquiring language, the child enters a world that is already there (*déjà faite*). This is not an alien world, but one which comes naturally to the child. As Taine observes correctly, the child enters the linguistic world as part of a succession of others *like* him or her. But—and this is the second theme—the child is a "génie original," an original genius, also in the sense that, if language were not available, he or she could recover it or produce an equivalent. With this second suggestion we are close to the root of the problem exemplified in what follows: abilities which *are* natural and which act as a fundamental force in our development and socialization as human beings are misrepresented. We could diagnose what happens in Taine's second claim with reference to McDowell's insistence that the natural bifurcates, that part of what comes naturally to us is really *second*-natural, *made* natural by the fact that language, culture, and tradition are already in place.

What Dilthey called the "central regions" of psychology belong with this already made world and cannot be recast as a mobile telescope to be used everywhere there is a psychological question. Early development presents us with this kind of difficulty. What needs to be resisted in this case is not the humanization of the undisputedly human infant, but the confusion between its original genius and the original genius of Taine or Darwin, its representation as an athlete *in utero*, its transformation into a miniature version of James's Ballard.

III

I signaled above that I will make my case by way of example. I now turn to one of the most ambitious research programs in contemporary developmental psychology, one which has resulted, recently, in a comprehensive and manifesto-like vision of human nature. This program illustrates well the consequences of detaching regular concepts from their usual contexts of application and pushing them into explanatory roles in marginal areas. Moreover, the magnitude of this research enterprise (including its popular reception), and the fact it has at its center a seemingly technical notion, not the usual psychological concepts, make a case study opportune.

In a series of publications in the last two decades, Michael Tomasello and his (former) colleagues at the Max Planck Institute for Evolutionary Anthropology have introduced a new concept to cognitive developmental psychology: *shared intentionality*. This innovation was meant to provide the fundamental explanatory notion for a theory of early cooperative and communicative abilities. While the concept of shared intentionality is new to developmental psychology, related ideas are to be found in other areas and schools of psychology, for example, in social psychology or the earlier *psychologie des foules* (crowd psychology), and in other social sciences, like anthropology. More relevant to our purposes, the concept of shared intentionality, as used by the developmental psychologists, has its roots in recent philosophy of action.

The original philosophical source for Tomasello and colleagues has been Searle. It took more than a decade for Searle's paper "Collective intentions and actions" (1990/2002) to have an impact on the Max Planck team, and this only happened in the early stages through the filter of the sketchy account included in *The Construction of Social Reality* (Searle 1995). The idea, it would seem, influenced initially the work of Rackozy (2003), and then began its official career in a first important paper published by Tomasello and Rakoczy in *Mind & Language* (2003). Other philosophers became, during the following decade, recurrent references, as shared/collective intentionality was developing into a "cottage industry" (Searle 2010, 45) in philosophy. Among them, Michael Bratman, Margaret Gilbert, and Raimo Tuomella. More recently, the loop reversed direction, as philosophers became aware of the psychological fallout of their ideas and began referring to the work of Tomasello and colleagues (Bratman 2010a, 2010b, 2020, Searle 2010).

When, in 2005, the Max Plank group published what remains one of the most important papers of this corpus in *BBS* (Tomasello et al. 2005), even some of the more critical comments that accompanied the article did not question the notion of shared intentionality itself, as if it was reasonably clear what it meant and what kind of explanatory potential it carried. This was due, perhaps, to the fact that other concepts prefaced by "shared" had already made a career in developmental psychology, notably that of shared *attention*, which has been prominent in the literature on autism. The difficulties inherent in the notion of shared intentionality, the discussion of which forms the substance of the original philosophical literature, and the *additional* difficulties of applying it in the context of the rudimentary cooperative abilities of children were for the most part ignored or downplayed. This has not happened only in the discussion of this particular paper; it has been more or less the rule. As a consequence, a problematic theoretical construction was allowed, silently as it were, to play an increasingly visible role in developmental research. Shared intentionality has become the common interpretative halo of the experimental work of Tomasello and colleagues, and eventually the cornerstone of a grand theory that connects ontogeny and phylogeny—something that Piaget, for example, wished for, but deemed impossible (see e.g. 1971, 13). This is clearly visible in the triad of volumes Tomasello has published in the last years (2014, 2016, 2019). What began as a rather sketchy candidate for explaining the endearing cooperative play of children is currently considered the core of understanding human culture, that which makes our species unique in the animal world, the fact that we have parliaments rather than insect-picking sticks. In case the reader was not aware, "[t]oday, this puzzle is essentially solved" (Tomasello 2019, 3).

Despite its becoming common place when discussing the significance of experiments or when making general considerations about the evolution, ontogeny, and sociality of human beings, shared intentionality has had fluctuating descriptions, and remains an unnatural concept. I have already mentioned Lewis Wolpert's take (1992) on the valuable idea that it is in the nature of good science to be unnatural, to divorce common sense and ignore vulgar expectations. But this is not what has happened in this particular case. After significant quantities of learned writing, what shared intentionality should mean is not at all straightforward. Perhaps that needs not be settled in advance in order to capture a genuine insight into human nature. One cannot dismiss the possibility that ongoing empirical research may justify using the notion retrospectively, by gradually sculpting a meaning for it (its supporters seem to think this has already happened). Consistency and consensus can be manufactured, and the process of scientific discovery can be incremental. As things stand, however, the foundations for a meaningful construction are missing. One is not faced with a concept that is hard to grasp or elusive, but with one which is blurred to the point of being unusable. If this is so, there are obviously reasons to be skeptical about the explanatory potential of the concept of shared intentionality in the developmental context. Reasons, that is, to doubt that what we witness is a discovery in the making.

The background for the discussion that follows will be the idea that the inflation of cogwheel mentalism, typical of cognitivism and exemplified in this case by the disguising of a philosophical analysis of cooperative action as a cognitive-psychological piece of machinery, adds little in terms of explanatory scope or depth to developmental psychology. Monumental investments in systematic observation and experiment are hurt by this interpretative pressure to the point that real discoveries might be missed or their nature misconstrued. The larger forces at play in this process are those described earlier in this book. "Shared intentionality" is a neologism, certainly not part of the regular array of psychological concepts. But it was, at least originally, defined as a second-order notion designating particular structures of beliefs, intentions, and so on—the stuff that we do designate via regular notions. It was anchored, that is, in familiar territory.

Even if the target of the following criticism will be the explanatory language used by Tomasello and colleagues, I take it that the import of the problems discussed here is more than verbal. If this case matters, it is because here too we face the kind of gravitational pull documented in the previous chapters. This is to say that in this example of developmental psychology we see a recurrent problem, a philosophical conception turned into a philosophical misconception. It is an abstract view of what makes people tick that is worth a second thought here, not a particular set of experiments.

IV

I will begin with the conception, presenting and comparing the accounts of shared intentionality given by Searle and Bratman. Not only that these two philosophers have had the largest degree of influence on the relevant psychological work, but they exemplify a crucial disagreement about the treatment of the issue. This disagreement has been initially disregarded by the psychologists, and then summarily dismissed, and this is a mistake of consequence. It will also be important to take note of the fact that, although shared *intentionality* is invoked as an explanatory umbrella by Tomasello and colleagues, the philosophical debate illustrated by the ideas of Searle and Bratman deals only with shared *intention*. The two concepts differ at least in terms of scope, but more significant differences will become visible as we go on. The bottom line of this presentation will be that Searle fails to offer a defendable notion of shared intention, let alone one usable in empirical research, whereas Bratman's take on the subject is *not psychological* in the sense required in a developmental context.

In what regards the psychological research under discussion, it will not be possible in this context to give an exhaustive presentation of the work of Tomasello and colleagues. I will instead sketch a survey based on the more theoretically inclined texts of these scientists. The focus will be on what is taken to be the *explanandum* in the materials, and on the contribution shared intentionality is supposed to make once in the *explanans* position. Put in the interrogative: What are the explanatory needs the advertised theory serves? How does shared intentionality serve them?

The next step is to suggest that neither a Searlean nor a Bratmanian treatment provides an adequate conceptual apparatus for interpreting developmental research. Both are in fact particularly ill placed when it comes to understanding immature minds. Searle's notion of we-intention is primitive and set in terms of inner processes (it is "mentalistic"), and this would seem to suit the proposals made by the Max Planck psychologists. However, the notion is ill-constructed, obscure and, as Rakoczy and Tomasello (2007) have noted, curiously inclusive (it applies to us, and to some insects, for example). As charitable as one may be, it is hard to see what could count as a proper operationalization of Searle's proposal. Bratman, on the other hand, has a much clearer treatment, thus one that may be (and has been) operationalized (Tomasello et al. 2005, Moll and Tomasello 2007, Tomasello 2010). However, his notion of shared intention is reducible to familiar attitudes (it is an aggregate thereof), and, as such, is *not* a mentalistic construct. The latter remark is fundamental, since it indicates that the notion is inadequate for the explanatory enterprise of Tomasello and colleagues. It is hard to see how it could designate an *adaptation*, for example. What Bratman is doing is a kind of rational psychology that *presupposes* the mature exercise of the very abilities the emergence of which, in the developmental case, should be explained.

This leaves the option that, inspired by talk of the philosophers, Tomasello and colleagues have gradually introduced an *autonomous* concept of shared intentionality. Like everybody else, psychologists may very well play language games of their own. Almost two decades of empirical work and theory construction would back the notion up, and it would matter little if shared intentionality à la Tomasello had a homophonous counterpart in the philosophy of action. This option, however, collapses on a close reading of the relevant material (e.g., Tomasello and Rakoczy 2003, Tomasello et al. 2005, Tomasello 2008, Callaghan et al. 2011, Tomasello and Moll 2011, Tomasello 2014, 2016, 2018, 2019). The suggested analyses are vague, unstable between a Searlean and a Bratmanian interpretation, and they misconstrue rather than replace the philosophical concept. Eventually, they take a life of their own which disregards the fact that this original instability has never been solved, but merely glossed over. The recent exchange occasioned by a review of Tomasello's *Becoming Human* (2019) by Moll and colleagues (Moll, Nichols, and Mackey 2020) is telling in this respect. Some degree of skepticism is now manifested, so to say, from within.

A charitable strategy taken into consideration is to return to the more promising account available (Bratman's) and see if anything can be done to make it work in the developmental context. I will give a brief overview in the following, and return in a subsequent section to the details of the proposal. Bratman's analysis suggests itself because it posits a number of criteria that gradually approximate the nontechnical notion of cooperation. It can be seen as a case of conceptual reverse engineering aimed at analyzing a possibly interesting notion for further theory building. Since this approach sets checkpoints for genuine cooperation, it may be thought that these checkpoints are operationalizable as diagnostic "symptoms" for a distinct psychological process that underlies the ability to cooperate. The issue is not, however, if they ever could be so used, but whether they could in the specific context under discussion, that is, early development. And in this context Bratman's criteria could not target a specific psychological process, even if they could be given a psychological reading elsewhere (i.e., where his notion of shared intention does apply).

Operationalizing his criteria in a developmental context amounts, for all practical purposes, to changing the subject. This is because Bratman's treatment of the core notion in this theoretical family, shared intention, is based on an analysis of mature, common sense, unmistakable *planning*. This approach is inherited from his account of intention *simpliciter*. The resulting picture of shared intention is that of an aggregate *state of affairs*, kept together, essentially, by norms of rationality. Shared intention is not a previously unthought-of insular mental capacity, but *what emerges* when individual intentions, beliefs, and so on are rationally synchronized, and when there is a deliberate effort to keep them so.

When we turn to the story psychologists tell, we get a very different picture in terms of what they are aiming at. The eventual goal is something that should be recognizable to the historians of science: what about human nature makes us, well, *us*—different from all other animals. In other words, one tries to locate *the* source of what makes us distinct, mentally, from even close relatives, like the great apes. Their quest extends to both evolution (natural history) and ontogeny (development). In the 1990s (e.g., Tomasello, Kruger, and Ratner 1993) some of the same scientists thought the psychological key to our unique social abilities was the understanding of agents as being driven by *goals*. Now, that fundamental ability is thought to be shared intentionality. Surely, there must be some such mental switch that is turned on only in humans.

Now, if one bases one's understanding of shared intentionality on however loose Bratmanian ideas, the concept will not refer to a new mental faculty, even though what it purports to capture emerges from the human psychological makeup, the child's "original genius" here included. Shared intentionality could not be a novel mental faculty acquired in evolution under spiraling and species-specific adaptive pressures; at most, it consists in a resultant range of social aptitudes. The latter, of course, could very well be the proper objects of evolutionary history. But this does not change the fact that shared intentionality could not play the explanatory role Tomasello and colleagues want it to play. As it has been used and abused, I suspect that this conceptual artifact stands in the way of a proper interpretation of an impressive body of empirical work.

This failure is informative. A heavily mentalistic developmental theory as that proposed by Tomasello and colleagues can be attacked on the usual grounds that attributing mental states liberally is cheap and confusing. I think such a criticism is partially justified, but my skepticism is more specific. Not only that Tomasello and colleagues attribute complex mental states to young children with debatable justification. They attribute a social aptitude, shared intentionality, which, to the extent that it has a stable meaning, is not the kind of thing that *can* be attributed as a novel kind of mental apparatus. The developmental theory of shared intentionality mentalizes what is better seen as a social and normative achievement. This is not a mark of progress in psychology, but an old mistake.

V

Let us now return to the main philosophical sources and try to reconstruct a genealogy of the conceptual dead end that I think we now witness in the thread of developmental literature I referred to above. The concept of collective or shared intentionality is present in most of Searle's writings on "social ontology" published since the 1990s. It is one of the central elements of what he has called "a philosophy *for* the social sciences"[4] (2010, 5). Fuller—but substantially similar—accounts are given in one early paper, "Collective intentions and actions" (1990/2002), in an essay that prefaces a volume dedicated to Searle's philosophy of action and society (2007), and in *Making the Social World* (2010). Shorter sections are included in *The Construction of Social Reality* (1995), in *Mind, Language and Society* (1999), and in *Freedom and Neurobiology* (2008); collective intentionality, though not discussed there, is also part of the conceptual infrastructure of *Rationality in Action* (2003b).[5]

"Collective Intentions and Actions" is Searle's first attempt to argue for the notion of collective intentionality, or, more to the point, for that of collective *intention*, and it has remained the most substantive. There is agreement among commentators about this (e.g., Smith 2003, Zaibert 2003, Gilbert 2007, Ludwig 2007). Contrasting the individualistic account defended in *Intentionality* with that of CIaA, Barry Smith notes that this latter publication is a "crucial turning point" (2003, 14). We will find the ideas of this paper in everything else Searle has written on the subject, despite some interesting variations present in the more recent texts. I will thus focus on CIaA and then briefly note the consequential departures from its line of argument.

The paper is structured around five theses, the middle triad (theses 2, 3, and 4) containing the claims that matter:

> Thesis 1: There really is such a thing as collective intentional behavior which is not the same as the summation of individual intentional behavior.

> Thesis 2: We-intentions cannot be analyzed into sets of I-intentions, even I-intentions supplemented with beliefs, including mutual beliefs, about the intentions of other members of a group.

> Thesis 3: The thesis that we-intentions are a primitive form of intentionality, not reducible to I-intentions plus mutual beliefs is consistent with these two constraints (methodological individualism and methodological solipsism—see below).

> Thesis 4: Collective intentionality presupposes a background sense of the other as a candidate for cooperative agency, i.e. it presupposes a sense of others as more than mere conscious agents, but as actual or potential members of a cooperative activity.

> Thesis 5: The notation, and hence the theory, of *Intentionality* together with a certain conception of the role of the Background can accommodate collective intentions and actions. (Searle 1990/2002)

The first thesis is the easiest to accept, at least on a neutral reading. If some people cooperate in doing something, they are not doing the same thing as in the case where each of them independently performs an action, and their actions *happen* to add up to the same result as in the cooperative case, even if they may go through the same "movements" in both situations. Even if this seems uncontroversial, getting the details right is essential. For example, the difference might arise because of the socio-communicational context of the actions and/or due to their being part of longer chains that include counterfactual and future ramifications. Alternatively, the divide could be understood mainly in causal (psychological) terms. In any case, the problem, as Searle himself notes, is to give an illuminating characterization of this difference.

Searle thinks that an action can be parsed into mental and behavioral (roughly, body movements) components. Since a person or a group can go through exactly the same "movements" in performing collective versus individual actions, the difference between the two must be "mental," in the sense that the two situations diverge in their recent history of psychological causation: "So if there is anything special about collective behavior, it must lie in some special feature of the mental component, in the form of the intentionality" (Searle 1990/2002, 91). What makes actions collective in the robust sense specified by the first thesis is the intentionality "behind" them. Searle thinks this intentionality is of a distinct variety, which he calls "collective intentionality." The special character of collective actions is thus inherited; it is collective *intentionality* which makes the difference. This means that we are now in a position to rephrase the problem raised at the end of the previous paragraph as follows: what is the nature of collective intentionality, and what in this nature confers the special character mentioned above to some actions performed in social contexts?

To ask this question is to enter the territory covered by the second thesis, the one we need to focus on. The claim that the intentional component of collective actions does not reduce to regular individual intentions—together with the somewhat rhetorical claim that such non-reductivism is compatible with methodological individualism (thesis 3)—gives Searle's approach its specific profile. There are no group minds, but each individual mind can think in the plural, *literally*. Let us try to spell out what this latter aspect amounts to, since it has proven to be seductive.

While Searle switches liberally between intentionality and intention, the discussion in CIaA only concerns collective or we-*intention*. Indeed, as mentioned earlier, this is the case with the philosophical literature on the subject generally. Socially coordinated *action* is what these philosophers want to understand, and this explains their interest in intention and planning. There is comparatively negligible attention to other attitudes, such as belief, and only nodding gestures to bodies of literature defined by other priorities, such as that on common knowledge (Vanderschraaf and Sillari 2009). So, while collective intentionality may be an important topic, the material is at most an argument for there being *intending* in the plural. We will have the opportunity later on to ask if the lessons carry over, and whether that should matter.

Let us focus then on collective intentions. Searle maintains that at the basis of collective action there are intentions of the form *we intend to do X*. Collective or we-intentions are thus given a first syntactic identification. This form may seem harmless, as it may be acceptable to describe actions performed by groups in such terms.[6] What makes the position substantive is the claim that collective intentions do not reduce, that is, the idea that they are a special *type* of intention: "The real distinction between the singular and the collective case is in the type of intention involved, not in the way that the elements in the conditions of satisfaction relate to each other" (Searle 1990/2002, 102).

The characteristic element of Searle's account is an attempt to show that a certain logical form typifies collective intentions. The idea that formal properties individuate attitude types is continuous with the account defended in *Intentionality*. A more important idea taken from that source is the distinction between *prior intention* and *intention-in-action* (Searle 1983, 84–98). The latter concept captures the idea that genuine action has a contemporary intentional component. Intention in this sense is concomitant with, and part of, the doing. The former concept overlaps more or less with the everyday use of "intention"; that is, it refers to the idea that intention anticipates and prepares *subsequent* deeds, and also to the idea that intention may *fail* to result in action. This way of speciating intention involves debatable commitments, but it is a step that should be kept in mind in order to understand Searle's account of collective intention.

While Searle mentions once collective prior intentions in CIaA (1990/2002, 104), this is without any explanation; he is only discussing collective *intentions-in-action*, and it is not clear whether what he says about this notion is supposed to carry over to prior intentions. Indeed, given that prior intentions are supposed to cause intentions-in-action (à la *Intentionality*), and that in CIaA Searle explicitly rejects the idea that collective intentions work by causing other intentions, the extension of the account seems even more dubious, and the mentioning of collective prior intentions, like the mentioning of collective beliefs and desires in other writings (Searle 1995, 23, 2008, 85, 2007, 12, 2010, 43),[7] gratuitous. This is one of the important contrasts between Searle's treatment and that developed by Bratman, who focuses, as we will see, on *prior* intentions. The picture so far is the following: Searle mentions collective intentionality, but his analysis covers exclusively collective intentions-in-action. Even if the analysis is correct, which is unlikely, it would not deliver a concept of collective or shared intentionality.

Let us now move to the theory proper. Searle proposes to analyze collective intentions on the model of the singular intentions-in-action that involve operators like "by way of" or "by means of." The driving idea here is that when people cooperate there must be something like each of them intending to do his or her share. In the singular case, I can, for example, intend to fire the gun *by means of* pulling the trigger, or I can intend to vote *by* raising my arm. Searle calls these "the causal by-means-of," and "the constitutive by-way-of" relations. Analogously, it is suggested, some collective goals are achieved *by means of* individual acts (we start a car by means of me pushing and you releasing the clutch). Some other are *constituted by* individual acts (we play a duet by me playing the piano and you the violin).[8] Again, the operators are meant to capture the idea of doing one's share.

In the individual cases, we have the following formal rendering,[9] where "i.a." stands for intention-in-action:

> i.a. B by means of A (this i.a. causes: A *content of A*, causes: B *content of B*).

To use another of Searle's examples, I can intend (B) to fire the gun by means of (A) pulling the trigger (1990/2002, 102). This will be analyzed as:

> i.a. B by means of A (this i.a. causes: A trigger pulls, causes: B gun fires).

The locution outside the parentheses specifies the type of intention, while the part inside stands for the content of the intention. One should note that, even in this benign case, the formalization induces an inflation of intention types. As Searle says about the example above, "it isn't just any old type of i.a., it is an achieve-B-by-means-of-A type of i.a." (1990/2002, 102). Analogously, in the case of collective intentions, we get the following formalization:

> i.a. collective B by means of singular A
>
> (this i.a. causes: A *content of A*, causes: B *content of B*)

According to Searle, this would translate as follows (filling in yet another example of his):

> I have a collective intention-in-action, B, which I do my part to carry out by performing my singular act A, and the content of the intention is that, in that context, this intention-in-action causes it to be the case, as A, that the car moves which, in that context, causes it to be the case, as B, that the engine starts.
>
> (2007, 19)

We are now at some distance from the first identification of collective intentions as those of the form "we intend … ", and a few questions are in order. The first one is how does this analysis further, as opposed to hinder, our understanding of cooperation. The second and related question is what could motivate such a cumbersome structure.

The first problem is easier to answer. In its everyday use, the notion of intention is linked to that of control. If I can exert no control over a process, I cannot intend the outcome of that process, though I might desire it. I cannot intend to win the lottery tomorrow, unless I rigged it. Now, the relevant philosophical analyses inherit and take seriously this restriction, since they are, after all, analyses of the common notions, or at most of extensions thereof. This is the case for both Searle and, as we will see shortly, Bratman. The problem, in this context, is that once one begins talking about *collective* intentions, the overlap between the scope of intending and that of control evaporates, since one's intention suddenly extends beyond one's own actions, and beyond one's control over one's own body. If I literally intend that *we* do such-and-such, and this is not taken as expressing an order to you, as referring to a communicational or conventional device, something needs to be said about how such an intention determines *both* me and you to do such-and-such.

The formal analysis offered by Searle tries to answer the above as a question of intentional causation. Here are two examples: "[T]he puzzle is, how does this collective intention cause anything?" (1990/2002, 100); "How could *our* collective intentionality move *my* body?" (2007, 17, 2010, 50). The suggested solution is that although the intention is collective, it "bottoms out," from the individual's perspective, in singular acts. This is why, according to Searle, collective intentions can guide actions; this is what explains causation by we-intentions. Roughly, *only the goals are collective*, that is, beyond the individual; all one does is one's part as a means to achieve the goals. It is the collective profile of the goals that typifies the intentions. So, while we started with a difficulty expressed in terms of scope, that is, about *what* one can intend, we are given a solution expressed in terms of *how* one can intend.

This is seen in the formalization, where the only thing that changes in the collective case is the nature of the goal B, not the structure of the content of the intention. The move that multiplies the types of intentions and which makes collective intention *sui generis* was, as mentioned, already taken when operators such as "by means of" were represented not as part of the *content* of the intention, but as modifiers of the attitude kind itself. If one accepted the analysis of complex intentions presented in *Intentionality*, one might as well accept this one, in form. This will not, however, mitigate the offense of having *collective* goals modify the category of intention, even if one accepted intending-by-means-of in the original individual setting. This will be seen if we compare two translations of the formalization.

It would be mistaken to think that Searle is telling us that, when we act collectively, I intend that we do such and such, and you intend that we do such and such, and so on. This would mean that I can intend, in certain conditions, what I *could* not do by myself, and one would have to analyze away the eventual difficulties with such a formulation in terms of the scope of intention, to which one may add ordinary communicative coordination, justified expectations, and so on. What we are in fact told is that I *we-intend* to do such and such, where we-intention takes the by-means-of or by-way-of analysis, and the question of scope is hereby eliminated. Searle says, in effect, that if one intends *in the right way*, the question of scope does not arise.

Suppose for now that we can make sense of a notion of intending in a special way, and this could solve the "mystery" of acting collectively. Let us turn to the second question: Why would anyone think that this is the way things actually work? Searle's does not offer an independent argument in this case, but claims that the alternative theories have less to offer. One such alternative is the idea that psychological attributes can be directly and literally ascribed to groups. The point depends on one's views about the nature and implications of such attributions. But let us side with Searle for the time being and accept that, for example, an orchestra might play a symphony by acting masterfully, but an orchestra is not the kind of thing that intends.

The other alternative is reductivism, and this has been, as Searle observes, the default position: collective action is a genuine phenomenon, but its intentional aspects can be analyzed as *aggregates* of individual intentional aspects. Social synchrony is explained by complex architectures of regular beliefs, assumptions, expectations, intentions, desires, fears, and so on (embedded in a social and cultural matrix which is already in place). The symphony is successfully played because each member intends to play his or her part in the knowledge that others have similar attitudes, fearing collegial reproach, and so on. Searle needs to show that this will not do, while accepting that "there aren't any agents except individual human beings, and somehow intentional causation has to work through them and only through them" (1990/2002, 100).

Resisting reductive analyses in this case is understandable, at least if we take seriously the familiar *feel* of seamless social interaction. In the social sciences, theorizing this resistance has been a foundational issue, one which continues to trouble the waters. The motivation Searle puts forward to move away from the default of reduction is centered on the notion of cooperation. The difficulties with his account are instructive in our context, given that the notion of cooperation also plays an important role in the empirical work discussed later in this chapter.

Searle claims that reductive analyses fail to specify sufficient conditions for collective intentions. Either, he argues, collective intentions are *built into* the notion of doing one's part of a collective action (since we are talking about doing one's part toward a *collective* goal), or the conditions for collective action will allow for counterexamples[10] in which groups of people act, but not collectively in the proper sense. The general problem, we are told, is this:

> The notion of a we-intention, of collective intentionality, implies the notion of *cooperation*. But the mere presence of I-intentions to achieve a goal which happens to be believed to be the same goal as that of other members of a group does not entail the presence of an intention to cooperate to achieve that goal. One can have a goal in the knowledge that others also have the same goal, and one can have beliefs and even mutual beliefs about the goal which is shared by the members of a group, without there being necessarily any cooperation among the members or any intention to cooperate among the members.
>
> (Searle 1990/2002, 95)

The problem with this claim is that it is circular, if an intention to cooperate is itself a collective intention. Alternatively, if an intention to cooperate is just an "I-intention," then sufficient conditions can be after all specified. Just add the required intention to cooperate. Searle cannot be suspected of ignoring such a simple point, so perhaps something else is aimed at. It remains nonetheless hard to understand what cooperation might mean in this context, a problem aggravated by later hesitations. Take, for example, what is, perhaps, the most important paragraph in the relevant CoSR chapter:

> There is a deep reason why collective intentionality cannot be reduced to individual intentionality. The problem with believing that you believe that I believe, etc., and you believing that I believe that I believe that you believe, etc., is that it does not add up to a sense of *collectivity*. [...] The crucial element in collective intentionality is a sense of doing (wanting, believing, etc.) something together, and the individual intentionality that each person has is derived *from* the collective intentionality that they share.
>
> (Searle 1995, 24–5)

This way of putting things is confusing if one considers that in CIaA Searle placed within the *non-intentional Background* a "sense of *us* as possible or actual collective agents" (1990/2002, 104). Whatever this "sense" may be, besides the intuitive appeal of the notion, if it is part of "the Background," then it can hardly be the "crucial element in collective intentionality," though it belongs to its conditions of possibility.

Also confusing is the phrasing used in SO. For example, we are told that:

> I have objected to [the reductive] analysis on the grounds that the way that the problem is posed reveals a fallacy. The fallacy is to suppose that, because all intentionality exists in the brains of human and animal individuals, that therefore it must always, in thoughts and utterances, take the grammatical form of the first person singular. There is no reason why you could not have intentionality in individual heads that took the form of the first person plural. I can have in my head and you can have in your head the answer to the question, What are we now doing? which is of the form, *We* are doing such and such. Where "doing such and such" involves doing something that is *essentially cooperative*.
>
> (Searle 2007, 12)

"Essentially cooperative" refers perhaps to actions that can *only* be performed by groups, such as playing a symphony (why use "essentially" otherwise?). But this again changes direction since the point was to analyze actions that are cooperative *simpliciter*, not essentially so, as indeed Searle's examples make clear. One was after an understanding of situations in which one may either act cooperatively *or not*. Roughly, this was because one hoped to capture what happened when one moved from acting alone to cooperation—while keeping all else equal. The point of the analysis, in such contexts, was to block the reduction of cooperative scenarios to familiar intentional elements, since the failure of reductivism was the only justification for introducing collective intentions to begin with.

Finally, in MSW, the case from CIaA is reiterated (Searle 2010, 47–58) with some additional comments, some of them quite puzzling. Again, the idea is that the presence of cooperation blocks reduction, but this idea gets a number of different expressions. First, Searle uses an example from CIaA, of business graduates who, *in mutual knowledge*, aim at the *common goal* of improving the world by being relentlessly selfish (they are disciples of a misunderstood Adam Smith). They will, of course, not cooperate, and Searle thinks this shows there is no collective intentionality in their case. If they made a *pact* to behave in the same manner, there would have been cooperation, therefore collective intentionality. The implication is, as per above, that common goals and mutual beliefs are not enough for genuine cooperation. Since in the formalization of collective intentions it is exactly the collective goals that make the difference, a supplementary *differentia* needs to be introduced. Searle's answer is to suggest that there is an *assumption* of cooperation "specified in the form of the collective intentionality" (2010, 53). In other words, "collective B" somehow implies that others are cooperating with the agent, not only that there is an overlap between goals. The *differentia*, now, switches from the intentions to the epistemic positioning of the actors (their relevant assumptions). To spell out what cooperation means, Searle introduces a representation of this kind of belief as part of his analysis of collective intention. The general form is:

Bel (my partner in the collective also has intentions-in-action of the form (ia collective B by means of singular A (this ia causes: A *content of A*, causes: B *content of B*))).

A few observations are in order. If cooperation dissolves into such reciprocal assumptions, then it cannot act as *differentia*. Indeed, it seems to become a vehicle of *reducing* collective intentions. The only element that is not reduced in the above intention + belief representation is "collective B." This is the route already described, where common goals typify intentions. What is more damaging is that one arrives at an analysis of collective action in terms of intentions *and beliefs*, after insisting that any such analysis would not do. Finally, the circularity mentioned before returns to the enterprise: whenever the question arises as to what justifies a non-reductive notion of collective intentionality, cooperation comes up. But when one asks what is meant by cooperation, one is referred back to collective intentions and beliefs.

A bit later in MSW a distinction is introduced between, on the one hand, collective intentionality in the strong sense of collective intentions, and, on the other hand, collective *recognition*, a lesser form of collective intentionality (e.g., we merely acknowledge the existence of a social institution). The difference is given in terms of there being a "collective intention to cooperate" (Searle 2010, 58) in the former case, but not in the latter. This indicates that there is an inherent instability in Searle's analysis. The claim just mentioned would mean that cooperation does *not* dissolve in reciprocal beliefs, nor does it enter the structure of collective intentions as an additional regular intention; it is already there in the collective form. This means it cannot be part of an analysis of collective intentions or of collective intentionality generally. We are back, in fact, to the hesitations about what is part of the Background and what part of the analysis proper.

The notion of collective intention, then, stands on an unconvincing manner of rejecting reductivism. Searle claims that all reductive attempts have counterexamples in which *something* (cooperation, intention to cooperate, feeling of collectivity) is missing. But we have seen that one can accept that all kinds of things need to be in place for cooperative action to be possible (roughly, what Searle calls "Background"), without thereby accepting that these conditions of possibility require the introduction of novel *psychological* categories, notably that of collective intention. Since no other example of collective intentionality is discussed in any detail, this latter notion remains at best vague. So, without denying the common reality of collective actions or their specific phenomenology, it makes little sense to accept Searle's conceptual apparatus as an analysis of an otherwise familiar kind of social happening. One can have an appreciation for the intuitive motivation for a theory without accepting the theory itself.

If we look further and consider the applicability of Searle's theory to empirical research in psychology, the conceptual difficulties with the notion of collective intention translate into problems with its operationalization. It is not at all clear why one would choose to operationalize a notion that does not have clear explanatory benefits. Even if there was a motivation to attempt operationalization, there is the difficulty of not knowing exactly *what* to translate into testable dimensions. Of course, Searle's hesitations can be leveled and his account can be seen as suggestive of a certain way of conducting empirical research—as we will see when discussing the hypotheses of Tomasello and colleagues—but this is not something which can be done with resources Searle himself offers. If it is done, it must be done from without, and with an independent justification.

Searle, let us remind ourselves when considering the usability of the notion of shared intentionality, offers only the following: first, a vague and unstable characterization of the relevant concepts; second, circularity when it comes to establishing a *differentia* for collective as opposed to regular intentions; third, a contrast between a formal, if unconvincing, treatment of collective *intentions*, and a liberal use of collective *intentionality*. The consequence is that operationalization cannot begin on such a foundation. Since the criteria for applying the concept of collective intentionality are not available (and if they just are the common criteria for cooperation, then the discussion is without object), one cannot arrive at a set of symptoms for the putative special mental apparatus at work in cooperative action. One does not know what to look for. We see cooperation around us, but this is not what we have been sent to look for.

We need to keep in mind also that Searle distributes freely collective intentionality to most social interactions and to the social animals (1995, 23, 2007, 13, 2010, 43). This may have some intuitive appeal, given perhaps by the idea that there is some special flavor to social synchrony in general. The problem is that this makes the notion suspicious for psychological theorizing. What plausibility could have any *psychological* reading of the claim that we share collective intentionality with the ants? For a psychological theory that looks for the roots of *characteristically* human traits, like language, morality, and institutions, Searle's approach seems distinctively unpromising. And this is precisely the kind of theory that Tomasello and colleagues have proposed. As we will see in the following, Rakoczy and Tomasello (2007) openly confronted this difficulty of translating Searle's account into a tenable psychological model with testable predictions, without however arriving at an acceptable solution.

VI

Michael Bratman's work on shared intention and shared action, like Searle's, has had an important influence on the research program of Tomasello and colleagues. There have been, in this program, a few recognizable attempts to operationalize the Bratmanian concept of shared intentionality (e.g., Tomasello et al. 2005; Moll and Tomasello 2007). It is then of some significance to have a good understanding of what Bratman proposes. The starting point is not, however, his work on group action and the mental states that underlie it, but his analysis of intention.

Bratman presented an extensive account of intention in his book *Intention, Plans, and Practical Reasoning* (1999d), which he continued with a number of further elaborations and expositions (see also Bratman 1992). The theory is situated well within the functionalist camp; it belongs, to be more precise, to the "platitude" variety of functionalism (Stich and Nichols 2003), which theorizes over the usual psychological concepts. Bratman notes that the common conception of practical reasoning and of ensuing rational action involves a notion of intention. He proposes to say what the notion is by asking what *roles* the mental states that fall under the concept play. The notion is to be made good by having it cover states that play a distinctive set of roles; this allows the concept of intention to make a distinctive explanatory contribution.

The core claim of this theory is that intentions are elements of hierarchical "partial plans." By keeping an eye on the reasonably transparent concept of planning, one can delineate a proper contour for the notion of intention. Planning takes time and energy (no "frictionless deliberators"), and, since such resources are always limited, plans must be arrived at in reasonable time and must not be abandoned easily. Planning requires a degree of stability over time, which is enforced by a series of constraints; this inertia of planning mirrors the intuitive understanding of intention as involving commitment. To return to a terminology that is shared by Searle and Bratman, the appeal to planning means that intention-in-action, the immediate intentional component of an action, is *not* the concept analyzed in this context. Plans sometimes conclude with actions, but they are neither instantaneous, not concomitant relative to acting. The notion of intention relevant here is, then, that of prior intention.

Inherent limitations in planning will also mean that plans remain at each moment partial or incomplete.[11] This is not damaging their role in controlling action over time since plans have a hierarchical structure. For example, means for achieving a certain subgoal can be filled in as one acts in the direction of achieving a major goal. Not everything has to be decided in advance. Stability, too, will be distributed hierarchically, with lesser elements being more open to change. Planning, characterized as such, is essential for coordination—of each individual on the longer term, and also of one individual with others.

Viewed from this angle, there is a division of labor in practical reasoning that justifies positing intentions as independent mental states. Bratman goes against the Davidsonian analysis of practical reasoning as weighting of belief-desire reasons (Bratman 1999a, Davidson 1963/2001). Intention and desire are both pro-attitudes, but there are distinct roles to be played by each. One tier of practical reasoning is indeed Davidsonian in the above sense: it involves the evaluation of motivations consisting in beliefs and desires. But, according to Bratman, there is a second layer that acts as a framework for the first. The introduction of this supplementary stratum is based on the idea that practical reasoning is constrained in terms of *what appears at each moment as a problem* for deliberation—there is (prior) selection of problems; and the process is constrained historically by what was already decided and by commitments that are already in place, that is, by prior intentions.

The following overall picture of intentions results: they are pro-attitudes distinguished from desires (but also choices, etc.) by their ability to control conduct,[12] by their stability, and by their forming of hierarchical structures—partial plans—subject to requirements of consistency and coherence. These features allow them to play their characteristic roles within practical reasoning: they select problems for further practical reasoning, allow for long-term intelligent action, and make possible intra- and interpersonal coordination.

Before moving on to Bratman's views on shared intentionality, let us stress what the theory sketched above does. It looks at what it takes to be a shared, unelaborated conception of human reasoning and acting—that is, *typical, mature* reasoning and action—and then it offers an analysis of the notion of intention that is allegedly a part of that conception. It does *not* question the validity of the common conception. It does *not* attempt to extend it to atypical or marginal situations.[13] This is the perspective from which the notion of shared intention is to be seen.

Let us now consider how a conception of shared intention grows out that of intention *simpliciter*. A selection of Bratman's work on collective actions and the kind of reasoning that they involve was published in his collection *Faces of Intention* (1999b). There is also a significant stream of more recent texts (e.g., Bratman 2010a, 2010b). The starting point of this project has been the idea that agency can be "unified" and "coordinated" not only within a given individual, but also among individuals. This much is similar with what Searle proposes, and indeed constitutes a point of wide agreement in the field. The substantial and debated issue is how to conceive of the nature of such a unified but trans-individual agency. Bratman's contribution is centered on the notion of shared intention. Together with some less significant gestures toward "common knowledge," this is the fundamental element of Bratman's account of shared *intentionality*.

Searle provides an instructive background against which Bratman's proposal can be clearly distinguished. Searle's core notion, let us recall, is that of we-intention, which is a specific kind of mental attitude attributable to an individual, even if that individual was alone (and delusional). Bratman's notion of shared intention has *neither* of these characteristics. A shared intention is not a novel, distinctive kind of attitude, for it is not an attitude to begin with, but an aggregate of regular attitudes (essentially individual intentions and beliefs)—a "state of affairs," as Bratman himself puts it (1999f, 111, 123). Moreover, given the way the structure of the aggregate is specified, no single individual can form a shared intention. Shared intentions are emergent *group* phenomena.

Now, this is not a straightforward concept of intention, or a natural extension of such a concept. Shared intention is, at least at a first glance, quite different from intention proper, even if Bratman's reconstruction of individual intention is correct. To call such a structure intention needs justification, and this is given on the lines of the planning theory of intention. From a planning point of view, the intentional actions of groups, under certain conditions, bear significant *analogies* to those of individuals. They are, for example, coordinated across periods of time, they track goals, and there is commitment to reach goals. Such features, if any, justify attributions of intention, to the point that it matters less that such an intention does not fit the regular practice of conceiving intentions as psychological phenomena that, ultimately as it were, can only by attributed to individuals. Thus, there is a place for a notion of intention at this level, even if there is no group mind that entertains an intention separate from those of the individual members of the group. As Bratman puts it, his approach is individualistic *and reductive* (1999f, 108, 129). His effort is concentrated accordingly on specifying the constitutive elements of shared intention and their interrelations. Such a specification is meant to contribute to the understanding of group action.

There are some variations in the way Bratman describes the functional architecture of shared intentions. For example, an emphasis on the normative aspects involved in the construct is clearly visible in the more recent texts. I take it to be both methodologically more adequate (Tomasello and colleagues refer mostly to the earlier texts) and charitable (their normative load makes the recent elaborations unlikely candidates for operationalization in developmental research) to take the more modest formulations as paradigm, while at the same time noting their later developments.[14] Here is such a formulation from "Shared Intention" (Bratman 1999f). We have a shared intention that we, say, go hiking together *if*:[15]

1 (a) I intend that we go hiking and (b) you intend that we go hiking.
2 I intend that we go hiking in accordance with and because of 1a, 1b, and meshing subplans of 1a and 1b; you intend that we go hiking in accordance with and because of 1a, 1b, and meshing subplans of 1a and 1b.
3 1 and 2 are common knowledge between us.

This construction, as advertised, lists a number of individual intentions and epistemic states (to the extent that "common knowledge" allows such an analysis), and a scheme of their relations. (1) presents the most difficult conceptual challenge for the theory, while (2) requires most unfolding.

The problem with (1) is one we have already encountered. The intentions it mentions have bizarre contents; expressing them that way does not sound right. To repeat the point made when discussing Searle's notion of collective intention, at least on the common understanding, I can only intend my own actions. So how can I intend that *we* do something? Note that one is not after situations in which one group acts under the (despotic) control of one individual, but after situations in which agency is "unified" freely and, ideally, in a spontaneous manner. Bratman's response is that the notion of me intending that we do X is salvageable, since I can include in my plans what you will do—indeed, I may *have* to do so in certain cases. In the relevant (~cooperative) situations, this does not mean that my control literally extends over your own actions—your agency is not bypassed (you can still decide to opt out)—but only that you are reasonably *predictable*,[16] so that I can plan around your reasonably predictable decisions and actions. Moreover, I can take steps to increase your predictability through communication and other means. Bratman insists that the fact that I can count on you in intending that we act together should not be conceived of as a background condition for my intention, or as making my intention conditional (I'll do it if you do it). The correct reading should stress that it is part of the *content* of my intention that its achievement *goes through* your doing certain things intentionally.

It is (2) that spells out this latter element, the intertwining of intentions. The "meshing," as Bratman calls it, happens as one goes down the hierarchy of planning. To speak of shared intention, there has to be a certain *deliberate harmonization* in terms of how the actors propose to act on their individual intentions. This need not cover all the depth of the hierarchy—indeed, it *could* not, since at every moment plans are unsaturated or partial—but the process should indicate some active or deliberate preservation of coherence. As we plan along, we try synchronizing our moves, and our willingness to do so should also cover some counterfactual territory.

The meshing condition is easier to grasp than the symmetry imposed on the efficacy of the intentions specified by (1). If I intend to raise my arm, a common story (which includes Searle's views) about the reflexivity of intention would go, then I intend to raise-it-because-of-this-very-intention. But if we look at (2), we see that there is an extension: an intention of a different individual comes to have an instrumental role in my acting on my own intention. Again, this is not something in the background of my coming to have this intention and of acting on it. It is part of my intention. What I am sensitive to, to put it in another manner, is what the other individual intends, not her standing in some sense in my way. Perhaps the clearest way to see what Bratman wants from this requirement is his insistence that the link between the agents is not merely *cognitive*. The common knowledge or "cognitive glue" added by (3) is not enough; shared intention should also include a kind of interconnectedness that only the *commitments* manifest in intention can generate. Not only should I know what you are about to—in making my mind about what I myself am about to, I should be committed to having significant parts be up to you.

The common knowledge condition (3) has its own share of complications, but, given the aims of this chapter, I will not discuss them. One thing however is worth emphasizing. Shared intention is a psychological phenomenon only in the sense of being *conditional* on the presence of certain mental states in those involved: multiple individuals will have to intend and believe regular stuff. Shared intention is not itself such a state, an extra bit of the stuff. What is common knowledge between the participants, then, is the presence of the constitutive *individual* mental states and their relations. There is a gradation of complexity in moving from individual to group agency, but no additional understanding of things mental must be involved.

To conclude the discussion of the notion of shared agency let us summarize the roles that, according to Bratman, are performed by structures such as that described above. (It is after all the functional niche that motivates the introduction of the notion of shared intention.) The roles are primarily varieties of coordination—in action, but also in planning, and in the dynamics of roles. Moreover, such a structure acts as a framework for bargaining. Bratman's argument, in brief, is that there are "states of affairs" which in collective action play roles that are similar to those played by intention in individual action. Such shared intentions are constituted by suitable *patterns* of intentions and beliefs of individuals, and are the unifying force of group agency.

Bratman's analysis of collective actions and his extension on functionalist lines of the notion of intention is thought-provoking. He proposes a perspective from which it seems that an analogy between individual and group action in terms of intention becomes possible. His willingness to bite the bullet and talk about shared intention not as a thing—*a fortiori*, not as a mental thing—but as a relatively stable pattern in the dynamics of groups is also a stance about the interpretation of folk psychological notions and their use in further theorizing.

Bratman exemplifies the attempt of detaching the use of concepts such as *intention* from the assumption that the core naive psychological notions inherently reify, that they should be understood as referring to entities. That one *tries* to detach the relevant notions from regular use could itself be seen as symptomatic of the view that, usually, psychological talk *is* talk of entities. If one does not start by, as it were, mentalizing the psychological, then one would have no need to de-mentalize it for further use. This point remains moot, but even if we restrict our attention to the collective intentionality literature, we will find that the idea of de-mentalizing whatever is collective, shared, or joint in the intentionality of groups has found adepts. David Velleman (1997), for example, follows a different route to arrive at a notion of intention that needs not be "psychological." This kind of tactical analysis of patterns of interaction in social contexts, for all its problems, seems more promising than looking for some elusive bio-psychological essence of sociality. In this case we may have a passable candidate concept of shared intention and a procedure—exploitation of functional analogies—that could be tried on the other attitudes. This may justify a more general notion of shared intentionality

One needs to note, however, that it is not clear how this conception will be particularly relevant for developmental psychology. We should remind ourselves of the fact that the theory is designed to account for the dynamics of group agency in the case of competent adults acting in non-institutional, non-hierarchical contexts; it is a theory of "modest sociality," as Bratman calls it, but not so modest as to be applicable to rudimentary social interaction. Even if we suppose that the theory can also be applied to the quite different dynamics of social interaction in developmental situations, this application should be compatible with the central observation made above: ascribing shared intention to a number of individuals captures a certain *arrangement* of ordinary, non-collective attitudes manifested by the individuals that form the group; if one thinks that a psychological notion must thereby be mentalistic, then shared intention does not even count as psychological. It is not a mental faculty; it is not a property of individuals in any sense; it makes no sense to say that it evolved in the same sense as opposable thumbs evolved.

To sum up what the two last sections did in terms of evaluating the applicability of Searle's and Bratman's treatments of collective intentionality to developmental psychological research, we find ourselves in the following situation: Searle's account is unusable due to internal instability; we have a number of alternatives to Searle's views, of which I explored the one which seems the clearest. Bratman's initial analysis should, for example, be more promising for empirical research than a heavily normative theory, such as that proposed by Margaret Gilbert (2009). This suggests that we may use Bratman as background when we evaluate, next, the claims of Tomasello and colleagues.

The point, I want to emphasize, is not to determine whether the way psychologists talk about shared intentionality matches the details of a particular philosophical point of view. (By now, it clearly doesn't.) It helps to keep the details and the motives of what Bratman is doing in mind, but what matters is the general approach. What we are after is loose conceptual compatibility. We are after such relative consonance because the kind of approach Bratman proposes seems, if one is charitable, reasonably intelligible in its original context. One may ask whether it might also make sense elsewhere.

VII

We are now in a position to return to the research program of Tomasello & Co. in order to complete the sketch I gave of it earlier and to reflect on what it has done with the concept of shared intentionality. This notion seems to have begun its career in the Max Planck group with the attempts of Hannes Rakoczy to apply elements of John Searle's theory of intentionality, including his conception of irreducible "we-intentions" as the basis of collective action, to developmental psychological problems. This effort is one of the theoretical pillars of Rakoczy's unpublished PhD dissertation, *The Development of Performing and Understanding Pretend Play: A Cultural Learning Perspective* (2003). Its conceptual apparatus then finds expression in a first important paper, coauthored by Rakoczy and Tomasello (2003). Some of the papers that followed (e.g., Rakoczy and Tomasello 2007, Tomasello, Carpenter, and Liszkowski 2007) echoed this Searlean influence, Tomasello's book-length treatment of the development of human communicative abilities (2008) being an example of mixed influences. An important moment was the BBS paper coauthored by Tomasello and colleagues (2005), which signaled a branching of the interpretative dimension of the project. In this case, the main philosophical influence is Bratman's account of cooperative action, specifically a version of his set of criteria for joint intention and action. Felix Warneken's unpublished doctoral dissertation, *The Origins of Helping and Cooperation* (2006), and papers from this period (e.g. Rakoczy 2008a, 2008b, Tomasello and Moll 2010) are some other instructive examples of using the adaption of Bratman's criteria pioneered in the 2005 BBS paper for developmental research. Traces of this approach, especially in what regards the significance of role reversal, joint goals and commitments (see below), are also found in the aforementioned 2008 book by Tomasello, and in the same author's similar volume *Why We Cooperate* (2009). Bratman's analysis maintains a similar influence in Tomasello's recent natural histories (2016, 2014), but it is only declaratively included in his more ambitious ontogeny volume (2019).

While this research program expanded (and as it was challenged), the imports from the philosophy of action diversified, and there has been a further focus on understanding the normative dimension of cooperation at early ages (e.g., Rakoczy, Warneken, and Tomasello 2008, Rakoczy 2008a, Gräfenhain et al. 2009, Schmidt and Tomasello 2012, Tomasello and Vaish 2013). This can be seen, in its more recent embodiments, in the context of the current popularity of naturalistic-evolutionary accounts of the fact the humans live in worlds set on moral and epistemic norms. In addition to Searle's thoughts about the nature of institutional reality, or to Bratman's discussion of commitment, some other positions, such as Margaret Gilbert's view about obligations inherent in joint action, thus came to inform the work of Tomasello and colleagues. While acknowledging all these ramifications, I will focus on the influences I have described earlier. This is a way to keep things manageable, but, as I tried to suggest at the end of the previous section, it is also principled.

Before we look at samples of the relevant material, a few general remarks are in order. The justification for paying attention to this particular theory is, in one vulgar word, size. A concept which is not properly explained, that of shared intentionality, became the *bon mot* in a way of talking that extends from unpublished doctoral dissertations, to countless research papers, chapters, books, keynote addresses, and popular media appearances (for an early example, see Scobel and Tomasello 2008). This is indeed much ado. Influence aside, two other things should be noted. First, as I stressed earlier in the book, what I criticize is bad *philosophy*; not a particular group of scientists. The way the Max Planck psychologists have chosen to conceptualize their numerous findings seems detrimental, first of all, to *their own* theorizing. The critical dimension of what I am proposing is to show that the reliance on the dubious concept of shared intentionality has little justification. If there is a constructive part to what is done here, it is to suggest that psychologists *need not* talk like this. Second, I want to counter the idea that once again hard scientific work has to endure philosophical hair splitting. We needed to see what philosophical discussion there is on the relevant notions, since that is the only kind of detailed discussion there is which does not take for granted that shared intentionality is a (mental) thing. Moreover, the two philosophers discussed earlier in this chapter embody two very different ways of thinking about the subject. One has to keep these differences in mind not because one would want scientists to solve quirky philosophical disagreements, and not because psychologists should keep exact track of what philosophers think, but because psychologists, too, need to keep good track of what they themselves think. What is confronted, then, is philosophy as practiced by some psychologists, and as manifest in a manner of presenting their empirical research.

Another element that we need to keep in mind is the "general geography" of the theory we are discussing. The background against which the notion of shared intentionality began to play an explanatory role in this area of developmental psychology is constituted by a founding question and by certain constant preferences in structuring one's research program which survive the model's details, changes, and even putative counterexamples. The founding question, as I have already mentioned, is one of historical proportions: how to conceive of human nature in such a way as to explain the striking differences between humans and intelligent social animals in a framework that also takes into account the natural history of our species. The focus of the research program in question is on communicative and cooperative abilities at very young ages (the first few years of life), the guiding idea being that such abilities underlie all the distinctive human accomplishments: language, morality, and a society with institutions.

In terms of preferences in constructing a model for the development of these abilities, the choices of Tomasello and colleagues in structuring their explanations have had the tendency to remain constant even when the conceptual architecture of, and the putative evidence for, the theory changed. The most important seem to be the following: (i) there is a discontinuity between human and animal communicative and cooperative endowments, and this gap is essentially the result of a discrete adaptation that occurred in recent evolutionary time; (ii) this adaptation can be described in the jargon of psychological competence; that is, the effect of the adaptation was that our ancestors became better at manipulating mental states of various complexities, and also better at reasoning about such states; they became (better) naive psychologists—a stronger interpretation would suggest that mentalistic chess was what the adaptation was *for*; (iii) small children typically develop the rudiments of the relevant normal adult abilities at very early (pre- and proto-linguistic) ages, and one can theorize about these emerging skills in roughly the same explanatory language as in the adult case ("rich," as opposed to "lean," explanation).[17]

Within this perimeter, Tomasello and colleagues have attempted in the last decades to explain the origins, architecture, and the first stages in the development of the extraordinary psychosocial abilities that people normally have, and which their ape cousins lack. This is a generic specification of what the research program tries to accomplish under the conceptual constraints mentioned above. *Some* decisive (and, in an admittedly loose sense, discrete) psychological breakthrough is the cornerstone of the model. In this context, the notion of shared intentionality has come to designate such a turning point.

The approach of the Max Planck group has been based on systematic comparative studies, which is natural, given that their main question is one of origins in evolution and in ontogeny. A small part of these studies focuses on the differences between typical and autistic patterns of development. Perhaps the best represented are the studies that compare the abilities of children and those of great apes (chimpanzees in most cases). Yet another kind of research explores differences between children in different age groups. All this work is done with an eye to paradigmatic adult abilities, as it will become clearer with a few examples.

Consider the following situation. An adult and a child play in a room. Suddenly, from behind a curtain a puppet appears. The child shows surprise and points, alternating looks between the puppet and the adult. The child seems to like it when the adult alternates looks and manifests emotion too. And the child seems happy with just that; she does not seem to require the puppet (Tomasello, Carpenter, and Liszkowski 2007). Take another case. The child and the adult clean up a room by putting toys in a basket. The adult holds the basket and the child picks up toys. Then the adult is giving the basket to the child and picks up a toy. The roles are switched. The child reacts by holding the basket so that the adult can place the toy there (Moll and Tomasello 2007). Or this one. The child and the adult take turns at playing with some toys. Then the adult suddenly stops participating in the game. The child tries to reengage the adult (the child gestures, hands objects) and sometimes performs the adult's missing turn of the game (Warneken, Chen, and Tomasello 2006). A bit more laterally, consider the situation when an adult is looking for an object necessary to complete an action, for example, a hole-puncher to be used on a sheet of paper. The child observes the scene and helpfully points to the object the adult is looking for (Liszkowski et al. 2006).

These observations in some of the founding studies in this "tradition" are meant to show that even pre- and proto-verbal children are communicative, like to do things with others, are flexible about what roles they play in the activity, and are helpful. Given such results, some questions seem to follow naturally: what explains the character of the children's behavior in these situations? What should we say about their understanding of the actions they perform, alone or with others? And what of their understanding of their own, and others', mental states? If agency is unified in some sense in these interactions, how is the constitution of this union to be read?

Questions like the above give a first specification of the explanatory needs the theory we are discussing proposes to answer. A second specification can be given in terms of inter-species differences. The comparative studies offer a series of systematic counterparts that are supposed to shed phylogenetic light on the ontogenetic points of controversy. To keep things in the concrete, in the kind of situations exemplified above, apes—even human-raised, adult apes—would *not* behave like children. Certainly, in this context, it is important to say why this is so. The claim we need to evaluate is that these findings are to be explained in terms of shared intentionality.

Since the corpus of publications we deal with has grown large with time, let me note a limitation and then select a few focal points for what follows. The limitation is that I will not discuss what might be called the first version of the psychological theory of shared intentionality. This is the theory exemplified by a paper by Tomasello and Rakoczy (2003); it proposes a distinction between shared and collective intentionality which is based on the Searlean distinction between social and institutional facts. This approach has been, as far as I can say, dropped. As for the focus, I will discuss next only two early papers that I take to be representative (Tomasello et al. 2005; Rakoczy and Tomasello 2007). The choice illustrates the persistence of the Searlean outlook and the misunderstanding of Bratman's views. Both problems seem endemic in the relevant writings of the Max Planck group from this period.

"Understanding and Sharing Intentions: The Origins of Cultural Cognition" (Tomasello et al. 2005) has been a turning point in the explanatory discourse used by these psychologists. While the Searlean vocabulary had already been adopted, the previous landmark paper (Tomasello and Rakoczy 2003) did not part with the idea that the human developmental path was unique due first of all to the understanding of others as intentional agents. This had been the key concept of Max Plank psychology in the 1990s (Tomasello, Kruger, and Ratner 1993, Tomasello 1999), and it certainly was *not* a concept of the "sharing" variety. What the 2003 *Mind & Language* paper did was to superimpose a series of notions from Searle's social ontology on the existing agenda. The already mentioned attempt to draw a distinction between shared and collective intentionality as some sort of Piagetian distinction of developmental stages that would also mirror some of the implications of Searle's distinction between social and institutional facts injected ambiguity into the text and bought little in return. The 2005 BBS paper solves at least some of this ambiguity by breaking with the agenda.

What changes is the conceptualization of the difference between human and ape social abilities. The apes too seem to have an understanding of others as intentional agents driven by goals. So this cannot be what separates us from the animals. The solution is to reconstruct the concept of shared intentionality as a new dividing line by building into it *more* than understanding of others as intentional; this understanding will still be required, but the profile of the concept will be determined by other features. Let us try to see what these features are.

Keeping to the landscape pictured in the first part of this chapter, the BBS paper can be considered an essay in Bratmanian psychology. It starts with a general view about what acting intentionally is which makes use of the planning theory of intention developed by Bratman. Given this general outlook, it tries to specify a hierarchy of understanding of actions. Its three steps are the understanding, first, of animacy; secondly, of the pursuit of goals; and finally of the selection of plans. The time horizon for these accomplishments is the age of about 15 months. Once this hierarchical structure is climbed, the argument goes, children will be in a position to engage in shared intentionality, since they would have understood enough about other minds to successfully manipulate them. They would have taken, in other words, the decisive step in becoming social creatures in the specifically human sense.

The concept of shared intentionality, we are told, "refers to collaborative interactions in which participants have a shared goal (shared commitment) and coordinated action roles for pursuing that shared goal" (Tomasello et al. 2005, 680). Those involved, moreover, need to be

> engaged with one another in a particular way. Specifically, the goals and intentions of each interactant must include as content something of the goals and intentions of the other.
>
> (Tomasello et al. 2005, 680)

Recognizably, this is inspired by Bratman's conception, as the authors themselves make explicit. The profile of shared intentionality, then, is given on the lines of Bratmanian shared intention: things are put together in the right way; the right way is analyzed in terms of the *content* of individual intentions. This is not, however, the notion the authors actually put to work. Throughout the text—and this will be a constant in the corpus—shared intention is said to bifurcate into cognitive-interpretative and *motivational* elements (indeed the emphasis is often on the latter). We are told, for example, that human beings are uniquely motivated "to share psychological states" (Tomasello et al. 2005, 688). "Motivations for shared intentionality" will in the next years become a trope in this body of literature. Such an approach presents a serious structural problem.

Surely, Tomasello and colleagues are right that something on the lines of "intention-reading" must be a part of an analysis of the notion of shared intentionality they present on Bratmanian lines. One has to understand what others intend in order to enter in the complex game of deliberately distributing and adjusting control over group action. But this is not what the shared element consists in; what is shared has to do with the *content and interplay* of intentions. This analysis has little to do with motivation, a motivation to share psychological states here included. One could, for example, understand quite well what others are up to and even interact cooperatively with them while entertaining a *diversity* of motivations. Human children may be much nicer than their ape counterparts, much more disposed or motivated to pay attention to others and their wants. This may very well be a fact about their psychological makeup. But the *interlocking* of mental states putatively at work in "collaborative interactions" is not a fact about the psychology of any of the *individuals* involved. Either we keep to a concept of shared intentionality based on the description of the "meshing" of states, as Bratman's calls is, or we give the notion a motivational reading. The two are not compatible. Shared intentionality as a pattern of group dynamics *presupposes* motivational elements in the individual involved; it is not itself a kind of motivation.

The curious situation of the BBS text is that it struggles to adapt the structural view imported from Bratman, while being continuously inclined to mentalize the view—that is, in a sense, to give it a Searlean reading. This is quite clear in the use the authors give to the criteria Bratman proposes for what he calls "shared collaborative agency" (SCA) (Bratman 1999b). We need to note from the beginning that SCA is *a more demanding* notion than shared intention. It presupposes shared intentions, but it has its eyes on the "joint actions" that shared intentions make possible. As Bratman makes clear, his analysis is not only of the *attitudes* that need to be present in SCA (essentially, the intention + belief structure of shared intentions we discussed previously), but also of the other elements that must be present in order to arrive at a diagnosis of SCA: the fact that the action takes place (it is not merely intended), and the fact that there is mutual responsiveness in action (and not just in the meshing of plans). This is how Bratman presents the structure:

(1)(a)(i) I intend that we J.

(1)(a)(ii) I intend that we J in accordance with and because of meshing subplans of (1)(a)(i) and (1)(b)(i).

(1)(b)(i) You intend that we J.

(1)(b)(ii) You intend that we J in accordance with and because of meshing subplans of (1)(a)(i) and (1)(b)(i).

(1)(c) The intentions in (1)(a) and in (1)(b) are not coerced by the other participant.

(1)(d) The intentions in (1)(a) and in (1)(b) are minimally cooperatively stable.

(2) It is common knowledge between us that (1).

[…]

For cooperatively neutral J, our J-ing is a SCA if and only if

(A) we j,

(B) we have the attitudes specified in (1) and (2), and

(C) (B) leads to (A) by way of mutual responsiveness (in the pursuit of our J-ing) of intention and in action. (1999e, 105–6)

And this is how this structure is represented by Tomasello and colleagues:

> According to Bratman (1992), joint cooperative activities, as he calls them, have three essential characteristics that distinguish them from social interaction in general (here modified slightly): (1) the interactants are mutually responsive to one another, (2) there is a shared goal in the sense that each participant has the goal that we (in mutual knowledge) do X together, and (3) the participants coordinate their plans of action and intentions some way down the hierarchy— which requires that both participants understand both roles of the interaction (*role reversal*) and so can at least potentially help the other with his role if needed.
>
> (2005, 680)

The point here is not to ask whether the latter represents the former well. The question is one of emphasis. Responsiveness in action and role-reversal are prominent in the criteria presented by Tomasello and colleagues. But these elements are not part of the original analysis that deals with the *attitudes* involved in SCA. Of course, one should not be forced to follow a particular proposal to the letter. But let us recall how we arrived here: the promising feature of Bratman's analyses is that they might remove the putative strangeness of saying that people can put their minds together when in social contexts. He focuses on social *action*, therefore, on the concept of intention. Tomasello and colleagues, on the other hand, are after a psychological dividing line. They think the notion of shared intentionality can have such a reading. If we model Tomasello's notion of shared intentionality on Bratman's concept of shared intention then the result is arguably dubious, but this is not the main problem in this context. Rather, when we get to the details of what Tomasello and colleagues think they can operationalize from Bratman's analysis, they *switch* from the analysis of shared *intention* to one of shared *activities*, and they focus on exactly those elements that are largely *irrelevant* for the meshing of intentions.

Let us look at the metric applied to the evidence, as this should make the criticism above clearer. Once the criteria for joint activities are laid down, Tomasello and colleagues claim that they can be met once children are able to participate in "collaborative engagement" (2005, 682–3). The kinds of "engagements" the children are said to be capable of mirror the hierarchy of understanding mentioned above. The supposition is that an understanding of planning and the choice of plans amounts to a sophisticated understanding of intention, and that allows the child to become a more active and flexible participant in increasingly complex interactions. This is collaborative engagement. Such interactions are to be seen through the lens of SCA. Finally, this is taken as an argument to the effect that shared intentionality must be what permits the child to be so engaged, since shared intentionality—in the form of shared intention—is after all the characteristic element of SCA.

What is the evidence that one may indeed apply the notion of SCA to what children do? Here, responsiveness and role reversal come into play. For example, one of the important pieces of evidence in the 2005 paper was a study by Malinda Carpenter and colleagues (Carpenter, Tomasello, and Striano 2005) which showed that when a child plays with an adult even some one-year-old children could take on the other role if the adult switched. There are a number of things to say if one supposes this could count as evidence for SCA. First, it says little about the claimed meshing of intentions in the relevant sense; the context is just too limited and dissimilar when compared to the original examples. Second, and this is fundamental, even if one proved that SCA can be applied to such interactions, what would be thereby *gained*? Not the psychologically novel capacity Tomasello and colleagues are looking for. To the extent that the psychologists have a point, the point is not about shared intentionality and SCA, but about, for example, the effects of understanding complex intentions, or of "collaborative engagement." In a sense, the fact that the child can engage in something like SCA is, if established, quite striking, and therefore exactly what needs to be explained; it cannot at the same time constitute the *explanans*.

Perhaps the prospects are a bit better with another category of studies, which explore the fact that when an adult and a child play together, the child will try to *reengage* the adult if she suddenly stops participating (e.g., Warneken, Chen, and Tomasello 2006). The interpretation is that a "shared goal" has been established, and that what the child does is an expression of the pressure to maintain that goal. Again, with all the charitable assumptions one may make, it is hard to see what shared intentionality adds to this discussion, if it is not given the *motivational* reading mentioned above. Suppose, however, that we assimilate shared goals as presumably established by this series of experiments to shared intentions as described by the authors themselves. We have the same situation as above; what controls and thus explains what the children do is not the "shared goal," but the fact that the child wants some things and that he understands some aspects of what the other is doing. He satisfies the psychological conditions for shared intention, let us say, but the explanation would still have to focus on the way these conditions are satisfied, for example, on the extraordinary interpretative achievement of the child. This way of telling the story is *too* charitable in the sense that it is already at a large distance from the story the authors themselves tell, and from the way their central concepts are introduced.

One should not obscure, with inflationary suppositions, the fact that the data presented is not evidence for shared intention, if one takes what the authors themselves say about the concept seriously. Neither should one ignore the fact that even some of the evidence said to motivate the analysis in the first place is stretched beyond the reasonable. For example, interpreting the results of the "rational imitation" series of studies—(a paper by Gergely, Bekkering and Király 2002) is mentioned in this context—as showing that children understand the choice of plans is doubtful, if by this one implies that the view of planning agency on which Bratman's concept of (shared) intention is build can be applied to the results. That in both cases one talks of plans is a verbal similarity, nothing more.

What we witness here is the already mentioned tendency to force a Searlean (mentalizing) reading onto the structural analysis taken from Bratman. We move next to a text in which this tendency manifests itself fully when Rakoczy and Tomasello confront Searle in "The Ontogeny of Social Ontology: Steps to Shared Intentionality and Status Functions" (2007). The critical thread of this paper is what matters in our context. The main worry of Rakoczy and Tomasello concerns "Searle's promiscuous attributions of collective intentionality" (2007, 114). If Searle is ready to go as far as talking about collective intentionality in social insects (1999, 121), then clearly one cannot use a concept advertised as similar to Searle's in order to account for the differences between humans and chimpanzees. But the strategy Rakoczy and Tomasello use to rescue Searle from his promiscuity is strange—and telling. They propose to show why humans are unique in their cooperative, communicative, and social learning skills, and that this uniqueness is captured in the by-now-known terms of shared intentionality. To do this, the authors tell us that they will use "either Searle's own definitions and concepts explicitly, or reasonable extensions or operationalizations of them" (Rakoczy and Tomasello 2007, 114). This does not happen, and, if the above discussion of Searle is even roughly correct, it *could* not happen. What happens instead is that Rakoczy and Tomasello use their own reading of Bratman's analysis of SCA as an instrument of weakening Searle's claims. Here is an informative excerpt:

> Tomasello et al. (2005) recently adapted this analysis for interpreting preverbal collaboration, attempting to operationalize Bratman's criteria. First, if in collaboration the participants pursue a shared we-intention, then if one

participant simply stops doing her part, the other(s) should be displeased with this and attempt to *reengage* her in the joint project. Second, if in pursuing their shared goal the participants grasp the roles that each participant plays (including themselves), then they should be able over repeated enactments of the joint activity to *reciprocate and reverse roles* as needed.

(Rakoczy and Tomasello 2007, 116—emphasis added)

The problem with this manner of approaching the issue is that the difference between Searle's views and Bratman's is not one of strength or scope. I have tried to make it clear that the disagreement is conceptual; the two views place the notion of shared/collective intention in different categories. It is not as if Bratman's structural analysis presents us with a somewhat *less* primitive notion of collective intention. The structural analysis is not of an individual's psychological property to begin with, *a fortiori* not of one that can be more or less primitive, species specific, and so on.

Rakoczy and Tomasello are aware of this issue. They claim that they agree with Searle that necessary and sufficient conditions for collective intentions cannot be given in terms of regular attitudes, but at the same time they criticize Searle for blackboxing the notion of we-intention. The criticism is, however, tributary to the misunderstanding described in the previous paragraph. Bratman's analysis is one given in terms of sufficient conditions, but not sufficient conditions for the presence of a mental property in an individual. That aside, the conditions that Rakoczy and Tomasello use to distinguish between coordination and collective intentionality proper are conditions that are in no sense operationalizations of Searle's views and, more importantly, cannot be simply *added* to these views to make them more precise or adequate. There is no connection between role reversal, reengaging reluctant partners, or social pointing on the one hand, and the autonomous category of collective intentions-in-action that Searle talks about on the other. What would be needed is a *trace* of switching mental gears between intending and we-intending, and one may safely wonder whether there is any such trace to be had.

The thing to keep in mind here is the attractiveness of Searle's intuitive approach for the psychologists. Searle claims that there is something *special* about minds—about what goes on *inside* each individual head—that makes seamless social interaction possible. This matches the general quest of Tomasello and colleagues. They, too, think in terms of there being something special about human minds—some feature inherited from an evolutionary breakthrough that explains our extraordinary sociocultural achievements in one broad move. But since Searle is not interested in offering clues about how to *test* for the presence of collective intentionality, the psychologists seem to have thought that an analysis which specifies criteria, as that of Bratman, can perform the required work. It matters perhaps less that they went for the irrelevant elements of the analysis. The main error is that they have ignored what the analysis is an analysis *of*—what it was meant to explain, and in what terms.

Let me conclude this section by pointing to a reply that Tomasello and Moll (Tomasello and Moll 2011) wrote in response to comments somewhat similar to those I made here (the comments came from Hans Bernhard Schmid). The critique in that case pointed out that *none* of the philosophical conceptions of collective intentionality that Tomasello and colleagues appeal to (Searle's, Bratman's, Gilbert's) are adequate for what they are doing. The response to this criticism went as follows:

> We do not consider ourselves compelled either to refute each of these conceptions, or to have to choose between them, because the views represented there can be used adequately in different parts of the theory of evolution and development. [...] Bratman's account, to our mind, is especially well suited to describe the early stages of this development [of collective intentionality—my note], when individuals face the challenge of understanding each other in a recursive way. All things considered, Searle is right in the assumption that, in the life of contemporary adults, the collective intentions which are constitutive for norms and institutions appear *qua primitivum*, and one does not depend on the individual recursive mental back-and-forth. In any case, considering the decisive goal of reconstructing evolutionary and ontogenetic sequences, we hope to be able to combine different theoretical pieces eclectically, rather than choosing a winner in the debate about the appropriate conception of collective intentionality.
>
> (Tomasello and Moll 2011, 164–5)[18]

There is nothing essentially new in this reply. For example, the idea that Searle's conception of primitive collective intentions can be justified at some stage of development when painstaking recursive dissecting is no longer necessary appears in a similar phrasing in Tomasello (2008, 95–6). The merit of this passage, however, is to give a clear and concise expression to what is mistaken in the way Tomasello and colleagues think about these issues. What they are asked is to say what the concepts *they* use amount to, not to designate the winner of a philosophical debate. It is not necessary to waste time with conceptual debates, but it is necessary to grasp what these debates are *about* if one is to use the very concepts that started the debates. This does not happen. There is no reason to think that the incompatible conceptions of shared intentionality originating in philosophy can serve different explanatory needs within one and the same cognitive-developmental theory. And it is false that they can be combined into an eclectic hybrid; one will not cure a Searlean disease with Bratmanian medicine.

One last attempt at a response still needs to be blocked. I used Searle and Bratman as cardinal points in trying to make clear the different treatments of the concept of shared intention. One might claim, however, that the eclecticism mentioned in the quote above means that out of the different pieces a *new* concept has been forged, so that the whole discussion of what the philosophers think is irrelevant. This response can be dismissed briefly. First, let us repeat that the pieces do not belong together. What we observe is not eclecticism but inconsistency. Second, there is no textual evidence that the authors propose to introduce a separate notion; on the contrary. What they try is to find ways to tone down existing notions, as we saw in the operationalization of Bratman's criteria for SCA. Third, the departures from the initial notions, for example, the motivational reading of the analysis of commitment, are still conceived of within the original framework, as performing the explanatory roles specified in that framework. To keep to this example, talking about motivations to share mental states does not *revise* the concept of shared intention; it *misconstrues* that notion.

VIII

It is perhaps a good sign, given the picture I painted above, that in recent years some of the same psychologists seem to have taken a certain distance from the tendency to force attributions of sophisticated concepts, like shared intentionality, and even of regular interpretive concepts, at very young ages. For example, shared intentionality does not seem to play a major role in Warneken's current research (Hepach and Warneken 2018, Warneken 2018, Lee and Warneken 2020). Rakoczy has suggested that claims that infants understand false beliefs need to be taken with a grain of salt (Poulin-Dubois et al. 2018, Dörrenberg, Rakoczy, and Liszkowski 2018). Notably, Moll has criticized Tomasello's use of the notion of shared intentionality (without rejecting the notion as such) (Moll 2016, Moll, Nichols, and Mackey 2020)—see also Tomasello's reply (2020). Perhaps the most interesting piece in this debate (or "tension") is a paper coauthored by Moll and philosopher Andrea Kern (2017). The main characters are those I have also discussed here—Searle, Bratman, and Tomasello—and the main suggestion is that the "additive" account of shared intentionality present in all these authors needs to be replaced by a "transformative" view. Shared intentionality is not an *extra*-feature of individuals, but something attributable to "the human form of life." Explicitly, we are in the vicinity of the second-natural tradition—the "Aristotelian-Wittgensteinian tradition," as the authors call it—with McDowell and Wittgenstein, obviously, mentioned as inspirations. The authors

> stress that collective intentionality is not just one of many capacities that its bearers happen to acquire in their ontogeny. Rather, it is a capacity which characterizes the manner in which mature bearers of such a form of life possess and actualize any of their capacities.
>
> (Kern and Moll 2017, 11)

This is close enough to what I have suggested, even if I do not share the authors' optimism about projecting the "transformational" view into usable cognitive-developmental explanatory lingo. As I explained at the very beginning of the chapter, I am not without doubts about my own views. This turn is, in any case, proof of lucidity, and a strong signal that ideology can be shaken.

What I have tried above amounts to criticizing a way of talking that became solidified into ideology. I do not think, for example, that one would lose explanatory power if one stopped describing the cooperative talents of small children in terms of shared intentionality. Even if talking of shared intentionality is just another fashion in psychology, it reveals a *philosophical* view of human nature that transcends fashions. This is the tendency to stipulate mental faculties for all the things we find ourselves capable of doing.

In the 1990s, we were told by Tomasello that the adaptation which makes us what we are is the understanding of other's intentions:

> My attempt is to find a single biological adaptation with leverage, and thus I have alighted upon the hypothesis that human beings evolved a new way of identifying with and understanding conspecifics as intentional beings. [...]
>
> It is important to emphasize that this uniquely human form of social cognition does not just concern the understanding of others as animate sources of motion and power, as hypothesized by Piaget (1954) and Premack (1990), which is a type of understanding seemingly possessed by all primates. Rather, this new form of social cognition concerns the understanding that others make choices in their perception and action and that these choices are guided by a

mental representation of some desired outcome, that is, a goal.

(1999, 204–5)

As we have seen, the story has then changed:

Following Vygotsky (1978) and Tomasello (1999), the general proposal here is that the human gap is best explained in terms of, ultimately, social (or cultural) factors. That is, human beings are especially sophisticated cognitively not because of their greater individual brainpower, but rather because of their unique ability to put their individual brainpowers together to create cultural practices, artifacts, and institutions—underlain by skills and motivations for shared intentionality …

(Tomasello and Moll 2010, 331)

Underlying humans' uniquely cooperative lifeways and modes of cultural transmission are a set of species-unique social-cognitive processes, which we may refer to collectively as skills and motivations for shared intentionality (Tomasello, Carpenter, Call, Behne, & Moll, 2005). These involve such things as the ability and motivation to form shared goals and intentions with others in collaborative activities, and the ability and motivation to share experience with others via joint attention, cooperative communication, and teaching. Skills and motivations of shared intentionality arose as part of a coevolutionary process in which humans evolved species-unique ways of operating, indeed cooperating, within their own self-built cultural worlds (Richerson & Boyd, 2006).

(Tomasello 2011, 6)

The account of human evolution on which we rely is that of Tomasello et al. (2012; see also Tomasello 2014, 2016), which focused on the evolution of human cooperation and how it enables species-unique processes of cultural coordination and transmission. For precision, the account borrows theoretical tools from philosophical accounts of shared intentionality (Bratman 1992, 2014; Searle 1995, 2010; Gilbert 1989, 2014). In this view, humans' abilities to cooperate with one another take unique forms because individuals are able to create with one another a shared agent "we," operating with shared intentions, shared knowledge, and shared sociomoral values. The claim is that these abilities emerged first in human evolution between collaborative partners operating dyadically in acts of joint intentionality, and then later among individuals as members of a cultural group in acts of collective intentionality.

(Tomasello 2019, 7)

What should be disconcerting here is the persistence of the idea that a discrete adaptation is what one should look for, *and* that this adaptation is to be described in terms of psychological competence—indeed, as a mental faculty. Perhaps this was an informed bet Tomasello and colleagues thought they were entitled to make. Our capacities are after all natural capacities and they must have *some* natural history. But if it is a genuinely difficult question how to go about in reconstructing this history, there are some mistakes that one can avoid. One such mistake is the misinterpretation of the everyday explanatory language we use to make sense of ourselves and of others "citizens of the realm of reasons." The inflation of mentalistic speculation that plagues the account of the origins of cooperation proposed by Tomasello and colleagues is a consequence of a readiness to reify what is essentially the everyday, cultural-embedded explanation of action. Perhaps the authors thought this is the signature of good science, but, on reflection, the signature seems rather that of a traditional and misplaced philosophical allegiance.

To conclude with an analogy with returns us to the parallel between psychology and medicine, the introduction of the concept of shared intentionality in developmental theorizing is not the result of a discovery or of stepping over old misconception. Early shared intentionality is not similar to infant *pain*, for example. In this case, too, there has been a long debate on whether babies feel pain—therefore on whether anesthetics should be used in neonatal surgery (Anand and Hickey 1987, Times 1992, Anand and Scalzo 2000, Pattinson and Fitzgerald 2004, Anand et al. 2006). Until relatively recently, behavioral and physiological signs of pain trauma in babies were ignored, because it was thought that their unmyelinated nerve fibers cannot transmit pain signals to the brain. In part, this was not only a medical blunder (unmyelinated fibers *can* relay pain signals), but also one about what pain *means*; of course, an infant is not capable of *all* the paradigmatic manifestations of pain, but this does not make the cases of trauma following surgery without anesthetics terribly ambiguous.

Things are quite different with shared intentionality, though this is also, in part, a problem of using concepts meaningfully. In this latter case is not as if we finally realize that children have been capable of shared intentionality— in miniature form—all along. We do not overcome embarrassing blindness to the facts, but make ourselves blind to the facts by extending to babies an already fragile conceptual innovation which, *at best*, is applicable to some adult achievements.

7

Psychosis as Margin

I

In a blog post dated April 29, 2013, the director of the National Institute of Mental Health, Dr. Thomas R. Insel, wrote as follows about the fifth edition of the *Diagnostic and Statistical Manual of Mental Disorders* (DSM-5), which was published soon after (May 18, 2013):

> While DSM has been described as a "Bible" for the field, it is, at best, a dictionary, creating a set of labels and defining each. The strength of each of the editions of DSM has been "reliability"—each edition has ensured that clinicians use the same terms in the same ways. The weakness is its lack of validity. Unlike our definitions of ischemic heart disease, lymphoma, or AIDS, the DSM diagnoses are based on a consensus about clusters of clinical symptoms, not any objective laboratory measure. In the rest of medicine, this would be equivalent to creating diagnostic systems based on the nature of chest pain or the quality of fever.
>
> (Insel 2013)

This was not, coming from such a source, mere criticism. As criticism, it would have been after all nothing new. The entrenched opponents of institutional psychiatry have been claiming the same for decades. There have also been dissenting voices coming from within the field. Indeed, Insel was not the first director of NIMH to express doubts about the DSM. His predecessor, Steven Hyman, was also skeptical about the scientific credentials of the manual (see Greenberg 2013). In a preface written in 2003 for a volume dedicated to some outstanding issues in the DSM, Hyman made the same point as Insel, but about the previous edition of the DSM—the revised fourth:

> If a relative strength of DSM is its focus on reliability, a fundamental weakness lies in problems related to validity. Not only persisting but looming larger is

the question of whether DSM-IV-TR truly carves nature at the joints—that is, whether the entities described in the manual are truly "natural kinds" and not arbitrary chimeras.

(Hyman 2003, xii)

Without denying the classificatory achievements of these "chimeras," Hyman went on to warn against reifying[1] diagnostic labels. They were, he suggested, the result of stipulative consensus, not of scientific discovery. In the absence of solid knowledge of the etiology of mental afflictions, symptomatology acts as a proxy that makes possible some degree of clinical management and therapeutic intervention. But one should not mistake arrays of symptoms with natural kinds—disease entities carved, as in the more mature branches of medicine, causally. Given this interim status of the DSM categories, they should not be allowed to (monopolistically) control research, for example, by determining and segmenting sample clinical populations. Alternatives should be considered and explored.

Insel reiterated this stance, but went one step further by drawing an institutional conclusion. The NIMH will "re-orient" its research, that is, its support and funding, away from the DSM framework, in an effort to place psychiatry on the same scientific basis as the rest of "precision medicine" (Insel 2011). NIMH will focus on an alternative framework—the "Research Domain Criteria"—aimed at pathogenesis rather than at symptoms (NIMH 2011). This framework, the advertisement went, would allow for research in neuroscience, brain imaging, or cognitive psychology to be conducted independently of the DSM categories. For example, experimental populations would not be selected based on DSM diagnosis, if there are biological markers that suggest alternative (cross-DSM-diagnostic) groupings. Even if, for practical (clinical and insurance) purposes, the DSM will be in place for many years to come, Insel's decision presents itself as a way out of what Hyman has called more recently DSM's "unintended epistemic prison" (Hyman 2010) (see also First 2012, Greenberg 2013). Given the decades-long dominance of the DSM system and its associated mode of thinking about mental illness (financially supported so far by the NIMH), this initiative has been and will continue to be intensely debated.[2]

This particular debate originated, it should be stressed, *within* professional psychiatry, that is, in a "camp" otherwise committed to its consensus that mental illness is biological in nature, not different in kind from kidney failure or cancer, only more complex, because of the complexity of the underlying organ, the brain. If one were to consider an issue in psychiatry while expanding the horizon of discussion to areas touching on psychiatry but not necessarily covered by its biological consensus—clinical psychology, neurology, medical ethics, intellectual history, pharmaceutical economics—things would be exponentially harder to adjudicate.

This tale stands at the beginning of this chapter as a reminder. Even in this brief illustration one can easily see that the important debates in psychiatry *immediately* raise a plethora of difficult questions—what counts as science; what counts as (scientific, medical) evidence and explanation; what are the entities that may be invoked in explaining phenomena (illness in this case); what is the significance of concepts like *diagnosis* and *treatment* in this context; how to balance public elements (~socially embedded behavior) and probable causal antecedents (~brain conditions) in accounting for human (de)feats; how to set a meaningful threshold in an area where nature and culture have both things to say, as is the case with the normal vs. abnormal (functional vs. dysfunctional) distinction—and so on. Moreover, the fact that the "young science" rhetoric of psychology has an analogue in the "young medicine" rhetoric of psychiatry should not obscure the fact that questions like the above turn out to be as pressing today as they have been for the founders of psychiatry—and, *mutatis mutandis*, throughout the cultural history of madness. The controversies elicited by the publication of the DSM-5 in 2013 provide by themselves abundant food for thought, but many other examples could be brought in support of this claim.[3]

By highlighting from the very beginning the question marks I do not intend to introduce alarmist suspicions only to have them dissolved at a later point by applying universal philosophical solvents. It makes in fact little difference if one cares, in respect of tradition, to call questions like the above "philosophical." As we have just seen, they constitute first of all public concerns. What makes a difference is that these puzzles are unlikely to be settled in any one move; faced with them, one has to balance costs and avoid the worst. We are entering a minefield, and the aims of what follows are, accordingly, modest. The reminder, however, cuts both ways. Epistemic authority in this region remains fragile and, accordingly, not only philosophical opinion, but also the claims emanating from the relevant scientific communities need to be taken with a grain of salt. The latter should not automatically displace or replace the former.

As in the previous chapter, in the following we will move from discussing a series of theoretical proposals to one central detailed engagement—with the account of schizophrenic symptomatology suggested by Christopher Frith and continued by Rhiannon Corcoran. Similarly to Tomasello's explanations of the development of communicative and cooperative skills in early childhood, Christopher Frith's ideas about the delusions and hallucinations experienced by psychotic individuals were born and became influential at a confluence of psychological and philosophical thinking. His suggestions have been influential in regions of philosophy and psychology, but, given the fault lines between clinical psychology and psychiatry, were more or less ignored by the latter. The philosophical interest attests, in this case too, that Frith's suppositions brought to surface themes that have been the object of long-standing conceptual concern. So while we will engage in some detail with this particular theoretical stream, this must be read, as in the previous chapter, against a larger background. Some time will be spent discussing this background.

One aim, then, is to raise doubts about what psychologists of historical importance, like Freud and Milton Rokeach, have done, and also to question recent efforts, such as those of Richard Bentall and Frith. Dealing with Frith's account especially is of some importance on its own, but, one may say, also somewhat tardive, given the extensive discussions of his ideas in philosophical circles. Moreover, there seems to be no urgency to the matter, as Frith's view of schizophrenic symptoms, inspired by cognitive psychological models of autism, had a modest impact in mainstream psychiatry, and thus on the ill. But, as with Tomasello's proposal, Frith's theory of schizophrenia should be seen in context. Once we place it in a larger current in psychology that sees psychosis as explainable in the sense of *understandable* in terms of reasonable reactions to unreasonable circumstances, this theory manifests its genuine significance and historical pedigree. That is to say, it can be illuminated as an instance of *assimilating* cases of abnormality or ambiguity to paradigmatic human thought and behavior. The exploration of this perspective is the second aim of the chapter and its main junction with the rest of the book.

If successful, the contextualization will place the discussion, admittedly loosely, under the umbrella presented at the beginning of the book. This, too, is similar with the previous chapter. However, the repositioning of psychosis— to the naïve observer the very antithesis of rationality—in the realm of typical reason-giving explanation makes this kind of theorizing of madness a *clearer* case of conceiving the margins in familiar terms than that of early childhood. Clearer not in the sense of a stronger example situated on the same scale, but, the paradox be excused, independently stronger. The assimilation considered in the following overlaps with the one exemplified in the previous chapter only from an abstract point of view. Madness is obviously not *like* a normal developmental stage, and it does not differ from the paradigm of mature, socially competent individuals in the same sense as early childhood. One does not become mad as one grows up. These two instances of the margins of psychology exemplify two divergent directions of assimilation to the paradigm; nonetheless, they are not completely unrelated, and their structural and motivational resemblances constitute one of the more interesting facts about them.

Between the larger perspective which forms the loose common thread of this essay and the move against Frith's theory which is central to this chapter, there is a middle layer of context which, as mentioned above, situates the present discussion in a particular explanatory current in psychopathology. This is where we begin, with two historical portraits and one contemporary example from Frith's immediate theoretical vicinity.

II

The asylum at Sonnenstein, on the Elbe (figure 3), could be seen as both landmark and metaphor for psychiatry—and perhaps for the history of science and medicine generally. It seems to emanate a fitting ambiguity, a mix of idealistic humanism and ideological, murderous madness. In the darkness of the early 1940s, Sonnenstein was one of the scenes for the so-called *Aktion T4*,

Figure 3 Bernardo Bellotto (Canaletto), *Die Festung Sonnenstein über Pirna vom Hausberg* (Sonnestein fortress), 1754–5 © Gemäldegalerie Alte Meister, Staatliche Kunstsammlungen Dresden, photo by Elke Estel/Hans-Peter Klut.

the programmatic extermination of people, often children, deemed mentally ill or otherwise defective not by uneducated bullies, but by Nazi doctors and eugenicists. Many thousands were gassed and cremated in what turned out to be a pilot study and training ground for the death camps.

This was the same Sonnenstein that in the nineteenth century had been acclaimed as one of the most progressive mental institutions in Europe, and this in a world in which German psychiatry was, by all measures, the queen of the field (Shorter 1997). The same Sonnenstein in which, just a few decades before the butchery of 1940–2, the most famous psychiatric patient of all times, Daniel Paul Schreber, wrote a brilliant and uncanny book rendered in English as *Memoirs of My Nervous Illness* (*Denkwürdigkeiten eines Nervenkranken*—1903).[4] This is not the place to dive into the details of Schreber's story—it is, after all, abundantly researched and discussed. But precisely because this case is a much-discussed classic, it brings into relief long-standing explanatory and interpretive tendencies in psychopathology. In this role it helps highlighting the common conceptual commitments of verbally dissimilar theoretical constructions. This is why a brief return to Schreber is in order in this context.

Among those diagnosed with various mental illnesses, it happens less often that psychotics write readable, book-length autobiographical material. Still, there are well-known examples, including older material—besides Schreber's volume, one could mention the at least equally bizarre three tomes written by Alexis-Vincent-Charles Berbiguier (1821), and possibly even anti-asylum memoirs such as those published by Ebenezer Haskell (1869) and Charles Merivale (1879). Closer to us, one can think of Joanne Greenberg's *I Never Promised You a Rose Garden* (1964/2009), Elyn Saks's *The Center Cannot Hold* (2007), or Emsé Weijun Wang's *Collected Schizophrenias* (2019). Even if not negligible, this output is hard to compare with that coming from the other side of the Kraepelinian grand division, from people with mood disorders. This is especially true in our age of depression epidemics and "survival" narratives. Melancholy, to use the anachronistic label, has—and has had—a more vocal and respectable presence in our culture.[5] This relative rarity would be reason enough for paying attention to the *Denkwürdigkeiten*.

It is not, by far, the only reason. Schreber's book, unaided, as the more recent comparable texts, by professional editorial interference (though it was mutilated by censorship),[6] remains perhaps the most authentic such document we have access to. Moreover, there is no denying that Schreber, even at his most bizarre, is an accomplished writer. His is considered by many the best book of its kind there ever was. And certainly, one may very well look for and observe symptoms, but what one *reads* is eloquent prose.

Schreber owes his fame not only to the obvious merits of his book, however, but to the interest the book elicited in psychiatry and in the larger culture. In 1911, the year Schreber died after a third and final return of his illness, Freud published one of his few studies on schizophrenia—"Psycho-Analytic Notes on an Autobiographical Account of a Case of Paranoia (Dementia Paranoides)" (*Psychoanalytische Bemerkungen über einen autobiographisch beschriebenen Fall von Paranoia (Dementia paranoides)*). This article is remarkable not only because it deals with a topic, (paranoid) psychosis, Freud otherwise systematically avoided, but because Freud wrote about a patient he never met: Schreber. A fairly complex explanation was put forward solely on the basis of a speculative reading of Schreber's book. That in this case, too, Freud was more preoccupied with his favorite narratives than with the nature of the available evidence is of interest, but it is not what matters in the current context. What does matter is the manner in which Freud explained Schreber's symptoms, the nature of the narrative. Typically, the uncanny and the bizarre in Schreber's writing are seen as surface manifestations, as a *code* in which a series of perfectly intelligible underlying themes *express* themselves, breaking, as it were, through the ice of repression and convention. We will see this structure at work again and again, in different terminological clothing, at other authors.

To put it bluntly, for Freud, Schreber, as other paranoiacs, was a repressed homosexual. His emotional investments, originally related to his "eminent" father,[7] and his uneasy masculinity, later translated into a delusion of being transformed into a woman, were unacceptable, impossible to live with. Schreber was after all a married man, a respectable Prussian judge, and an aspiring politician. The ensuing tension led to a psychotic breakdown. Specifically, *via* what Freud called "projection," Schreber's homosexual attachment was transferred to his first psychiatrist, Paul Flechsig, and its polarity got reversed: love became hate, the loved one became persecutor. No wonder, for Freud, that Schreber would accuse Flechsig of "soul-murder."[8]

Even if projection is described by Freud as a general psych(patho)logical[9] *mechanism* (compare: autoimmunity), its action is that of an *Enigma* machine. That is to say that it works with states that have semantic *content*, and it maneuvers that content in light of certain goals; its cogwheels *cipher* the intolerable in order to defend the integrity of at least some regions of the person's mind. As Freud sees it, once the mechanism that produces the symptoms is explained, the code is recovered and the symptoms can be understood. Indeed, they turn out to be rooted in the psychologically familiar.

The notion of projection deserves a parenthesis. It seems to develop from roots as old as psychoanalysis itself (from the Breuer–Freud conception of hysteria). To briefly sample this route, here is what Freud writes in the context of discussing the category of "defence hysteria" in 1894: "There is, however, a much more energetic and successful kind of defence. Here, the ego rejects the incompatible idea together with its affect and behaves as if the idea had never occurred to the ego at all" (Freud 1962b, 313).[10] One year later, in the so-called *Draft H*, which Freud sends to Fliess, we read: "The purpose of paranoia is thus to ward off an idea that is incompatible with the ego, by projecting its substance into the external world" (1966). Yet another year passes, and Freud published a case study about a patient he calls "Frau P." This encounter with paranoia is perhaps the best analogy[11] one can find in Freud with the Schreber case. Projection is already at the center of the interpretation Freud proposes: "In paranoia, the self-reproach is repressed in a manner which may be described as projection. It is repressed by erecting the defensive symptom of distrust of other people" (Freud 1962a, 403).[12] Finally, in the article on Schreber, we find a sophisticated account of projection which is essential in the explanation of paranoid symptoms, but which also has larger implications, since it is described as a process which does not belong by necessity to psycho*pathology*, but which is an integral part of *regular* mental life:

> The most striking characteristic of symptom-formation in paranoia is the process which deserves the name of *projection*. An internal perception is suppressed, and, instead, its content, after undergoing a certain kind of distortion, enters consciousness in the form of an external perception. In delusions of persecution the distortion consists in a transformation of affect; what should have been felt internally as love is perceived externally as hate. We should feel tempted to regard this remarkable process as the most important element in paranoia and as being absolutely pathognomonic for it, if we were not opportunely reminded of two things. In the first place, projection does not play the same part in all forms of paranoia; and, in the second place, it makes its appearance not only in paranoia but under other psychological conditions as well, and in fact it has a regular share assigned to it in our attitude towards the external world.
>
> (Freud 1958)[13]

Note how the anatomy of projection is centered on the notion of content (*Inhalt*), which covers both meaning and emotional valence. Note also the careful rejection of the idea that projection, *by itself*, triggers psychosis. It is crucial to keep in mind this kind of qualification which indicates a close continuity between regular mental life and unambiguous pathology/deviance. The processes which, in certain *circumstances*, produce psychosis are not themselves pathognomonic. The mental metabolism of the psychotic *is* displaced, it is moved, as it were, from an aerobic to an anaerobic environment, but it remains a metabolism nonetheless: it remains functional in the light of the circumstances (it supports after all a variety of mental life), and as such it invites functional (psychodynamic in this case) explanation. This way of thinking is common to Freud and, as we will see, to the more recent incarnations of the idea that mental illness is to be observed through a psychological lens.

What Freud writes about Schreber, then, is not revolutionary, but typical psychoanalysis (typical clinical psychology in fact), all the fascinating particularities of the case notwithstanding. More than in other places, the connection between paranoia, projection, and repressed homosexuality takes a special emphasis,[14] but the *interpretability* delivered by the concept of projection remains, for our purposes at least, the central aspect of the story. There is no need to emphasize this in commentary, since Freud himself is quite clear in this respect. Here is, for example, a contrast he presents early on in the study, after giving the "case history" of his "patient":

> The psycho-analyst, in the light of his knowledge of the psychoneuroses, approaches the subject with a suspicion that even thought-structures so extraordinary as these and so remote from our common modes of thinking are nevertheless derived from *the most general and comprehensible* impulses of the human mind; and he would be glad to discover the motives of such a transformation as well as the manner in which it has been accomplished. With this aim in view, he will wish to go more deeply into the details of the delusion and into the history of its development.
>
> (Freud 1958—emphasis added)[15]

And later:

> Thus in the case of Schreber we find ourselves once again on the familiar ground of the father-complex. The patient's struggle with Flechsig became revealed to him as a conflict with God, and we must therefore construe it as an infantile conflict with the father whom he loved; the details of that conflict (of which we know nothing) are what determined the content of his delusions. None of the material which in other cases of the sort is brought to light by analysis is absent in the present one: every element is hinted at in one way or another.
>
> (Freud 1958)[16]

Freud clearly thinks that he can understand Schreber, and that he can make Schreber understandable to a reader willing to see the case through the psychoanalytic interpretive lens. Now, the thing to say about this is not that Freud is very likely mistaken or that he builds his case on a methodological mess. Both are true, I think, but this is less interesting as observing the authentic puzzlement presented by the case as well as by the interpretation. It is too easy to regard Freud's speculations as brilliant but empty wordplay, completely unrelated to the "real" case. The puzzlement comes from facing a situation in which there *are* connections, connections that, however, do not quite add up or hold as Freud wanted them to.

Was it not natural for Freud—and for later writers, as we will see—to bring into the picture Schreber's father Moritz, an authority on scientifically disciplining young children, and the creator of such *über*-Prussian devices as the *Geradehalter*?[17] Was it not perfectly reasonable to focus on one of the dominant themes of Schreber's book, his transformation into a woman, initially to be raped by his soul-murderers, and, in a later development of his delusions, to be impregnated by divine seed? Was not Schreber's often expressed emotional ambiguity toward his psychiatrists, notably toward Flechsig, inviting explanation?

Given the quality of Schreber's writing, interpretation irresistibly invites itself in, and with that there is no problem. Nobody should want to say that Schreber utters noises, that what one reads is random gibberish. But this is not the same as saying that the strangeness of the *Denkwürdigkeiten* is less apparent or that it is reducible, that what it may *respond to*, to use a medical analogy, is a kind of enlightened literary criticism. One moment we follow Schreber talking about familiar things—history, politics, literature, philosophy, law—the next he abruptly switches to rays, hierarchies of nerves, fleetingly improvised men, nerve-language, and God dealing best with corpses. Here he manages to win himself, in court, the liberation from the asylum, there he writes to Flechsig an open letter in which he mentions the "overwhelming amount of proof" (Schreber 2000, 8) in favor of his views on "religion" in the same breath in which he all but openly accuses his former psychiatrist of malpractice. The reader is caught in a vortex, the text clearly has substance, one reaches out and feels the pressure of its matter, but at the same time it flows like sand when one tries to grasp it, to hold it steady in focus.

Freud, as all good interpreters, does not speculate without any basis. Often, what Schreber writes seems to be illuminated by Freud's account. Isn't there an "aha" moment when looking at fragments as the one below after reading Freud?

I can also "picture" myself in a different place, for instance while playing the piano I see myself at the same time standing in front of a mirror in the adjoining room in female attire; when I am lying in bed at night I can give myself and the rays the impression that my body has female breasts and a female sexual organ [...]. The picturing of female buttocks on my body—*honi soit qui mal y pense*—has become such a habit that I do it almost automatically whenever I bend down.

(Schreber 2000, 211)

But what to do with so many of the other themes that populate Schreber's multiverse? What about the traces of racism and German nationalism in which many have seen the echoes of a toxic surrounding culture, or the dominant figure of the supposedly proto-Nazi father? What about the elaborate theodicy? What about the omnipresence of "nerves" in the writing of a psychiatric patient in an era when research psychiatry was often neuroanatomy? Is the repressed homosexual writing the following?

The souls to be purified learnt during purification the language spoken by God Himself, the so-called "basic language," a somewhat antiquated but nevertheless powerful German, characterized particularly by a wealth of euphemisms (for instance, reward in the reverse sense for punishment, poison for food, juice for venom, unholy for holy, etc. [...] God's chosen peoples in history—as the most moral at a given time—were in order the old Jews, the old Persians (these in an outstanding degree, about whom more will be said below), the "Greco-Romans" (perhaps in ancient Greece and Rome, perhaps also as the "Franks" at the time of the Crusades) and lastly the Germans.

(Schreber 2000, 26–7)

Is Schreber reproaching Flechsig his lack of romantic interest, or, with a heartbreaking mix of lucidity and delusion, his professional misconduct?

There would then be no need to cast any shadow upon your person and only the mild reproach would perhaps remain that you, like so many doctors, could not completely resist the temptation of using a patient in your care *as an object for scientific experiments* apart from the real purpose of cure, when by chance matters of the highest scientific interest arose. One might even raise the question whether perhaps all the talk of voices about somebody having committed soul murder can be explained by the souls (rays) deeming it impermissible that a person's nervous system should be influenced by another's to the extent of imprisoning his will power, such as occurs during hypnosis; in order to stress forcefully that this was a malpractice it was called "soul murder," the souls, for lack of a better term, using a term already in current usage, and because of their innate tendency to express themselves hyperbolically.

(Schreber 2000, 9)[18]

The question, again, is whether one, say an experienced scientist using special technical means, can arrive at an explanation that evaporates the bizarre character of Schreber's text—and of what he claimed to have experienced. The question may start from Schreber or any other comparable case, but its import is general. It should reinforce skepticism about a *kind* of explanation. What must be doubted, as always at the margins, is the familiarity Freud tellingly mentions, the idea that one can move from being puzzled (*Verwunderung*) to understanding (*Verständnis*). In doubt are not the details of Freud's proposed explanation, or the details of the accounts we will meet in the following, but the availability of *any such* explanation. If this essay moves in the right direction, then one should not *expect* an explanation of delusion that reveals it as finally intelligible—elicited by aberrant peripheral conditions (disturbed perception, adverse environment, emotional vulnerability, childhood trauma, etc.), but motivated by recognizable motives, oriented toward recognizable aims, responsive to recognizable constraints, cohering in the familiar way with other elements of psychic life, carrying an (admittedly peculiar) reasonableness.

The case of Schreber shows with extraordinary clarity what this expectancy involves—an understandable hypnotic fascination that continuously tries to claim for itself an untenable epistemic authority, voicing itself not as sophisticated semi-fiction, but as science or philosophy. The list is long. Psychoanalysts like Niederland and Schatzman took over from Freud's speculations and sketched a monstrous picture of Moritz Schreber (Schatzman 1971). Canetti felt the need to discuss Schreber in relation to Hitler's regime in his analysis of power (1981). Eric Santner compared the phantasms of Schreber with those of the collective madness of National Socialism (1996). Han Israëls documented the lives of the two Schrebers to arrive at a more nuanced picture of their relation. Zvi Lothane openly attacked the "defamation," misunderstanding, and persecution of Schreber by psychoanalysts and psychiatrists (1998). Louis Sass suggested that a particularly satisfying interpretation of Schreber is accessible through the philosophy of Wittgenstein (1994). Quite the kaleidoscope.

These attempts are not similarly written or equally persuasive; the fact that there are debates on this topic is not without grounds (there can be debates about any biography, after all). But there is something these authors have in common— the commitment to the idea that there is an interpretation to be *adjudicated*, a fundamental lesson to take home. This is a far stronger and far more problematic stance than seeing cases such as Schreber's, and marginal cases in a larger sense than the psychological, as constituting objects of necessary, soul-enriching reflection. With the latter I can only agree.

III

Schreber spoke for himself; the interpretative avalanche started by his book is a filter that can, at least in principle, be set apart. This is not the case with the second hero of our tale; somebody else tells his story, though he is allowed to talk from time to time. To the best of my knowledge, the real name of this person remains confidential, so I will use the pseudonym under which he entered the history of psychology: Leon Gabor. His is, at least in the eyes of this reader, one of the great tragic stories told in our time by scientific observers of the mind's breakdown, the only comparable equivalent I am familiar with being the better known tale of Leonard L., recounted by Oliver Sacks in *Awakenings* (1999). Leon Gabor was one the three "Christs" the social psychologist Milton Rokeach assembled in 1959 at the Ypsilanti State Hospital in Michigan for a surreal experiment. This is how these three people introduced themselves on July 1st of that year, with Rokeach's commentary:

Joseph was fifty-eight and had been hospitalized for almost two decades. [...]

My name is Joseph Cassel.

- *Joseph, is there anything else you want to tell us?* -

"Yes. I'm God."

Clyde introduced himself next. He was seventy and had been hospitalized for seventeen years. [...]

"My name is Clyde Benson. That's my name straight."

- *Do you have any other names?* -

"Well, I have other names, but that's my vital side and I made God five and Jesus six."

- *Does that mean you're God?* -

"I made God, yes. I made it seventy years old a year ago. Hell! I passed seventy years old."

Leon was the last to introduce himself. Of the three, he looked the most like Christ. He was thirty-eight and had been committed five years before. [..]

"Sir," Leon began,

> it so happens that my birth certificate says that I am *Dr. Domino Dominorum et Rex Rexarum, Simplis Christianus Pueris Mentalis Doktor.* [This is all the Latin Leon knows: Lord of Lords, and King of Kings, Simple Christian Boy Psychiatrist.] It also states on my birth certificate that I am the reincarnation of Jesus Christ of Nazareth, and I also salute, and I want to add this. I *do* salute the manliness in Jesus Christ also, because the vine is Jesus and the rock is Christ, pertaining to the penis and testicles; and it so happens that I was railroaded into this place because of prejudice and jealousy and duping that started before I was born, and that is the main issue why I am here. I want to be myself. I do not consent to their misuse of the frequency of my life.
>
> (Rokeach 2011, 4–6)

These three people, all diagnosed schizophrenics, found themselves in the same room because they all claimed to be Christ. Rokeach, who would play the puppeteer for two years with the three men, was not a psychiatrist, but a social psychologist. He designed his experiment in order to test the view that there is a hierarchy in "belief systems," "primitive" beliefs, like those about one's identify or the constancy of the world, being extremely hard to revise. Research in this thematic region, amplified by Cold War fears about brainwashing,[19] was very popular in the social psychology of this period (Festinger's landmark cognitive dissonance theory is also a creature of the late 1950s).[20] Rokeach was trying to find a situation in which "primitive" beliefs would be contradicted, and to study the role of authority in such a context. This was not an easy task, because of the obvious ethical scandal of experimenting with someone's identity: "Social scientists cannot, for ethical reasons, conduct 'thought control' experiments or violate primitive beliefs in children or even adults for prolonged periods" (Rokeach 2011, 31). Fortunately, there was a way to circumvent this barrier:

> Suppose that the primitive belief to be violated is one that has no social support instead of one that has unanimous social support. This would be the case for a psychotic with a mistaken belief in his identity. Suppose we brought together two or more persons claiming the *same* mistaken identity? […] In confronting the three Christs with one another, we proposed to bring into a dissonant relation two primitive beliefs within each of them: his delusional belief in his identity and his realistic belief that only one person can have a given identity.
>
> (2011, 31–2)

This is, at its core, the theoretical motivation of the experiment—and the explanation for its taking place in an asylum. Rokeach was aiming at understanding the dynamic of belief in normal or typical individuals, but he had to make do with psychotics. This, it must be stressed, was *not* a theory-driven choice, but an administrative artifice that made possible an otherwise illicit experiment. That the subjects were mentally ill and had been institutionalized for at least five years counted *against* the rationale of the study. But, in order to get the experiment off the ground, Rokeach had to treat the situation of his subjects as nothing more than a source of noise of the kind one must deal with in any empirical study. Fundamentally, from its very beginning the study carried the assumption that delusions are beliefs—that "delusional" is an adjective that attaches to beliefs or belief systems (compare: "reasonable") without thereby altering their nature in such a way as to render the experiment useless. Rokeach is unequivocal:

> It should be clear [...] that the research with the three delusional Christs evolved as a result of a theoretical concern, not with psychopathology as such, but with the general nature of systems of belief and the conditions under which they can be modified. Because it is not feasible to study such phenomena with normal people, it seemed reasonable to focus on delusional systems of belief in the hope that, in subjecting them to strain, there would be little to lose and, hopefully, a great deal to gain.
>
> (2011, 32)

It was not beliefs, but people that were "subjected to strain" in the two years of the study. As for the driving theoretical concern of the experiment, this was conveniently fluctuating. Even if the project started as described, aimed at an area of typical psychology, Rokeach would in the course of time often speculate about the delusions he witnessed, and he would conclude his book deeply in that territory. Indeed, with its focus on Leon as the most articulate, strange, and *resisting* of the three Christs, Rokeach's study would effectively integrate an impressionistic version of the schizophrenogenic mother theory. If Moritz Schreber had been Daniel Paul's demon, Leon Gabor was nothing else than what Mary, his religiously obsessed mother, made of him.

> Mary was a religious fanatic and was reported to hear voices. Her own priest, whom we interviewed, said she spent too much time in church. In a broken accent he told us:
>
>> I tell her, "Go home." I say to her, "See me, Father, I say Mass half hour; see the Sisters, they go to Mass half hour. Then we go work—it's enough." And then I

look and she back saying rosaries. Leon, every day worse. She not cooking for boy, crackers and tea, not food for a boy growing. She not cleaning her house, praying, praying, all the time praying.

(Rokeach 2011, 46)

Upon directly observing Mary during her last attempt to meet her son (she died soon after), Rokeach writes:

She gives the impression of a defeated woman approaching the end of life, who realizes that all she has valued most highly has turned out badly, but who has not the faintest idea why. Least of all does she show any awareness of the part she herself played in her own bitter defeat.

(2011, 100)

Rokeach did not arrive at such observations—note the *théâtre de la cruauté* in the latter example—in an intellectual vacuum. In 1948, building on her earlier criticism of the "the dangerous influence of the *undesirable domineering mother* on the development of her children" (quoted in Hartwell 1996), Frieda Fromm-Reichmann explicitly designated a certain kind of mothering as the etiological root of schizophrenia. It is noteworthy that the concept of schizophrenogenic mother appears in an article which defends the idea that expressions of delusion are *communicative* acts, that therefore schizophrenia should be responsive to psychoanalytic interventions, contrary to the orthodox Freudian reticence[21] on the matter (no rapport, therefore no transfer, therefore no therapeutic vehicle). The intrepid analyst, Fromm-Reichmann claimed, *will* be able to break the code of psychosis:

It is now generally recognized that the communications of the schizophrenic are practically always meaningful to him, and potentially intelligible and not infrequently actually understandable to the trained psychoanalyst. It was not the nature of the schizophrenic communication therefore that constituted an obstacle to psychoanalytic psychotherapy with schizophrenics.

(1948, 263–4)

To understand the nature of this kind of "communication," it was necessary to keep in view the nature of the illness itself. In dealing with the schizophrenic, the analyst had to compensate for a disease process that had been acting in the biography of the ill person like a massive object, progressively warping the emotional fabric of her or his life. What was the anatomy of such a disaster? It had to do, primarily, with incompetent, controlling, power-hungry, role-ignorant mothers:

> The schizophrenic is painfully distrustful and resentful of other people, due to the severe early warp and rejection he encountered in important people of his infancy and childhood, as a rule, mainly in a schizophrenogenic mother. During his early fight for emotional survival, he begins to develop the great interpersonal sensitivity which remains his for the rest of his life. His initial pathogenic experiences are actually, or by virtue of his interpretation, the pattern for a never-ending succession of subsequent similar ones. Finally he transgresses the threshold of endurance. Because of his sensitivity and his never satisfied lonely need for benevolent contacts, this threshold is all too easily reached. The schizophrenic's partial emotional regression and his withdrawal from the outside world into an autistic private world with its specific thought processes and modes of feeling and expression is motivated by his fear of repetitional rejection, his distrust of others, and equally so by his own retaliative hostility, which he abhors, as well as the deep anxiety promoted by this hatred.
>
> (Fromm-Reichmann 1948, 265)

As with Freud's, Fromm-Reichmann's divination is brilliant, for all the terrible ethical and political consequences it had.[22] Faced with a clearly damaging parent, like Leon's mother, on the one hand, and with the terrible state of someone like Leon on the other, who would not pay attention to what Fromm-Reichmann is suggesting and connect the dots? Drawing the line seems to make sense. From a number of possible stories, it is surely not the worst one (compare: demonic possession). But of course that is by far not enough for an *explanation*, and a very thin ground for talking about understanding and curing people. As with the early responsive behavior of children, the very fact that the interpretive effort targets delusions essentially as instances of *communication* should immediately raise skepticism, since it indicates serious misunderstandings about what it means to understand language and symbolic behavior generally. (The phrase "meaningful to him" is, in this sense, pathognomonic.) Here, too, it makes a difference when one pushes interpretation far beyond the limits of regular, socially maintained accord and convention—beyond what makes adjudication of any interpretation possible. Freud tells a believable story about projection, Fromm-Reichmann one about bad mothers; explanatorily *nothing* is thereby settled. As Lothane says in the context of discussing attempts to decipher Schreber, "let every interpreter beware: *de te fabula narratur*, the story is about you" (2010).

Given the influence of psychoanalysis in (especially American) postwar psychiatry, the ideas of Fromm-Reichmann would continue to haunt the conceptual landscape in which Rokeach was writing, producing such ad hoc machinery as the influential double-bind theory of Gregory Bateson, nothing less than a (semantic) theory of psychosis openly modeled on communication theory (conflicting messages interpretation and management) (Bateson et al. 1956/1987, Bateson 1969/1987). The fact that, after spending years in their company, Rokeach, too, thought he understood his subjects, and elaborated freely on the nature of their maladies, was no greater sin (unlike the experiment itself) and should not come as a surprise.

Just as in the Schreber case, if one considers what Leon says and does—even through Rokeach's authorial filter—interpretative pretentions evaporate in a fog of irreducible ambiguity. Leon oscillates from incoherent ramblings to sustained polemical engagements. Most times, he hovers somewhere between these poles. Concluding a report of the November 8, 1959 meeting of the Christs, Leon writes:

> Read about item called "We're looking for people who like to draw" from a magazine section of DETROIT NEWS.
> Complete information according to instrumental "Devine Habeas Corpus cosmic parchement in front of the face, and in front of this parchement of paper. Closed meeting singing 4th verse of America.
>
> Sincerely;
> Dr. Rexarum. (Rokeach 2011, 116)

In stark contrast stand his protests against Rokeach's brutal interference. They are not as eloquent as Schreber's exposé of Flechsig, but they are similar in structure, a mix of delusional themes and cutting lucidity. They may, in fact, remind more of Berbiguier perorations against the *infâme* Pinel (1821). It is always quite transparent that Leon is opposed to Rokeach's "warped" and "frictional" psychology. His resistance, embedded in a vaster paranoid stream, manifests itself clearly from the very first meeting:

> *Why do you gentlemen suppose you were brought together? –*

> Leon said: "Sir, I sincerely understand pertaining to reading between the lines, and stay behind the scenes. And I realize that those people who bring patients together to have one abuse the other through depressing—is not sound psychological reasoning deduction."

> (Rokeach 2011, 11)

Things aggravate with time:

> On one occasion, following an argument, Leon abruptly stood up and said that he didn't want to discuss the matter any further, and that he was wasting his time here. With a little effort he was persuaded to stay, but as he sat down he proclaimed: "I know what's going on here. You're using one patient against another, and this is warped psychology."

> (2011, 52)

Later, after Leon had offered an uncanny picture of his humiliating situation by changing his name from *Rex* ... to Dr. Righteous-Idealed *Dung*, he protested as follows to Rokeach's making the Christs read a magazine article about themselves and his study of them:

> "Sir," he said on finishing the article, "there's indirect warped psychology here because I respect manliness as Jesus Christ and that's missing out of this [...] When psychology is used to agitate, it's not sound psychology anymore. You're not helping the person. You're agitating. When you agitate you belittle your intelligence."

> (159–60)

Rokeach, who would later count himself as the fourth delusional "god" of the story, did not see reason enough to stop the experiment in such remonstrations. On the contrary, his aggression on Leon's ruined mind reached an unspeakable zenith when he took over Leon's delusion of having a wife and made it real by writing letters[23] to the patient and proposing meetings at which no one showed up. It was decided, after all, that Leon stood little to lose.

But what was *gained* by having one unfortunate man pay such a cost? Nothing in terms of explanation of belief—or delusion. If Rokeach's study is important, this is because of its careful and abundant collection of firsthand material, and also because it reveals in bright light the porous border between ideology and the putative science of man. With the gentlemanly figure of the alienist replaced by something probably worse, this is, if anything, a Foucauldian *mis-en-scène*, the epistemic pretensions thoroughly penetrated by asymmetries of power. Leon and his co-sufferers are, even when compassion is claimed, under the gaze of a safely detached observer, *sous le regard d'un savoir permanent*, as Foucault might have put it (1975, 192). And as this perspective would have it, such knowledge remains mostly about archiving a life in vivo. The explanatory speculations are entirely forgettable and unoriginal, illustrating from Rokeach's particular cultural location the long-standing conceptual commitment we have explored in this book. Early in his volume he notes:

> It is clear that these three psychotic men, like all men, were stimulated by their environment and responded to it. Like all men, they immediately perceived their personal and social situation, were affected by it, tried to understand it, *thought* about it, and formulated hypotheses designed to explain it. The three Christs were, if not rational men, at least men of a type we had all encountered before; they were rationalizing men. (52–3)

When he reaches his conclusions Rokeach goes even further:

> The present study represents, in Helen Merrell Lynd's words, "a search for ways to transcend loneliness" and a refusal to accept the "finality of individual estrangement." [… W]e have also learned: that if we are patient long enough, the apparent incoherence of psychotic utterance and behavior becomes increasingly more understandable; that psychosis is a far cry from the happy state some make it out to be; that it may sometimes represent the best terms a person can come to with life; that psychotics, having good reasons to flee human companionship, nevertheless crave it. (331)

Recognizably, this is the basic theoretical stance we have met, in psychoanalytical clothes, in Freud and Fromm-Reichmann, and it is also one that informs some areas of contemporary clinical psychology, from the antipsychiatric immoderations of Richard Bentall to the meticulous reconstructive architecture of Christopher Frith. Psychosis is familiar ground; once the "schizophrenogenic traumatization" (Fromm-Reichmann 1948, 264) is identified, the delusional person can be seen "like all men" are seen: struggling to express an inner world, acting, given the circumstances, for good reasons.

In what may be read, perhaps, as a revealing negation, Rokeach concluded his study referring to the cannon set by Freud's interpretation of Schreber and suggesting that the science has since evolved: Leon was not to be seen as a repressed homosexual, but as confused about his sexually and ultimately about his humanity (2011, 324–30). But this difference is minor compared to the element of continuity referred to above, one that we need to confront in all these theories, and in ourselves: the idea that understanding can outrun itself by illuminating madness as a degenerate kind of rationality, the idea that delusion is (analogous to) belief, and manifestations of delusion attempts to communicate beliefs, the idea that the loneliness of the psychotic is circumstantial, waiting for the truly benevolent to share a world. If one succeeds in seeing in such a stance a perpetual but misleading attractor, then Rokeach's diagnostic for Leon—"suffering not so much from a delusion of greatness as from a delusion of goodness" (2011, 327)—can be seen on the lines suggested by Lothane, as describing the psychologist himself, and his philosophical camp.

IV

The ideas exemplified by Freud's portrait of Schreber, and by Rokeach's speculations about Leon Gabor, are still with us, even if in the meantime psychoanalysis suffered an intellectual bankruptcy (e.g., Borch-Jacobsen 2000, Meyer 2005, Borch-Jacobsen and Shamdasani 2012), and clinical psychology developed other intellectual envelopes. Experiments like Rokeach's are no longer possible, and the era of the asylum—a fragment of which he captured as it was beginning to fade—is over. In psychiatry, after the watershed marked by the third edition of the DSM (1980) (Mayes and Horwitz 2005), diagnosis moved clearly away from psychodynamic notions to a new focus on reliability which revived the Kraepelinian approach to mental illness, with its emphasis on symptom clusters, course, and prognosis. A consensus about the biological nature of mental illness associated itself with this reorientation.

Naturally, there has been opposition. The "second biological psychiatry," as the historian Edward Shorter called it (1997, chapter 7), had to confront antipsychiatry, which peaked in the late 1960s and in the 1970s. And, to this day, psychiatry, always preoccupied to attest its scientific and medical credentials, remains in an uneasy professional relation with clinical psychology, the latter sometimes seeing itself as the last barrier in the way of excessive medicalization. Incursions in the territory of psychiatry have come, as we are about to see, even from friendlier regions of psychology, from people that have not necessarily been targeting in a direct fashion the reigning biological consensus about mental illness. Christopher Frith's cognitive psychological theory of schizophrenia is such an example. It illustrates the more neutral tendency of modeling psychosis on non-delusional cases at the psychological level, without thereby contesting explanations in terms of biological mechanisms. Indeed, such models are built on assuming a *division of labor* between levels, as philosophical functionalism and cognitive scientific theorizing à la David Marr have taught. This is a philosophical choice and, as such, it is resisted by psychologists who think biology is orthogonal to the issue, and that psychological explanation is fine on its own in typical, *and* in clinical cases. Before we move to discussing Frith, it helps, for reasons of contrast, to briefly illustrate this counterpoint.

Richard Bentall, as Frith, is well known in both psychological and philosophical circles. He is one of the most uncompromising contemporary critics of psychiatry. To the biological and genetic models preferred by psychiatrists, and to the Kraepelinian consensus that has dominated psychiatric nosology in the last decades,[24] Bentall opposes a model of madness entirely on the lines we have just discussed.[25] Psychotic delusions, for examples, are not to be seen as "empty speech acts," but as "abnormal beliefs [which] are nearly always about their [the ill persons'] position in the social universe (Bentall 1994) or core existential concerns" (Bentall 2004, 199).

The most substantial presentation of Bentall's account of madness came with *Madness Explained*, a volume that the British Psychological Society saw fit to recompense in 2004 with its Book Award. A popular and more canonically antipsychiatric version arrived in 2009 with *Doctoring the Mind*.[26] As his intellectual predecessors, Bentall aims at presenting an account that explains the manifestations of psychotic mental illness by showing them to be understandable reactions to circumstances. Once this is done, the alien character of these cases either disappears or is circumscribed to a phenomenological or emotional periphery that, it is thought, does not threaten interpretation.

In applying this treatment to delusions, in the twelfth chapter of *Madness Explained*, Bentall begins with the tragic story of his own brother, who committed suicide:

> Of course, Andrew had always been different. At school, he had constantly been at loggerheads with his teachers and his peers. He had dropped out from formal education without achieving qualifications, and had drifted in to a life of drug-taking and unemployment. From the comfortable perspective of a professional clinical psychologist, some of his behaviour could be described as schizotypal. He complained of flashback hallucinatory experiences that he attributed to his experiments with LSD. He sometimes professed strange and magical beliefs, at one time telling my mother's elderly neighbour of his ambition to absorb all the knowledge in the universe. And yet, this kind of diagnostic labelling does not seem to do justice to the story of my brother's life. He might have been "schizotypal," for want of any better word, but he was not schizotypal in a vacuum.

(2003)

It is hard to bring this example into discussion within the limits of decency, and it is not my intention to criticize Bentall at this point; quite the contrary. The reader should keep the example in mind for the same reasons as in the cases we have considered above—precisely for its difficult and unsettling character. What *else* to do in such a case than look for an explanation, for reasons, for an answer to a haunting *why*? We do this as doctors and therapists, as friends and family, as survivors and sufferers; we face such questions with others, and we sometimes face them with ourselves, because occasional bizarre thought and even the breakdown of thought is not the monopoly of psychotics, and psychosis itself is not an all-or-nothing situation, but characterizes parts of a person's life story. What I criticize here does not target *that*, but the hope for a definitive, epistemically authoritative answer. The proposed horizon is, as before, that of inescapable ambiguity.

Bentall aims at a clear explanation of psychosis delivered in the vocabulary of psychology, and this is what places him in the intellectual lineage sketched above. He suggests that delusions are *reactions* to major, but not unheard-of stressors, circumstances Bentall prefers to call "the trials of life" (2003) or "the ordinary miseries of life" (2010, 40). Most adults will understand, I think, what such miseries mean, and the terrible shadows that they can cast on a life. The issue is what to make of this intuitive, non-problematic observation, in a clinical context. Bentall documents three classes of factors that can ignite psychosis: "family relationships, the general social environment, and traumatic experiences" (2003). Given a certain level of vulnerability—which may be itself environmentally determined—some people will become psychotic.

The defining element of the theory is, however, not this claim, but the idea that illness is not a mere causal happening; it does not work as a viral infection or a cancer, for example. In becoming psychotic, one *reacts* to one's environment (one's own weaknesses here included), one *looks* for a way out, or *tries* to defend whatever is left of one's life. The mentally ill person does what *anybody else*— what any thinking, reasonable being—would, in the given circumstances. This is the by-now-familiar element of assimilation, and it is also what opens the door to confident interpretation:

> The reader will recall that Karl Jaspers held all truly delusional beliefs to be ununderstandable, by which he meant that they are meaningless and unconnected to the individual's personality or experience. I have already

criticized this account for being far too subjective—the understandability of delusions seems to depend, to some extent, on the effort made to understand them. Indeed, when such efforts are made, it is apparent that the most common delusional themes observed in clinical practice, including most of those that I have just described, reflect patients' concerns about their position in the social universe.

(2003)[27]

Or:

The task for the clinician faced with the patient who lacks "insight" is not to dispute the patient's explanations for his symptoms, but to understand these explanations, to explore their origins, and to respect them as genuine attempts to account for experiences that are puzzling and frightening. By a process of empathetic understanding and skilful negotiation it is usually possible to find a way forward that allows the patient to work towards his life goals without causing harm to others.

(2010, 180)

The first thing to remark here is the imperative of empathy built into these fragments, and the gesturing toward the ideas that I discussed in the first part of the book (note: "empathetic understanding"). This is the kind of humanism one hopes for in a clinician. But it is also more than that. In this dismissive light, there seems to be something lazy and supercilious about the Jaspersian view. The point Jaspers was making, however, had little to do with medically inclined psychiatrists being cold, and refusing to accept tortuous interpretation as part of their job description. It had to do with the nature of interpretation itself— with its limits, to be precise—and he had in that the historicist–hermeneutical tradition on his side. Remember, for example, Dilthey's comments about the native territory of "descriptive" psychology.

One could also note, to keep to examples in this book, how such passages are reminiscent of Frieda Fromm-Reichmann's encouragements to try harder (the results, in her case at least, are notorious), but I leave that aside. The fundamental conceptual commitment expressed by them (intelligibility/interpretability) is by now familiar. It is also shared by Christopher Frith, in a different form, so I will be dealing with it again in the following. The point to make before we move on is that Bentall's criticism is set aside by the fact that it develops as part of a larger offensive against the conceptual roots of current psychiatry. Not only the present nosology is rejected,[28] but the very idea of mental illness as circumscribable pathological entity is questioned. These two strands of criticism are logically independent, but Bentall puts them together.

They are independent because, on the one hand, to claim that the syndromes which form the DSM system are arbitrary does not mean that the strategy of looking for "natural" clusters of symptoms is thereby invalidated. It may very well be the case that neo-Kraepelinian psychiatry failed to identify an adequate segmentation of mental illnesses. The *possibility* of such a classification remains intact. Bentall seems to argue on these lines when he refers to studies that have identified alternative clusters of symptoms which are intra- or transdiagnostic relative to the DSM framework. On the other hand, there is the far more radical criticism which is rooted in the idea that there is a continuum of mental disorders ranging from pure depression to pure schizophrenia. The implication here is that *all* classifications will verge on the arbitrary. This means that not only the psychiatry of the day is rejected, but psychiatry *simpliciter*, since it is hard to conceive of a branch of medicine in the absence of *some* nosology.

The bottom line is that psychiatry can be safely nailed to the cross of two continua: the one between kinds of illness, which blocks classification, and that between the healthy and the ill, which is supposed to render illicit the disease or medical model of mental illness. The interpretive model Bentall proposes can then step in *not* as an explanation of madness at a separate (psychological) level, and *not* as a mere alternative or complementary humanistic account, but as *the* true theory of psychosis. This is why, even if Bentall's account itself is a (less jargonized) *cognitive* psychological theory, its philosophical aura situates it closer to psychoanalytic and antipsychiatric views than to the model we consider next.[29]

V

The characters of our tale so far—Schreber and Freud, Rokeach and the Christs—are all present in Bentall's writings, though obviously not the same lessons are drawn. Also present and debated with is the proponent of another major contemporary theory of psychosis, Christopher Frith. In a series of papers published since the late 1980s and notably in a book from 1992, Frith has put together a cognitive theory of schizophrenia that has been intensely discussed in both psychological and philosophical literature. Its influence on mainstream psychiatry has remained, it seems, peripheral. The popularity of the theory was a result of its appearing at a confluence of topics, the nature of psychopathology and the logic of psychological explanation being the two main ones.

Frith aimed to explain the key symptoms of schizophrenia by reference to a dysfunctional "theory of mind" in the individuals with this condition. This idea came up at a moment when it seemed that a breakthrough was taking place in a significantly different region of psychopathology—autism. A number of psychologists, notably Uta Frith and Simon Baron-Cohen, had argued that the core symptoms of autism, the so-called Wing triad,[30] could be accounted for by the fact that autistic children did not (adequately) develop a "theory of mind." These children were, to use Simon Baron-Cohen's expression, "mindblind"; they could not understand what other people were thinking or feeling.

As this strand of research looked promising, Frith's adaptation of its design to schizophrenia elicited interest for at least two reasons: psychosis had always been an important subject and any credible explanatory effort invited legitimate attention; and then "theory of mind" was itself a hot area of research. Frith's ideas, if valid, were likely to shed light on the *explanans* itself. Schizophrenia could have offered a second opportunity, alongside autism, to reverse engineer "theory of mind," to reconstruct the working whole from the broken pieces. Since getting a grasp on "theory of mind" has been seen by many as nothing less than understanding how we understand ourselves, philosophical interest was especially high.

This is not the place to contest the legitimacy of this wave of attention. This more or less historical note is here simply to illustrate the continuity of the philosophical dispositions we have dealt with a number of times in this book. By now in any case it is quite clear that Frith's model does not work—not as a comprehensive *explanation* of psychotic symptoms. As in the previous cases, this is not to say that the driving ideas of the theory are completely implausible. One should note, in fairness, that Frith and colleagues were always aware of the speculative character of their ideas. It seems nonetheless true that the interest these ideas have attracted was due in part to the promise of elucidating in some proportion the mystery of "the sublime object of psychiatry" (Woods 2011), schizophrenia. The hope of a comprehensive explanation was not one that the authors consistently sanctioned, but neither was it hard to read into what they said.

A dysfunction of "theory of mind" probably does not explain schizophrenia on the lines of Frith. One reason to continue to write about an issue that seems settled is that this is a case where sorting out what went wrong matters. In a sense, moreover, the issue is far from settled. A second reason to think about Frith's proposal is that research efforts that relate a "theory of mind" deficit to schizophrenic and other pathologies are not at all a thing of the past (indeed, they cannot be if we continue our infatuation with the idea of "theory of mind").[31] Bentall too, for example, while rejecting Frith's central explanatory tenet, accepts that "there is obviously something *theory-of-mind-ish* about persecutory delusions" (2003).[32] It is, however, Rhiannon Corcoran's work that is the clearest example of pushing Frith's theoretical framework to the limit.

At this point, even with a very fragmentary history of interpretive attempts to explain psychosis behind us, there are enough contextual elements to be able in the following to recognize Frith's theory as part of that intellectual heritage. But, as in the case of the developmental models proposed by Tomasello, this theory should also be seen in its technical detail and immediate conceptual context (the context that the author himself set it in). This means that we need to locate it at the intersection of computational cognitive psychology, cognitive neuroscience, and DSM-style psychiatry.

Let us begin with the latter. Current diagnostic systems, as the DSM-5 (American Psychiatric Association 2000) and ICD-10, make use of a concept of schizophrenia developed, under a different label—*dementia praecox*—by Emil Kraepelin, though we inherit the name from Eugen Bleuler, who thought of the condition in quite different terms. What holds together the signs and symptoms of schizophrenia, in the Kraepelinian view, is the fact that the illness has a certain long-term physiognomy described by probable *course* and *outcome*. The ability to predict course and outcome is thus the main support for the clinical validity of the diagnosis, and for the claim that schizophrenia is a disease entity in spite of its recognized heterogeneity (Shorter 1997, Winn 2000, Burns 2007). As things stand—and as they stood for the last century or so—the concept remains fragile and widely disputed. Bentall, for example, is quite forceful when pressing this point.

Prediction is invaluable for clinical practice, but it is clearly not enough while we do not understand what exactly allows us to predict. At least two other dimensions would be needed to stabilize the concept of schizophrenia. *Etiology* is by far the more important,[33] especially if one is interested primarily in explaining the signs and symptoms of the illness. *Intervention* is a second and related dimension. Selective treatment and a specific manner of intervention measure both the level of understanding of a condition and the utility of a diagnostic category. Biologically inclined psychiatrists of the founders' generation in the late nineteenth and early twentieth centuries, or belonging to the current revival of biological psychiatry, have hoped that a diagnostic system based on clinical experience would eventually be vindicated by discoveries in biology and medical science. Advances were made, especially in terms of intervention with the arrival of antipsychotics,[34] but it seems clear that psychiatric conditions are still poorly understood, if better cared for. Schizophrenia is paradigmatic for this uncomfortable situation.

One important difference between the first age of biological psychiatry, when people like Alzheimer and Wernike (and Flechsig!) made important contributions by focusing their microscopes on tissue samples from the brains of deceased patients, and research conducted nowadays is that more kinds of mechanisms can be studied and used in explanation and theory construction. In fact, there seems to be a fracture in this area of research between two families of explanations: biological on the one hand, cognitive on the other (Frith 1992, Winn 2000, Bolton and Hill 2003). This fracture is imperfectly, but consistently, mirrored by that between psychiatry and (cognitive) clinical psychology.

Cognitive neuropsychology, a research strategy that had a boost with the arrival of functional brain imaging, aims at bridging this gap. Cognitive models are correlated with indices of neural functioning, and this is meant to ground explanations that work on two inter-translatable *levels*. Frith's model locates itself here:

> Given this approach to the relationship between mind and brain, there are two clear components in any attempt to specify the neuropsychology of schizophrenia. First, a description of schizophrenic abnormalities at a psychological level, and, second, a specification of how this description maps onto abnormalities at a physiological level.
>
> (1992, 29)

Frith's approach, built on such familiar functionalist lines, made an impression. For example, in October 1999, *The Monist* had a special issue on "Cognitive theories of mental illness" (Smith and Proust), and, in February 2000, *Mind and Language* had a similar issue, republished in book format as *Pathologies of Belief* (Coltheart and Davies). Frith's ideas are discussed in almost all of the papers collected in these publications. Philip Winn sums up this mood:

> Frith has described a theoretical framework that attempts to embrace and account for all of the signs and symptoms of schizophrenia (Frith, 1992). It is too soon to know whether or not this will be successful, but the attempt has undoubtedly generated more interest in recent years than any other theory. Given the existence of a testable theory, it seems pointless to abandon the concept of schizophrenia now.
>
> (2000, 253)

Here is a somewhat more recent proof for the canonical status of Frith's model, from Jonathan Burns:

> In my earlier discussion of theory of mind in schizophrenia, I referred to Frith's (1994) model of impaired mental state attribution and faulty selfmonitoring and I believe this model is a good place to start in constructing a cognitive model of the disorder.
>
> (2007, 145)

These are unexceptional remarks, and a sketch of the theory will perhaps explain them. The first chapters of Frith's 1992 book contain a remarkable methodological effort. He evaluates the current state of affairs, summarizes what is known about schizophrenia and the range of theories meant to explain it, and discusses the tools of, and the manner in which, an adequate theory should proceed.

The methodological remarks are the more important, given that one finds in them not only the building blocks of a specific model, but the foundations of a whole research program. Early in the book, Frith notes that current practice and theory in psychiatry are largely classificatory enterprises. Classification is opposed to genuine *diagnosis*, since the latter notion would imply some amount of knowledge about the etiology of conditions, and such knowledge is lacking.

> I have already referred to studies showing that, with careful training in the use of standardised interviews, it is possible to achieve a high degree of reliability in the identification of schizophrenia in terms of some standardised procedure such as PSE-CATEGO (Wing et al. 1967). This, however, is not diagnosis, but classification. Traditionally, making a diagnosis has implications about aetiology. As the aetiology (or cause) of schizophrenia remains essentially unknown, this traditional approach creates many problems.
>
> (Frith 1992, 7)[35]

Frith may be right on this often made point, but of course consistency in classification is itself something to be explained. It may be an artifact of "careful training"[36] and DSM, ICD, or PSE orthodoxy, but given that none of the classification systems is arbitrary, consistency *may* indicate that something "real" is captured by such systems. But Frith is surely right that we should not mistake sociological consistency for explanatory consistency. Ideally, they would overlap, but, as historical and current debates indicate, it is not clear that this is happening. Frith notes that the validity of the notion of schizophrenia would be vindicated by a biological marker for the condition, but no such marker is presently identified.

The consequence is that the researcher is in an awkward situation. She tries to investigate the causes of a condition without being sure that she has the right means to identify that condition, or indeed that the condition exists. Moreover, as it will become clear, she is not sure where to look and what tools or explanatory language should be used. Frith has things to say on both issues.

Perhaps psychiatrists are trapped in an error of historical proportions in trying to define schizophrenia. But even if there is no such thing, the symptoms reported by those affected and the signs observed by clinicians are real enough. Surely *they* need to be explained. Thus Frith recommends that the investigator be blind to the diagnostic label—given its dubious status—and focus on the symptoms. This is a recommendation presently followed by a large number of researchers involved in the so-called trans-diagnostic studies of mental illness. The caution that informs this approach is, it seems, well justified. Frith's distinction between symptoms and diagnosis is similar to that between dimensional and categorical views of psychosis.[37] Frith is not interested in settling this issue and is content to take note of the vulnerabilities of the Kraepelinian categorical system; it is left open whether the categories are valid or not.[38]

While in the design of studies and in the extraction of patient and control samples diagnosis should be left aside, complete blindness is not possible. The questions about *schizophrenia* (as opposed to, say, paranoid delusions) are still looming large, and this cannot be ignored. Here the move is to work back from explanations of symptoms to clusters of symptoms or syndromes, that is, to the conditions as specified by the current DSM/ICD definitions. This could be done by using what Frith has called, in a slightly different context, a "theory-driven" approach:

> One way to reduce the influence of spurious associations is to adopt a theory-driven approach. This requires the construction of a detailed "story" in which associations are predicted rather than discovered.
>
> (1992, 26)

Roughly, this means that an explanation for a given symptom would predict the fact that the symptom tends to co-occur with other kinds of symptoms (and signs, etc.). In opposition to a descriptive attempt to collect symptoms, such a theory, if successful, would also explain *why* the symptoms cluster in some ways and not in others. In a latter paper, this emphasis on theory construction resurfaces as a distinction between descriptive and *mechanistic* approaches, the first trying to capture the "characteristic pattern of intellectual impairment," the second asking "what psychological processes give rise to particular signs and symptoms associated with schizophrenia and how do these processes relate to normal brain functioning" (Frith 1996, 619). These two distinctions—symptom vs. diagnosis, and descriptive vs. theory-driven approaches—form the roots of Frith's solution to the fragility of current diagnosis systems.

A second and more serious difficulty is that the researcher is confronted with a choice of jargon. Traditionally, schizophrenia has been considered a *functional* illness. Currently, it is inconsistent with a DSM diagnosis of schizophrenia that the patient have any clear physical dysfunction, such as a brain lesion. If this is taken seriously, explanations of schizophrenia—and of all other functional conditions—should be confined to the language of function, that is, to the language of psychology (Morton 2004, 21). The continuous search for a biological marker of the condition proves that this exclusion criterion matters only in clinical practice, where it is important to make sure that psychotic symptoms do *not* have known etiologies, such as amphetamine abuse. The problem of explanatory jargon arises because it is not clear how one should settle the relation between biological and psychological levels of explanation, indeed because the problem is seen as one of competing or complementary *levels*.

Frith, as others in the field, is aware of the difficulties inherent in working with two kinds of explanatory discourse. Like others in the field, he thinks that the tools forged by functionalism in decades of philosophical dispute are adequate for the challenge. The third chapter of the 1992 book contains the bulk of his attempt to tackle this issue. Here is what he says at the beginning of this chapter:

> For me the distinction between mind and brain concerns levels of explanation. Behaviour and experience can be explained in terms of mental processes or in terms of physiological processes. Both types of explanation can be formulated in such a way that each can readily be mapped onto the other. Philosophers call this identity theory, or, in a weaker form, parallelism. This attitude towards the mind-brain is much influenced by experience with computers.
>
> (1992, 25–6)

There are three ideas of interest here. The fundamental one places Frith firmly within generic functionalism and concerns, as announced, levels of explanation. The two secondary claims are those about completeness[39] of explanation at each level on the one hand, and inter-level mapping on the other. Now, "mapping" could be given an identity theoretical, that is, a *non*-functionalist reading, but this is far from customary, and Frith should not be taken at his philosophical word when he mentions "identity theory"; this is just one of a number of confusions. Frith continues by polemically situating his perspective:

> My main concern in the first part of this chapter is to establish that certain causal explanations for schizophrenic symptoms are simply not admissible. For example, I think it is wrong to say, "thought disorder is caused by supersensitive dopamine receptors", or "hallucinations occur when the right hemisphere speaks to the left hemisphere via a faulty corpus callosum". The doctrine of parallelism requires that complete explanations of these phenomena can be made in either the mental or the physical domain. My two examples are incomplete explanations in either domain. Two incomplete explanations in different domains do not make up a complete description.
>
> (1992, 26)

Frith clearly rejects at this point a pattern of explanation that makes use of *both* biological and psychological concepts in the same move. This we can rephrase thus: the connection between a psychological predicate and a biological predicate is not that between *explanandum* and *explanans*. Biology does not explain psychology. The connection must be thought of in some other terms. That Frith does not have a tenable solution to the traditional philosophical of "crossing the divide" between mind talk and brain talk is, of course, no fault of his own. What we should note here is how this problem and its conceptual aura inform a scientific project, not that it unsurprisingly remains unsolved.

To be precise, Frith contradicts himself on the issue throughout this book and in other writings. He may mention parallelism, as in the example above, but he is not a property dualist;[40] he and a majority of cognitive scientists think that what happens in the mind *is* caused, ultimately as it were, by what happens in the brain. And Frith often notes that whatever their relation may exactly be *explanation* has a lot to do with causation.[41] So the idea of a complete explanation at a level that nonetheless stands in causal relations to a neural substrate is somewhat unstable. We should not attach too much of consequence to it. There is no need, in any case, to insist on these quirks, even if their accretion in this book and in the kind of literature it belongs to is indicative of a certain conceptual fog—and eventually produces effects.

The way out of the philosophical moving sands is, as evident in the quote above, to ask for complete explanations in *both* psychological and biological jargons. This is a curious requirement. If one has arrived at a *complete* explanation of anything, why should one go for a second round? Immediately following the fragment above, Frith summarizes his project thus:

> My approach will be to develop as complete as possible an explanation at the psychological level. In parallel with this there should eventually be a complete explanation at the physiological level. Both explanations should be continuously modified so that mapping one to the other is made easier. By searching for commonalities between the two domains, what we know about physiology will influence our explanation at the psychological level and vice versa.
>
> (1992, 27–8)

This is a customary formulation in cognitive psychology, illustrating what we have previously seen with, for example, David Marr's explanatory strategy. Explanation of mental phenomena, according to this story, is a two-front war. We are striving for contact, that is, we eventually "map" one level onto the other. Even if things may seem settled within each level, one cannot stop there.

Of course, one should not give "completeness" such a strong reading, but this uncharitable interpretation is not gratuitous. It shows that there is a simple, known, and important reason for wanting double explanatory bookkeeping: a maximally complete psychological explanation, *by itself*, would still be perceived as unsatisfactory. This is because the "cognitive," construed as an ontological domain, remains conceptually fragile, so an eye must at all times be kept on biology for signs of vindication. This may seem an outrageous claim, but the fact remains that cognitive psychologists themselves are trying hard to ground putative psychological mechanisms in biological fact. Why should they care if the biological did not have, given their own conceptual lenses, priority? This paradoxical predicament— insisting on *functional* explanation, but suggesting that it must somehow be backed by *biological* hard currency—is a consequence of the regimentation of the regular interpretive vocabulary. Psychological concepts, partially uprooted from their common usage, seem to need grounding. But attempts to reconfigure them result, again and again, in inherently instable notions.

This is seen in Frith, too. On the one hand, the talk of separate completeness and parallelism invites the idea that there is a kind of symmetry between biology and psychology. But on the other, he points to the priority of biology. For example, in the context of making the distinction between symptoms and diagnosis Frith says the following:

> Demonstrating that schizophrenic patients have certain cognitive abnormalities does not "explain" schizophrenia. "Explaining" schizophrenia inevitably involves

saying something about cause. This leads us back to the mind-brain problem. The aetiology of schizophrenia almost certainly involves abnormal brain development. Cognitive abnormalities can tell us nothing directly about brain structure and function, let alone brain development. What studies of cognition can "explain" is not schizophrenia, but schizophrenic symptoms.

(1992, 33)

Schizophrenia itself, he continues, might be eventually explained by a faulty biological process. This is a dead end, a sign of conceptual confusions got out of hand. Schizophrenia just is, as a matter of definition, medical history, and history of use, an arrangement of symptoms. To have schizophrenia *means* to manifest certain symptoms. Add to this hesitation the fact that there is little connection between the more abstract observations made in this context, where the nature of psychological explanation is in question, and those made earlier, where a focus on symptoms was recommended for local methodological reasons (due to the fragility of diagnostic categories, not the etiological primacy of biology).

It should be stressed that the sample above is no accident, but a symptom, one which resurfaces in a number of other writings by Frith. For example, in the 1996 *British Medical Bulletin* paper already mentioned, we find these remarks:

[These studies] address the question of whether schizophrenia or certain signs and symptoms are associated with certain cognitive impairments. As is well known, such studies cannot address questions of causation and will always be unsatisfactory since an apparent link may be spurious, being mediated by some hidden factor. There is a sense in which schizophrenia will never be satisfactorily "explained" in terms of cognitive impairments. Nor can an explanation solely in terms of a gene or a particular form of brain abnormality be considered satisfactory. In contrast, it is possible to "explain" particular signs or symptoms in cognitive terms and then link these to brain abnormalities. Such an explanation involves the description of a cognitive mechanism that causes the symptom of interest.

(623)

Frith criticizes here studies that are merely correlational. While they cannot determine causation, positing "cognitive mechanism[s]" could. This seems wrong. Correlation *is* an imperfect evidence of causation. It is far from clear why a biological explanation would not be satisfactory, if one could be had, and it is dubious that it would be unsatisfactory for the same reasons as its "cognitive" counterparts. And if "cognitive mechanism[s]" do cause "the symptom[s] of interest," we are back to the problem discussed above. Why should there still be "a sense in which schizophrenia will never be satisfactorily 'explained' in terms of cognitive impairments"? What is that sense?

In another paper, coauthored in 2000, we find a further elaboration, which includes the notable addition of phenomenology as a separate explanatory level:

> In order to understand symptoms like delusions of control we require an explanation at least three levels. First, at the cognitive level, we must understand how the symptom arises in terms of a model of motor control that can be applied to normal and abnormal cases and which makes a distinction between those aspects of motor control which reach awareness and those which do not. Second, at the physiological level we need to consider how the cognitive components of the model relate to underlying brain function. Third, our explanation of the symptom should give us some insight into what it is like to have that symptom. We should gain some inkling of the experience that lies behind the patient's report.
>
> (Frith, Blakemore, and Wolpert 2000, 358)

The point here is not to deny the importance of phenomenology, and of paying attention to the testimony of the patients. It is to note that a philosophical idea about the need for concomitant explanatory levels persists.

A last and quite different example comes from another paper, also coauthored by Frith, defending the so-called dysconnection hypothesis of schizophrenia. In this case, the view is simpler: a biological problem at the level of molecular mechanisms controlling neural development and functioning causes a failure in the cognitive mechanism(s) of self-monitoring, which at its turn causes the core symptoms of the illness:

> This theory postulates that the core pathology in schizophrenia resides in aberrant *N*-methyl-D-aspartate receptor (NMDAR)-mediated synaptic plasticity due to abnormal regulation of NMDARs by neuromodulatory transmitters like dopamine, serotonin, or acetylcholine. We argue that this neurobiological mechanism can explain failures of self-monitoring, leading to a mechanistic explanation for first-rank symptoms as pathognomonic features of schizophrenia, and may provide a basis for future diagnostic classifications with physiologically defined patient subgroups.
>
> (Stephan, Friston, and Frith 2009, 509)

The hypothesis of dysconnection[42] was pursued by Frith in other places, too, and it seems clearly biased toward a biological explanation of schizophrenia. But note that *psychological* machinery plays an intermediary causal role in the explanation. Moreover, the machinery is quite specific: self-monitoring mechanisms. We will see it at work below. To anticipate, the postulation of such cognitive mechanisms smuggles back into the picture regular psychological concepts.

VI

Frith was inspired in constructing his model of schizophrenia by the "theory of mind" hypothesis of autism. In the case of autism, he suggested, the triadic symptomatology identified by Wing and Gould (autistic aloneness, abnormal communication, lack of pretend play)[43] is thought to be determined by a single cognitive deficit: a developmental problem with "theory of mind" (ToM) (Frith 1992, 118). Similarly, in the case of schizophrenia, the proposal went, a discrete cognitive breakdown was at work. The candidate revealed in the last chapter of Frith's book was the capacity to represent mental states, or "metarepresentation." Frith followed in this case Alan Leslie's view that metarepresentation is the fundamental element of ToM, so in effect his explanation of schizophrenia is parallel to that of autism.

In part for historical reasons ("autism" was initially used by Eugen Bleuler and his followers to name the social withdrawal characteristic for schizophrenia), many in the field were captivated by the idea that schizophrenia was essentially "late-onset autism." The inspiring model of autism, however, appeared at the confluence of two theoretical trends, and it did not survive their fading away. The first trend was defined by Leslie's ideas of metarepresentation and "decoupling" as key elements of social cognition, an idea strongly influenced by propositional attitude theory. The second element was the attempt to conceive autism primarily as a failure to think about mental states, that is, to metarepresent.

These ideas—that ToM is based on a specific logico-syntactic process, and that autism is caused by an impairment in that very process—were then applied to the long-known fact that schizophrenics suffer a devastating setback in their social skills. While this latter fact is indisputable, it is no longer a matter of wide agreement that metarepresentation is the core of social cognition, or that autism is a disorder of ToM understood on Leslie's cognitive-mechanistic lines. The confluence that inspired Frith's ideas is no longer there, but research relating ToM and schizophrenia continues.

Given his views on explanation, and on explanatory access to diagnostics as such, Frith's approach was symptom-based. Three clusters of symptoms were defined, based on co-occurrence, and then three different cognitive mechanisms were posited to explain each of the classes of symptoms. The mechanisms were: (1) impaired willed action, (2) failure of self-monitoring, and (3) disorders in monitoring the intentions of others. (1) putatively explained negative symptoms such as social withdrawal, (2) could do the same for positive symptoms like thought insertion, whereas (3) accounted for paranoid delusions. The crucial claim of the theory was that all these three mechanisms were instances of a more general breakdown: metarepresentational failure (Frith 1992, 115ff).

I will focus in the following on the second and third mechanisms. It matters less for our purposes whether the model covers *all* symptoms associated with a diagnosis of schizophrenia.[44] Before moving on, a side note is necessary. It is the *first* mechanism that is meant to explain negative symptoms, and it is the schizophrenics with negative symptoms who are most similar in terms of symptoms or behavior to persons with autism. The model makes here what seems to be a counterintuitive move, by making *positive*-symptom schizophrenia cognitively closer to autism, thus betting on theory rather than evidence:

> In many ways the behaviour of people with autism resembles that of patients with negative schizophrenia. Such patients show a version of Wing's triad: stereotyped behaviour, social withdrawal, and poor language [...]. However, I shall suggest that it is schizophrenic patients with certain positive symptoms, such as paranoid delusions and delusions of reference, who have difficulty inferring correctly the mental states of others.
>
> (Frith 1992, 121)

A transparent artifice is used to patch this difficulty. The negative symptoms are also explained as a breakdown in metarepresentation, and thus the tension evaporates. Frith does this by suggesting that impaired access to one's own goals might cause negative manifestations (i.e., not acting on said goals). He refers in this context, for support, to work by Perner, but this amounts only to a tentative explanation. In the book referred to, Perner argues against a Piagetian view of patterns in action at early ages. Perner explains why young children do not seem to mind repeated failure and why they engage in the so called circular reactions thus:

> In other words, young children, at best, have goals that enable goal-directed action, but they do not yet conceive of having goals. Without this conception children do not expect completion of the planned action to produce the goal. And without this expectation they do not experience failure or success.
>
> (1991, 207)

The distinction between having goals and conceiving of goals is what Frith is driving at. But it is of little help, since, supposing it makes sense, it explains patterns of acting, not a *failure* to act. At best it could explain repetitiveness or failure to correct errors in reasonable time—manifestations that *are* seen in some schizophrenics. Negativity essentially involves, however, *absence* of action. The distinction is of no help in this case. Avolition, for example, seems to imply the absence or impotency of goals, not a "lack of access" to them, as if they became unreadable sectors of a hard drive. A failure to act is not a failure to *reflect* on acting, though the second can have effects on the first. The negative symptoms, moreover, cover a large spectrum of manifestations that could hardly be related to such a mechanism (though, as mentioned, it matters less if not all symptoms can be forced into one explanatory schema). The bottom line here is that we witness the effects of a theoretical lineage that begins with using the concept of goal in a dubious manner (Perner), and ends with the claim that one can explain *lack* of action by reference to goals (Frith). This is not conceptual innovation, but something akin to losing one's train of thought.

A crucial inspiration for Frith's model was a theoretical view of action initiation and control. When we act, the story goes, there is *monitoring* of the planning and execution of the action (Frith 1992, 73). This is needed mainly for rapid, online correction of action prior to the observation of consequences. At least in some cases we do not need to make serious mistakes in order to correct our action planning, and this keeps the price of correction low. Some of the actions plans are filtered out early, being found faulty, some actions are adjusted on the way. The story suggests, further, that it is also by monitoring that we become *aware* of our actions. Monitoring is what supposedly allows us to recognize the actions that we initiate as our own. Schizophrenics are known to have problems in this area: they have difficulties with action initiation (lack of willed action), action execution, and recognition of authorship and/or ownership of actions. Given a commitment to the monitoring theory, one can connect the dots and blame faulty monitoring for such troubles.

Frith extended the scope of this argument to mental states. One should expect something similar to the malfunction of corollary discharge[45] to affect the representation of mental states in schizophrenics. Typically, it is claimed, we become aware of mental states because there is monitoring of them, too, not only of actions. Thought is thus conceived as a kind of effortful *action*, an effort which leaves a (phenomenologically) recognizable trace (Frith 1992, 81). We represent mental representations (thus the terminology of *meta*representation), and thus, by this reflective effort, we become aware of them: "metarepresentation is the crucial mechanism that underlies this self-awareness" (Frith 1992, 116).

In the case of actions, it has been argued that corollary discharge (or "re-afference copy") effectively labels willed actions (as opposed to what Frith calls "stimulus-driven" actions and reflexes) as originating in the subject—as "self." Since, according to Frith, there is not only monitoring of actions, but also of *intentions* to act, something similar would happen at this level. Now, if the labeling/recognition mechanism *fails*, symptoms like thought insertion might emerge:

> Patients say that thoughts that are not their own are coming into their head. This experience implies that we have some way of recognizing our own thoughts. It is as if each thought has a label on it saying "mine". If this labelling process goes wrong, then the thought would be perceived as alien.
>
> (Frith 1992, 80)

Moreover:

> Thinking, like all our actions, is normally accompanied by a sense of effort and deliberate choice as we move from one thought to the next. If we found ourselves thinking without any awareness of the sense of effort that reflects central monitoring, we might well experience these thoughts as alien and, thus, being inserted into our minds.
>
> (81)

One may very well doubt the assimilation of thought to action, or reject the image of thoughts as bits of stuff that can carry labels. One needs to note at least that, fashionable as the motoric theory of thought may be, there are strong arguments against this view. Fundamentally, thoughts are subject to semantic evaluation and arguably are logically connected to language; this is not the case with actions, though expression of thought implies acting, including via speech acts. Moreover, whatever one may think about the putative phenomenology of thought, it is hard to square with the description above. For example, we do not struggle to take the next step in a reasoning chain, we struggle to take the right step, and these are quite different efforts. And we are familiar with spontaneous or idle thought (both effortless), which normally have no alien flavor, quite the opposite.

To exemplify Frith's third mechanism, which deals specifically with knowledge of other minds, let us look at some of the things he says about the

communicative difficulties of schizophrenics in the sixth chapter of his 1992
book. These problems lie specifically in the domain of discourse or pragmatics;
schizophrenics are more likely than typical controls to break Gricean norms.
According to Frith, this is because they fail to take into account the communicative
intentions of their conversational partners.[46] This failure can manifest itself as
missing intentions that are there, but also as seeing intentions where there are
none. Withdrawal might result in the first case, paranoid beliefs in the second.

One needs to be careful with handling the model and its predictions here.
Autistic individuals paradigmatically have considerable difficulties with social
interaction, but they do *not* experience delusions or hallucinations. Indeed, as
Frith notes (1992, 122), their presence is an exclusion criterion for autism. There
is some hesitation here, but the solution to the puzzle is of some consequence for
what follows. The suggestion is that it is the dissimilar developmental histories
that make the difference. Most autistic persons never had "mindreading"
abilities, whereas the schizophrenic did not have serious problems "for the first
20 years or so of life." This will be a recurrent theme in the later developments
of Frith's model: the schizophrenic is trying to use an ability that is *no longer*
functional. This kind of explanation is anticipated by a telling passage Frith
quotes when discussing communicative problems in schizophrenia: "There is a
futile, but still persisting struggle to communicate adequately" (Bertram Cohen
quoted in Frith 1992, 105).[47]

Let us now ask how these three seemingly separate cognitive mechanisms
coagulate in the conceptual framework of metarepresentation and ToM. The
idea appears early in the book. For example, we are told that "[t]he difficulty
that many schizophrenic patients have with recognizing emotions may be part
of a larger problem with making inferences about mental states" (52). The last
chapter is where the model comes together:

> I shall suggest that all the cognitive abnormalities underlying the signs and
> symptoms of schizophrenia are reflections of a defect in a mechanism that is
> fundamental to conscious experience. This mechanism has many labels. I shall
> use the term metarepresentation.
>
> (116)

The reduction then proceeds roughly on the following lines. Negative symptoms
are caused by a lack of access to goals. Goals are a kind of mental states. Access
is conceived as the ability to represent goals. So what the patient cannot do
is to represent goals. He cannot represent a mental representation; that is, he

cannot metarepresent. Passivity—thought insertion, delusions of control, and the like—is caused by lack of self-monitoring, which blocks self-awareness. Monitoring is conceived as representing the states being monitored. Therefore metarepresentation must be the problem. Lastly, paranoid delusions reflect dysfunctional monitoring of other people's intentions. The patient cannot represent others' mental states. Metarepresentation is again faulty.

This schema is problematic both in detail, and in overall conception. For example, Frith moves freely from the idea of monitoring which inherited its meaning from the physiology of corollary discharge, to another understanding of monitoring, identical for all purposes to Alan Leslie's conception of a ToM module whose main job is to handle metarepresentation. Whatever the evidence for either, they certainly are not analogous.

It is also clear that, as it happens in cases of intellectual contagion, a peculiar concept was unreflectively allowed to take and keep center stage, despite its lack of convincing explanatory credentials. Metarepresentation seemed a promising idea at the time due to Leslie's arguments that it is central to the development of social cognition (Leslie 1987, 1992, Leslie and Thaiss 1992). Leslie saw metarepresentation at work early on in pretense and then in full-blown "mindreading." He also suggested that such a structure reflected the relevant logico-semantic properties of intentional language (notably opacity). Not much of these views have survived scrutiny, even within psychology. It makes sense to ask what happens to Frith's proposal if the nature and role of metarepresentation in social cognition are not the ones sketched by Leslie beginning with the mid-1980s. Especially so since the ToM theory of autism has had diminishing support, even from its founders (Baron-Cohen 2002, Baron-Cohen 2004, Hill and Frith 2004, Morton 2004). What Kim Sterelny says about this latter situation can also be applied to Frith's model:

> Theory of mind explanations of autism have lost considerable ground in the last few years. It once seemed likely that interpretative deficits could explain other aspects of the syndrome, but that hope now seems unlikely to be fulfilled.
>
> (2003, 213)

With all this ground lost the architecture of Frith's unification necessarily collapses, but the *motivation* for his approach remains largely intact. Social cognition was known to be defective in schizophrenics since the illness was identified as such, after all. This is the motivation to tell an intelligible story about psychotic symptoms, a story which gives a specific kind of *satisfaction*: it shows in familiar terms why they act as they act and especially why they believe the strange things that they seem to believe.

Gregory Currie (2000) argues that one can in fact read two theories into Frith's proposal: "While Frith sometimes treats metarepresentation as his central theoretical concept, there are places where he gives more emphasis to the notion of efference copying" (2000, 171). This is on the lines of the discussion above about the difficulties with "monitoring." Currie prefers the subpersonal interpretation of "efference copying" or corollary discharge. But his criticism of metarepresentation matters more in this context. Currie asks an important question: why is it that schizophrenic delusions and hallucinations have peculiar *contents*? Metarepresentation *might* at best explain how a thought can become "disattributed." But why should the thought have bizarre content?

This question connects the discussion of Frith's theory with our larger theme. It invites in the problem of interpretability and reasonability. Frith illustrates a general weakness from this perspective. It seems that in trying to design cognitive models of schizophrenia—and there are many (e.g., Winn 2000, 249–50)— one proceeds roughly on the following lines: first, a cognitive mechanism that underlies *typical* abilities is posited; second, a breakdown of the mechanism is indicated as cause of the symptoms to be explained; the *nature* of the symptoms (e.g., content of delusions, their being resistant) and their forming of syndromes is then explained by answering the question "What would a person do, believe or experience if she found herself in such a condition (e.g., if she perceived others in such a way)?" For example, Frith suggests that being unable to adequately reflect on the intentions of others makes these other persons seem mysterious and unpredictable, *therefore* threatening, *therefore* likely to conspire against the ill person. *Who* would not feel threatened being faced with an opaque other? Who would not become paranoid when feeling constantly threatened? We are not far from asking: "Who would not go mad with such a mother?" From speculations about mechanism, the argument moves then, tacitly, to the regular territory of interpretation. It invites the specific "aha" moment of grasping a point of view.

This pattern, if indeed typical, points to the fundamental error we have been tracking in this chapter. The pattern assumes that the ill person preserves in *some* sense intact rationality. When one asks, "What would a person do if such-and-such?" the question *must* be asked about a *typical* individual, one situated well within the space of reasons, because this is the only available world for interpretation and understanding. This must be an individual about whom the common conceptual connections between, say, perception and belief, or between belief, desire, and action hold. Otherwise, we cannot begin to answer the question, we would not know how to explore the counterfactual vistas in front of us. Now, the psychotic person, when laboring under delusions, is not such an individual. This is not to say that she is outside the humanistic concern of others, or of the scope of their care. She is not even outside interpretation as such, but in a region where it has limited traction, where at least some questions asked in regular terms must remain moot.

Various authors have already proposed similar criticisms. Langdon and Coltheart, for example, reject the idea that "delusions are meaningful hypotheses which have been generated by *normal* reasoning processes to explain aberrant perceptual experiences, such as hallucinations" (2000, 185–6). They also reject the idea that such phenomena should be seen as the result of a *bias* in reasoning (what I have called a theory of shift above). Even a large bias could be overcome by commensurate evidence or argument, or by a change of scenery. This is not the case, by definition, with delusions. To use the distinction which is by now standard in the literature, delusional individuals probably have *deficits* (versus biases) in reasoning. This erodes the plausibility of understanding, and the legitimacy of forcing psychosis, for explanatory extravaganzas, into a position internal to common interpretative practices.

The conceptual difficulties illustrated above bring us in the vicinity of what Derek Bolton and Jonathan Hill have called, in reference to the canonical work of Jaspers, "psychiatry's problem" (2003, xvii). In trying to explain the seriously bizarre one remains torn between recognizing it at such, and domesticating it by betting that it must be, under its mantle, already familiar. This is a predicament that comes with the territory, not an accident of our temporary ignorance. We can hope that a more mature biological psychiatry will soon give us a typical medical explanation of psychosis, and better therapeutic tools. Still, we cannot but search for meaning in madness, as we search for meaning in every corner of our life. That we remain puzzled in this quest should not worry us too much; it is better than unjustified certainty. Such puzzles are tests and training grounds of our moral constitution, and perhaps this matters most. Here, we can always do better. There is no reason to deflate the envelope of concern, as we have so often done, to the fluctuating cone of light of our understanding.

Conclusion

I

In 1511, Titian, who had just moved to Padua, was commissioned to paint three frescoes representing Saint Anthony's miracles. This was to decorate the main hall (*sala delle adunanze*) of the upper level of the *Scuola del Santo*, which had been added in 1504. The small building—due to its size it is known by the diminutive *Scoletta*—is adjacent to the dominating, domed mass of the *Basilica di Sant'Antonio*, which has at its core the tomb of the thirteenth-century Lisboan saint. In the *Scoletta*, Titian painted three of the more popular moral tales associated with Anthony: the *Miracle of the Jealous Husband*, the *Miracle of the Healed Foot*, and the *Miracle of the Newborn*, also known in English as the *Miracle of the Speaking Babe* (Graham-Dixon 2004, Messaggero 2017, Cole 2018). This last fresco, which I thought fitting for the cover of this book, has two counterparts inside the Basilica: a 1505 marble relief by Antonio Lombardo, and a smaller, but more famous, bronze relief by Donatello, finished in 1450. All three[1] are canonical representations of the dangers of gossip and mistrust, and of Anthony's ability to restore domestic harmony. The presence of the infant is merely a device that marks his performance as miraculous.

The story is roughly the following. A child is born in a family of noble standing, their first. The husband, giving a listening ear to gossip, unreasonably suspects that he is not the father, and vilifies his wife. Anthony enters the scene to solve this conflict, and he does that by taking a shortcut. He addresses the infant directly, an apparently absurd gesture, and asks him to speak—to say who his father is. The infant dutifully responds, calming the fears of his suspicious father, and protecting the good name of his mother. In Titian's painting, an astonished audience witnesses the scene, turning to one another to share and confirm the experience. One instance of disbelief triggering multiple of conviction.

The reader may suspect that I refer to this story to stress the same point I made when I suggested, in a previous chapter, that developmental psychology at times outbid itself into zealous bankruptcy. Newborns, barring miracles, do not engage in conversations. Etc. And yes, I think this bit of visual culture fits nicely into the picture I presented above. But there is also a more general moral here, and I would like to conclude this book in its vicinity.

Anthony's performance qualifies as a miracle because it punctures the natural course of things. Uncomfortable comparison, but in another of his feats, he makes a dead body speak. These voices settle dilemmas, they bypass the need for messy and perhaps inconclusive detective work, and provide (moral) clarity. Now, in the story of the speaking babe, it isn't even clear that the voice is the infant's own, borrowed as it were from a future self. There is, at least, a sense in which it isn't. Anthony's question is meant to dissolve the dispute, and how could the child be authoritative in such matters? The answer comes as if an artifact gave testimony of its creation, as if one asked, archeologically, a thing unearthed: "Who made you?" We do after all summon material traces as witnesses to their own conception long after the creators have been swallowed by time.

The clarity brought by such miraculous testimony is soothing. But for Titian's painting—and the story behind it—to work, it can as well remain moot whether miracles can be conjured, indeed whether a young man, many centuries ago, conjured them. The point is that the image carries a lesson, and that the viewer should act according to that lesson. In other words, the truth of the painting is pedagogical; it need not be historical, too. The viewer, familiar with this story and others like it, will reflect on the fact that ultimately ambiguities and misconceptions can be evaporated, as the temporary imperfections that they are.

In science, the counterpart of this hopeful moral horizon has been the kind of epistemic optimism embodied in the heritage of the *Lumières*, and in characteristically modern philosophies of science, such as positivism. The ethos of modernity, which has been constitutive to the emergence of psychology as a science, has been much maligned, and often for flimsy reasons. But psychology may just be one of the places where skepticism is not merely reactionary, where ideals of scientificity, as all ideals, can do damage. In part this is so because psychology cannot live up to such ideals, unless it is willing to endure the kind of violence that Skinner & Co. did to it. In any case, it is a discipline with a (recent) history that invites measured criticism as to how it has practiced its creed. I think this is seen quite clearly if one focuses on the fragments of human life in which said life is not yet, no longer, or not fully a life of the mind. There, we either change the subject (as the behaviorists did), or accommodate a perspective in which some ambiguities are permanent, built into the unavoidable concepts of the field. As with Titian's speaking babe, not even miracles would iron these wrinkles out fully, due to their outlier character.

In the previous pages I have tried to make a case for this view mainly via a series of ideas and examples involving explanation. In cases of incipient, defective, or partial rationality, we begin to observe explanation slipping, as long as explanation is thought of psychologically, that is, in the vocabulary of agents motivated by beliefs and desires (or mental states with semantically evaluable content in whatever description), directing their actions in an imperfect, but unmistakable, spotlight of reason (i.e., feeling the pull of norms). In the regions I called "margins of psychology," this way of looking at people naturally begins to fade away. At bottom, this is because the vocabulary in which we know mind is not extendable and precisifiable from the outside. We have seen such extensions fail with attempts to introduce apparently innocuous ideas, such as miniaturized versions of (false) belief understanding, rudiments of practical reasoning, or paranoid reasoning style from defective premises.

There is nothing new or extraordinary about these observations, or indeed about this state of affairs in which there is friction between norms and naturalization (for the latter, compare the troubled relationship between ideas of justice and legal practice on the one hand, and psychology and the social sciences applied to law on the other). But, as basic tenet, the idea that a kind of explanation eventually loses grip would not take us far. So I focused instead on threads and details which are colored by their particular setting and by larger commitments, but which put together I thought illuminating, accepting that they will coalesce slowly and with a number of loose ends. Things are lost from such a messy picture, but more would be lost if one took a strictly argumentative, ahistorical approach. How we think of ourselves is also a story that keeps unfolding, and it is part of this unfolding that we face recurrently slippery tropes.

Since scientific careers in the real world are not built on leaving everything as it is, it is certain that we will hear again about imminent revolutions concerning development, mental illness, or, to mention an area not covered here, animal minds. Of course, a more sophisticated psychology will find ever subtler rudiments of mind, or splinters of method in madness. If precedent is reliable, it will not be satisfactory to such a science to accept that there is a sense in which we *cannot improve* on the idea that what we see in early childhood—*especially* when we look harder, and at younger ages—are rudiments. "When I was Three/I was hardly me," as A. A. Milne put it. The same goes for the idea that some minds are just broken, no matter how refined the translation we subject them to.

It will not matter much, either, how concepts are used in familiar situations that at least we understand well, even if by now there is a long history of botched regimentations of the basic psychological vocabulary. For example, assuming reasonably that nonexperts are poor observers of infants or psychotics, it is nonetheless clear that we are abundantly familiar with switching in everyday life from belief-desire reasons to explanations centered on tiredness or distress—and back—when we are unable to put our thoughts in *order*. This is a tell-tale sign among others of instances of, as it were, transient marginality. A narrative of explanatory progress, which otherwise is respectable, has blocked and will continue to block the view here. To it, this book is a cautionary footnote.

I have shown it perhaps poorly in these pages, but I have written at times against my affinity for the lack of patience with traditions and foggy notions manifested by apostles of science, such as that truly divine marquis, Condorcet. And, while borrowing from the critical traditions, I have often been a disloyal fellow traveler. A philosophy of psychology may have the luxury of contemplating the parallels with explanation in history, for example. But a historicist turn is not in the cards for the psychologist doing her or his work in the lab. And why should it? Rumors of a dialogue between the kind of critical prose I have tried here and science are exaggerated. The psychologist may still be willing to accept, or so I hope, that, from the asymmetrical position of foil, philosophy can take part in setting, or indeed dismantling, the stage for her or his findings.

II

Discussing in their monumental study of melancholy the penetration in popular culture, during the Later Middle Ages, of the doctrine of the temperaments, Klibansky, Panofsky, and Saxl wrote as follows:

> The echoes of Aristotle among the learned scholastics, St. Hildegard's visionary descriptions, highly subjective and often horrifying, Hugues de Fouilloi's interpretations expressly designed "ad aedificationem claustralium", the subtle doctrine of the medical schools, always sceptical of, or downright inimical to, a schematic adaptation of pure humoralism—all this was not calculated to become part of the common stock of knowledge or to serve as a guide to medieval man [...]. What was needed was not so much a full or even a profound picture as one that was clearly defined. Men wished to know how the choleric, the sanguine or the melancholy type could infallibly be recognised, at what times each had to

be particularly careful, and in what manner he had to combat the dangers of his particular disposition.

(Klibansky, Panofsky, and Saxl 1979, 113–14)

This is a fragment of the history of medicine as much as it is one belonging to the history of psychology. It brings into light the intellectual compromises inherent in popularization, no less in medieval times than in ours, but it reminds us, in so doing, of a more serious danger. Not only that sophisticated attempts to answer hard questions can be disfigured by vulgarization, but that it may be forgotten that they are attempts rather than answers—that they carry countless assumptions, qualifications, and limitations, that they embody philosophical allegiances, and that these cannot go unquestioned. If brilliant metaphors—humors and temperaments, clockwork and computer—are allowed to hold the scientific imagination captive, their undeniable usefulness is lost, turned into ideological blindness. Mesmerized by the essential role of irrigation technology in their culture, the Egyptian priests of old, otherwise adept anatomists due to the routine of dissecting and embalming corpses were utterly wrong about the heart and the circulatory system: they saw the heart as the source of a vast irrigation system, and were never able to grasp the division of labor between the two types of vessels in that system (Amidon and Amidon, 2011). Simply because ours is an age of science, of bureaucratized epistemic authority, does not eliminate this kind of vulnerability, especially when we ourselves are the object of inquiry. This is a permanent cultural anomaly, and we can only hope to keep it in check. Philosophy has a role to play in this context, and, it should be emphasized, a responsibility to speak, since what usually goes wrong is a matter of philosophical compass.

This book, for better or worse, has been an effort to take this responsibility seriously by criticizing an influential set of ideas in historical and current psychology, essentially the view that psychologically ambiguous or marginal cases can be conceived of as explanatorily continuous with paradigmatic cases. This view amounts, in some recent psychological literature, as in that of the temperaments, to imposing an explanatory order at the expense of fullness and profoundness. Now as then, this is a dubious balance of trade to maintain.

The overall goal of the book, I should emphasize one last time, has not been to attack psychology, a school of psychology, or a number of psychologists. I tried to expose, rather, the philosophical commitments that keep infecting some regions of psychology (early development and psychopathology have been the examples of choice). Some of these mistakes, such as those emanating from machine functionalism, are specific to certain schools, like cognitive psychology; and then there are certain misconceptions that are endemic, recurring despite radical theoretical changes and reorientations. Such an example is the idea that psychology fixes "naïve" concepts like belief, motive, or intention, which are integral to venerable interpretive practices, and thus makes them *un*ambiguously applicable, as terms of art, to previously ambiguous cases. One cannot, however, have under one foot the pre-theoretical plausibility of psychological explanation, and under the other extensions which annul that plausibility. To think one can stand on both is an unnecessary philosophical error—unnecessary since the multifarious traditions which merged to create psychology should offer plenty of avenues of dealing with different cases in suitably tailored ways. This includes the admirable scientific position of being clear about what is not clear, or clarifiable with a given set of concepts. The credentials of the discipline should not be threatened by embracing these differences, and the limits of the kind of explanations that define it. On the contrary, the illusion that there are clear-cut answers to age-old puzzles about human nature is, if anything, an archetypal philosophical illusion, not a symptom of scientific progress. Geertz's dictum remains valid:

> As with all such enterprises, there are a good many more ways of getting it wrong than there are of getting it right, and one of the most common ways of getting it wrong is through convincing ourselves that we have got it right—consciousness explained, how the mind works, the engine of reason, the last word.
>
> (Geertz 2001, 28)

I am aware that in the current climate of normalized self-aggrandizing, the spoilsport habits of philosophical skepticism are likely to be ignored. But then on the long term everything is, including intellectual achievements far superior to what I was able to offer here. In this spirit, I still thought it worthwhile to remind the reader, and myself, of the unfortunate limits and forgotten strengths of our self-understanding.

Beyond the prolonged divorce of psychology and common sense, and its significance for what we take our basic psychological concepts to be concepts of, we should remember that perspectives emanating from this dispute should not have grand ethical consequences. A recognition of what we grasp hesitantly or not at all is not a license for moral hierarchies, or for failing our duties of care and concern. They are, if anything, more stringent at the margins—but this is something better left to expression in a way of living, rather than in words.

Notes

Introduction

1   I initially found this image in Clair (2005, 260).

2   See e.g. the fascinating history of Frederik Ruysch's "cabinet" (van de Roemer 2009, Hansen 1996).

3   The pose is canonical, and probably borrowed from painting—see e.g. the *Miniature of Lord Herbert of Cherbury* by Isaac Oliver, early seventeenth century, or *Sir Brooke Boothby* by Joseph Wright of Derby, 1781.

4   The translations that are not given a source are mine. In such cases, I will also provide the original: "La pose mélancolique donnée ici au fœtus [...] semble dire le dépit de l'anatomiste qui, tout en excellant dans la description du corps humain, demeure encore incapable d'en comprendre la formation et le développement. C'est une sorte de mélancolie 'pré-biologique'. La connaissance de l'anatomie ne dit rien sur la vie parce qu'elle ne traite que du cadavre."

   Comar notes that the term "biology" is introduced only in 1802 by Lamarck.

5   The reader could, for example, look at the debates on there being culture-specific emotions to form an opinion on this matter.

6   There is a thread of literature in psychiatry that investigates the so-called new religious movements (e.g., Hare Krishna, druids). Members of some such groups have similarities, statistically, with clinically delusional (i.e., diagnosed) individuals, though, unlike the latter, they are not distressed. A question that comes up in this literature is whether one can talk about delusional *subcultures* in such cases. I will come back to this question later in the book.

   More recently (e.g., in the 2016 and 2020 US electoral cycles, and during the Covid-19 pandemic), the explosion of conspiracy theories, and of the online communities built around them, has raised comparable problems. For an overview, see Butter and Knight (2020). For a rejection of the idea that mental illness plays a significant role, see Van Prooijen (2018).

7   On this analogy, see Chapter 6.

8   This is documented in Chapter 7.

9   Original: "Pour cette raison nouvelle qui règne dans l'asile, la folie ne représente pas la forme absolue de la contradiction, mais plutôt un âge mineur, un aspect d'elle-même, qui n'a pas droit à l'autonomie, et ne peut vivre qu'enté sur le monde

de la raison. La folie est enfance. Tout est organisé à la Retraite pour que les aliénés soient minorisés" (Foucault 1972, 509).

Original: "Et les juges n'y contredisent point, qui n'acceptent pas comme crime le geste d'un fou, qui décident de la curatelle en supposant toujours que la folie n'est qu'empêchement provisoire, où l'âme n'est pas plus atteinte qu'elle n'est inexistante ou fragmentaire chez l'enfant" (Foucault 1972, 227).

Chapter 1

1   The remark is unexceptional. To give another example, in his *Intellectual History of Psychology*, Daniel Robinson has this to say on the matter: "But in its current form, psychology is so various, so partitioned into separate provinces, that the nonspecialist might pardonably conclude that there is no unified subject at all" (1995, 3–4).

2   This may be true only of Anglophone academic psychology.

3   Skinner is the prime example; see Skinner(1971) for an extended presentation and Skinner (2005a) for a fictional portrayal. In a preface written to the latter ("Walden Two Revisited") three decades after the original publication, Skinner notes: "It is true that when the behavioral sciences have gone beyond the collection of facts to recommend courses of action and have done so by predicting consequences, they have not been too helpful. [...] From the very beginning the application of an experimental analysis of behavior was different. It was doubly concerned with consequences. Behavior could be changed by changing its consequences— that was operant conditioning—but it could be changed because other kinds of consequences would then follow. Psychotic and retarded persons would lead better lives, time and energy of teachers and students would be saved, homes would be pleasanter social environments, people would work more effectively while enjoying what they were doing, and so on" (2005b, viii).

    For vehement opposition, see Chomsky (1971), or, for a disturbing picture of the confident behavioral scientist in the planning rooms of the Vietnam War, Chomsky (1969). For a parallel—deducting sociopolitical consequences from *psychodynamic* theory—see Staub (2011) on brainwashing.

    A thread of literature which I do not discuss here is that which criticizes the role of psychology and psychiatry within the ensemble of Western science which was part of the imperial and colonial enterprise. The militant locus classicus is Frantz Fanon's work (1952, 2002); for a more recent take on the matter see Bhatia (2017). For a synthetic discussion of the notion of "indigenous psychology" see e.g. Okazaki, David, and Abelmann (2008).

4   To quote just one example, discussing learning theory, Stuart Shanker says: "Both [behaviorism and AI] proceed from the assumption that there is a continuum

leading from reflexes to reactions to concept-acquisition, and that the only way for psychology to explain the mechanics of learning is by having a uniform grammar of description [...]. This is why it is so often argued these days that AI is just a form of neo-behaviourism" (1998, 51).

5   On this analogy, see e.g. Greenwood (2009, xxiii, 7, 12) and Chomsky (2000, 84, 108).

6   Paradigmatic, as already noted in the Introduction, in the sense of normative measure of things.

7   See Greenwood (2004) for a study of what this difference meant for the evolution of social psychology in the United States.

8   E.g. "We impute our orthodox logic to him, or impose it upon him, by translating his deviant dialect" (Quine 1986, 81).

9   For a recent instance of what one might call "neuropesimism"—a view which shows how little we in fact know about the workings of the brain—see Cobb (2020).

10   "Let the psychologist tell us why we are deceived; but we can tell ourselves and him why we are not deceived" (Ryle 1949, 326).

Chapter 2

1   The astronomer who discovered the satellites of Mars in 1877.

2   As we will see later in the book, historicism is a big part of the picture here. For an overview, see Beiser (2011).

3   Original: "Le seul fondement de croyance dans les sciences naturelles est cette idée, que les lois générales, connues ou ignorées, qui règlent les phénomènes de l'univers, sont nécessaires et constantes; et *par quelle raison* [emphasis added] ce principe serait-il moins vrai pour le développement des facultés intellectuelles et morales de l'homme, que pour les autres opérations de la nature?" (Condorcet 1793–94/1822, 262).

4   I am leaving aside what is perhaps the most interesting element of Mill's conception of Ethology—that it is, as the etymology suggests, a science of *character*, or, to be precise, of character *formation*. One could thus draw not only a parallel between Mill's "moral sciences"—the translation of which is the origin of the German term *Geisteswissenschaften*—but also one between his Ethology and the idea of *Bildung*, which, with shifted connotations, will be placed at the core of the *Geisteswissenschaften* by Gadamer, a move of lasting consequence.

5   James, even without direct disciples, has been considered very influential (Miller 1983, Greenwood 2009).

6   Or, in a now anachronistic sense, "psychosis." James considers adopting this terminology later in the book (1890/1983, 185–6).

7   He refers to "machine-like" behavior (e.g., reflexes) which is nonetheless adaptive, functional, etc.

8   He returns to it, for example, at the beginning of chapter VIII (James 1890/1983, 197).
9   Ladd calls the latter "a 'mess of pottage', or little better" (1892, 51).
10 See also Ladd (1892, 50–1).
11 The analogy is James's, so "special science" does not have its current sense of roughly "natural science which is not physics": "Every special science, in order to get at its own particulars at all, must make a number of convenient assumptions and decline to be responsible for questions which the human mind will continue to ask about them. Thus physics assumes a material world" (1892a, 147).
12 He mentions in this respect the "modern doctrine of aphasia" (James 1892a).
13 See also: "Now the provisional value of such knowledge as this, however inexact it be, is still immense. It sketches an entire programme of investigation, and defines already one great *kind* of law which will be ascertained. The *order in time* of the nerve currents, namely, is what determines the *order in time*, the coexistences and successions of the states of mind to which they are related" (James 1892a, 152).
14 Of which James claimed he was able to cure himself, presumably due to his psychology (Greenwood 2009).
15 See also Watson (1917), where he denounces the American psychologists' "Freudian cult" (1917, 85) while accepting with a degree of reticence that there is truth in Freud.
16 James's text continues thus: "So the seeker of his truest, strongest, deepest self must review the list carefully, and pick out one on which to stake his salvation. All other selves thereupon become unreal" (1892/2001, 53).
17 In the following I refer to behaviorism in psychology, as practiced by psychologists, and not to its counterpart in philosophy, logical behaviorism.
18 "Experimental pedagogy, the psychology of drugs, the psychology of advertising, legal psychology, the psychology of tests, and psychopathology are all vigorous growths. […] At present these fields are truly scientific and are in search of broad generalizations which will lead to the control of human behavior" (Watson 1913/1994, 251).
19 Except in the "scientific" sense of delicate movements of the larynx.
20 The "circles" at work: in the *Plea*, James invites both the biologist and the philosopher to be psychologists. Nowadays cognitive science is an even larger melting pot.
21 Here is a sample of what he says about the psychology of ideas and meaning: "The practice may have been defensible when inquiries into verbal processes were philosophical rather than scientific, and when a science of ideas could be imagined which would some day put the matter in better order; but it stands in a different light today. It is the function of an explanatory fiction to allay curiosity and to bring inquiry to an end" (Skinner 1957, 6).

22 "[T]he basis of Behaviorism is just as philosophical as my criticism: Behaviorism grows on epistemological ground" (Köhler 1947/1992, 32).

23 Principles such as: *"Experienced order in space is always structurally identical with a functional order in the distribution of underlying brain processes"* (Köhler 1947/1992, 61—emphasis in the original).

24 Physics too assumed that the experience of an external world and the experiences of reading instruments were truthful. It was just that physics managed to "refine" more of its early qualitative observations into quantitative measurements.

25 They are undeniable in, for example, robotics; the question of how to model vision so as to *program* a machine to "see"—to mimic our abilities to interact with the visual world—is certainly a fascinating topic of research. There has been enormous progress in recent years in machine vision—whole academic programs are dedicated to it, and the job market will only accelerate this process. The question whether such a research program *explains* vision in animals remains a separate problem.

26 He died before the book was published.

27 See e.g. Morton's word recognition example (2004, 21–2), in which a cognitive unit called "logogen" was postulated to integrate stimulus and context so as to identify words. The logogen as a system of rules could be "realized" by a number of devices, from a single neuron to a computer.

28 Data structures that can be manipulated by a program.

29 It is also interesting to note the larger context here. Eye tracking is fashionable tech, and is now used in a variety of areas, many of them unrelated to academic preoccupations, from corporate studies on webpage optimization to on-board driving safety systems (are you paying *attention* to the road?).

30 Chapter 6 discusses developmental theories extensively.

31 There are, of course, even more sanguine proposals in *philosophy* that recommend equivalent maneuvers. They range in substance and style from Quine's psychologization of epistemology to recent experimental philosophy. Psychologists are not, by far, alone.

Chapter 3

1 Makkreel and Rodi, writing the introductory study for the revised translation of the *Einleitung*, justify translating *Geisteswissenschaften* as "Human Sciences" by the need to stress both that "interpretation and the circularity associated with it are inherent to both the natural and human sciences" (1989b, xiii–xiv), and that Dilthey's distinction between *Natur-* and *Geisteswissenschaften*—and explanation and understanding—is more nuanced than commonly thought (1989: xiii–xiv). In

his earlier monograph dedicated to Dilthey, Makkreel was of the opinion that for rendering *Geisteswissenschaften* in English, "the widely accepted expression 'human studies' remains the best translation" (1975/1992, 35).

2   Original: "Ich schließe mich an den Sprachgebrauch derjenigen Denker an, welche diese andere hälfte des *globus intellectualis* als Geisteswissenschaften bezeichnen. Einmal ist diese Bezeichnung, nicht am wenigsten durch die weite Verbreitung der Logik J. St. Mill's, eine gewohnte und allgemein verständliche geworden" (Dilthey 1883, 6).

3   See Makkreel (1975/1992—chapter 1) for extensive background.

4   Original: "Die Antworten Comte's und der Positivisten, St. Mill's und der Empiristen auf diese Fragen schienen mir die geschichtliche Wirklichkeit zu verstümmeln, um sie den Begriffen und Methoden der Naturwissenschaften anzupassen. Die Reaktion hiergegen […] schien mir die berechtigte Selbständigkeit der Einzelwissenschaften, die fruchtbare Kraft ihrer Erfahrungsmethoden und die Sicherheit der Grundlegung einer sentimentalischen Stimmung zu opfern, welche die für immer verlorene Befriedigung des Gemüths durch die Wissenschaft sehnsüchtig zurückzurufen begehrt" (Dilthey 1883, xvi).

5   This is not intended as a piece of Dilthey scholarship so I am simplifying. See Makkreel's studies for the important differences between *Erfahrung* and *Erleben*. What follows is significantly indebted to Makkreel's analyses (Makkreel and Rodi 1989a, Makkreel 2012, 1975/1992).

6   Original: "Alle Wissenschaft ist Erfahrungswissenschaft" (Dilthey 1883, xvi). Note the displaced echo in Köhler of this position.

7   Dilthey qualifies the idea of purposiveness as "indestructible."

8   Original: "Die Aufgaben einer solchen grundlegenden Wissenschaft kann die Psychologie nur lösen, indem sie sich in den Grenzen einer deskriptiven Wissenschaft hält, welche Tatsachen und Gleichförmigkeiten an Tatsachen feststellt, dagegen die erklärende Psychologie, welche den ganzen Zusammenhang des geistigen Lebens durch gewisse Annahmen ableitbar machen will, von sich reinlich unterscheidet. […] [S]ie ist demnach die erste und elementarste unter den Einzelwissenschaften des Geistes; […] Für die Psychologie selber aber ergibt sich aus ihrer Stellung im Zusammenhang der Geisteswissenschaften, daß sie als descriptive Wissenschaft […] sich unterscheiden muß von der erklärenden Wissenschaft, welche, ihrer Natur nach hypothetisch, einfachen Annehmen die Tatsachen des geistigen Lebens zu unterwerfen unternimmt" (Dilthey 1883/1990, 32–3).

9   Original: "Diese Metaphysik des Geistes (rationale Psychologie) wurde dann, als die mechanische Auffassung des Naturzusammenhangs und die Korpuskularphilosophie zur Herrschaft gelangten, von anderen hervorragenden Metaphysikern zu derselben in Beziehung gesetzt. Aber jeder Versuch scheiterte, auf dem Grunde dieser Substanzenlehre mit den Mitteln der neuen Auffassung

der Natur eine haltbare Vorstellung des Verhältnisses von Geist und Körper auszubilden" (Dilthey 1883/1990, 7).

10 Original: "Der Beweis wird versucht, daß eine allgemein anerkannte Metaphysik durch eine Lage der Wissenschaften bedingt war, die wir hinter uns gelassen haben, und sonach die Zeit der metaphysischen Begründung der Geisteswissenschaften ganz vorüber ist" (Dilthey 1883/1990, xix).

11 Here is the larger context: "In the human studies, to the contrary, the nexus of psychic life constitutes originally a primitive and fundamental datum. We explain nature, we understand psychic life. For in inner experience [*innere Erfahrung*] the processes of one thing acting on another, and the connections of functions or individual members of psychic life into a whole are also given. The experienced whole [*erlebte Zusammenhang*] is primary here, the distinction among its members only comes afterwards" (Dilthey 1977, 27–8).

12 The translation is mine. Original: "Nach den Objekten und nach der Natur des menschlichen Denkens sind die drei möglichen wissenschaftlichen Methoden: die (philosophisch oder theologisch) spekulative, die physikalische, die historische. Ihr Wesen ist: zu erkennen, zu erklären, zu verstehen. Daher der alte Kanon der Wissenschaften: Logik, Physik, Ethik;—nicht drei Wege zu einem Ziel, sondern die drei Seiten eines Prisma, wenn das menschliche Auge das ewige Licht, dessen Glanz es nicht zu ertragen vermöchte, im Farbenwiederschein ahnen will" (Droysen 1882, 11).

13 Which he also calls "constructive" to emphasize that it is a *tradition* that is criticized: "Sie würde mit dem Namen der konstruktiven Psychologie noch schärfer bezeichnet werden. Zugleich würde dieser Name den grossen historischen Zusammenhang, in welchem sie steht, herausgeben" (Dilthey 1894/1990, 139–40).

   Translation: "It would thus be more exact to designate it by the term 'constructive psychology'. This term also underscores the vast historical context to which it belongs" (Dilthey 1977, 24).

14 Original: "Ein Kampf aller gegen alle tobt auf ihrem Gebiete nicht minder heftig als auf dem Felde der Metaphysik. Noch ist nirgends am fernsten Horizonte etwas sichtbar, was diesen Kampf zu entscheiden die Kraft haben möchte. Zwar tröstet sie sich mit der Zeit, in welcher die Lage der Physik und Chemie auch nicht besser schien; […] Zudem hindert die Unlösbarkeit des metaphysischen Problems vom Verhältnis der geistigen Welt zur körperlichen die reinliche Durchführung einer sicheren Kausalerkenntnis auf diesem Gebiete. So kann niemand sagen, ob jemals dieser Kampf der Hypothesen in der erklärenden Psychologie endigen wird und wann das geschehen mag. So sind wir, wenn wir eine volle Kausalerkenntnis herstellen wollen, in einen Nebel von Hypothesen gebannt, für welche die Möglichkeit ihrer Erprobung an den psychischen Tatsachen gar nicht in Aussicht steht" (Dilthey 1894/1990, 142).

15 *Imperium in imperio* (Dilthey 1989, 58).

16 The translation is mine. Original: "erweitert Beobachtung der Lebensentwicklung und der krankhaften Zustände" (1883/1990, 15).

The context is the following: "On the other hand, I can start from the world of physical nature, as I see it before me, and perceive psychic facts ordered within space and time; I then see changes within spiritual life subject to external interference—natural or experimental—consisting of physical changes impinging on the nervous system. *Observation of human growth and pathology* can extend this standpoint into a comprehensive picture of the dependence of the human spirit on the body. This results in a scientific approach which proceeds from outer to inner, from physical changes to mental ones" (Dilthey 1989, 67).

17 "At both point of transition between the study of nature and that of the human world—i.e. where nature influences the development of the mind and where it is either influenced by or forms the passageway for influencing other minds—both sorts of knowledge always intermingle" (Dilthey 1989, 70).

18 Original: "der Naturzusammenhang auf die Entwicklung des Geistigen einwirkt" (1883/1990, 18).

19 Original: "Auf dem Grenzgebiet der Natur und des Seelenlebens haben Experiment und quantitative Bestimmung sich der Hypothesenbildung in ähnlicher Weise dienstbar erwiesen, als dieses im Naturerkennen der Fall ist. In den zentralen Gebieten der Psychologie ist nichts hiervon zu bemerken" (Dilthey 1894/1990, 145).

Note that the use of "frontiers" in the translation may misleadingly suggest that this is an area where one can push for further expansion—a doctrine of scientific "manifest destiny." This suggestion of progress is absent from the original, which refers merely to a "borderland."

20 Original: "Sie [die beschreibender Psychologie] hat die *Regelmäßigkeiten* im Zusammenhange des *entwickelten* Seelenlebens zum Gegenstand. Sie stellt diesen Zusammenhang des inneren Lebens in einem *typischen* Menschen dar" (Dilthey 1894/1990, 152—emphasis added).

21 The danger that Dilthey saw in his earlier work was subjectivism.

22 I refer the reader again to Frederick Beiser's comprehensive discussion of German historicism (2011).

23 Selections were published as *The Idea of History* in the mid-1940s (Collingwood died in 1943), and closer to our time (1999) as *The Principles of History*. Fragments from both volumes were intended as part of a unitary project begun in the 1930s and which was never completed.

24 "The new science of human nature was therefore envisaged as a science of human thought, or the rational part of human nature. [...] The proposal, then, was to replace logic and ethics, and their kindred economics and aesthetics, by a science covering the same ground but using naturalistic methods" (Collingwood 1999, 82).

25   Rather than, say, emergence or rise of psychology. Collingwood took note of what he saw as the *changed* role of psychology after the eighteenth century.

26   The likes of Locke, Hume, or Kant.

27   This is reminiscent of Wittgenstein's more famous dictum that in psychology "problem and method pass one another by" (Wittgenstein 1953/2009 II—§371).

28   Which was not particularly stable; see Dray and van der Dussen (1999).

29   For example: "But historical knowledge is not concerned only with a remote past. If it is by historical thinking that we re-think and so rediscover the thought of Hammurabi or Solon, it is in the same way that we discover the thought of a friend who writes us a letter, or a stranger who crosses the street. Nor is it necessary that the historian should be one person and the subject of his inquiry another. It is only by historical thinking that I can discover what I thought ten years ago, by reading what I then wrote, or what I thought five minutes ago, by reflecting on an action that I then did, which surprised me when I realized what I had done. In this sense, all knowledge of mind is historical" (Collingwood 1992, 219).

30   See Collingwood (1935/1999, 179–80); or consider such claims: "Over and over again, as we have seen, the [positivistic] principle has been denied, but those who denied it have never completely freed their minds from its influence" (Collingwood 1992, 175).

31   "Naturalistic" (Collingwood 1992, 155—remark on Frazer) or "physical" (Collingwood 1999, 92) anthropology, to be precise. See also Collingwood (1992, 224), and similar claims in the *Idea*, for example: "[A]s long as the validity of scientific thought in its own allotted filed of nature was left unquestioned, its prestige reacted on historical thought and twisted in into pseudo-scientific forms. Thus arose a number of hybrid sciences such as anthropology, *Völkerpsychologie*, comparative philology, etc., whose general principle lies in extracting historical facts from the context in which alone they are truly, that is historically, intelligible, reassembling them in a classificatory system according to their likeness and unlikeness, and attempting to lay down general laws governing their relations. These sciences have always been regarded with distaste by historians, because the historian […] cannot tolerate the substitution for any one fact whatever of another more or less like it" (Collingwood 1935/1999, 179–80).

32   Here Collingwood can be read as expressing a version of the idea of *Bildung*.

33   See especially Collingwood (1948).

34   E.g. "To speak of the psychology of reasoning, or the psychology of the moral self (to quote the titles of two well-known books), is to misuse words and confuse issues, ascribing to a quasi-naturalistic science a subject-matter whose being and development are not natural but historical" (Collingwood 1992, 231).

Or: "Psychology has always approached the study of thought with a perfectly clear and conscious determination to ignore one whole department of the truth, namely to ignore the self-critical function of thought and the criteria which that function implied. From this determination it cannot depart. It stands committed to it, not in its character as science, but in its character as psychology, a science which ever since the sixteenth century has been working out with a good of success methods appropriate to the study of feeling" (Collingwood 1948, 115–16).

35 But see Collingwood (1948, 117–18) for a criticism of Freud's *anthropological* speculations. For example: "[H]owever remarkable have been the triumphs of psychology when it has attended to its proper business, the study of feeling, its claim to have thrown light on the processes of thinking is incapable of surviving any critical inspection of the work done by psychologists when they deal with such matters as the nature and function in human life of religion or art; the aims and prospects, hopes and fears, of what is called civilization; or the intellectual structure of institutions which, because they are found in civilizations other than that to which the writer belongs, are called savage."

36 "To think that [historical events, actions] can be thus merely perceived is to think of them not as mind but as nature; and consequently sciences of this type tend systematically to dementalize mind and convert it into nature" (Collingwood 1992, 223).

37 Early in the book, Gardiner points to the systematic and law-like character of psychoanalytic tenets, but does not take a stance on their scientific validity. He also compares the use of concepts in psychoanalysis and in behaviorism—"the other school" of psychology (1952/1978, 20).

Chapter 4

1 In Collingwood's story, a haughty musician friend of the hypothetical traveler advises him upon reading one of the philosophers' papers: "there is nothing here about music at all" (Collingwood 1999, 90).

2 See the reference to Frederik Ruysch's in the Introduction.

3 For the so-called resolute reading and its precursors see Cerbone (2000), Conant (1991, 2000), Stroud (1965/2002), Putnam (2000), Cavell (1979/1999—chapter V); for a reply see Hacker (2001c—chapters 4 & 5). A more recent version of the debate is available in Miguens (2020).

4 "[I]f I say of someone that he is kind or cruel, loves truth or is indifferent to it, he remains human in either case. But if I find a man to whom it literally makes no difference whether he kicks a pebble or kills his family, since either would be an antidote to *ennui* or inactivity, I shall not be disposed, like consistent relativists, to attribute to him merely a different code of morality from my own or that of most men, or declare that we disagree on essentials, but shall begin to speak of insanity and inhumanity; I shall be inclined to consider him mad, as a man who thinks he

is Napoleon is mad; which is a way of saying that I do not regard such a being as being fully a man at all" (Berlin 1980, 166). I was led to Berlin's essay by Conant's comparison between the logical and the moral "alien" (1991—endnote 112).

5   Hanganu-Bresch and Berkenkotter (2019) document a few cases that are relevant for this topic. See also my review of this book (Tudorie 2021).

6   Is psychopathy a moral or a medical category? Should there be "screening" for psychopathy? See Seabrook (2008) for an example of debating this issue in the intellectual press.

7   Original: "Wie würde eine Gesellschaft von lauter tauben Menschen aussehen? Wie, eine Gesellschaft von 'Geistesschwachen'? *Wichtige Frage!* Wie, also, eine Gesellschaft, die viele unserer gewöhnlichen Sprachspiele nie spielte? [Vgl. Z 371.]" (Wittgenstein 1990a, 169—§957).

8   See below the discussion on Snell, Onians, and Jaynes.

9   Frazer himself describes the ritual this way: "The strange rule of this priesthood has *no parallel in classical antiquity*, and cannot be explained from it. To find an explanation we must go farther afield. No one will probably deny that such a custom savours of a barbarous age, and, surviving into imperial times, *stands out in striking isolation from the polished Italian society of the day*, like a primaeval rock rising from a smoothshaven lawn. It is the very rudeness and barbarity of the custom which allow us a hope of explaining it" (1890/2009, 14–15—emphasis added). See also Hacker (2001a, 74).

10 Therefore the terminology of "genetic explanation."

11 For comments on this point, see Cioffi (1998), Hacker (2001a), Bouveresse (2008).

12 Original: "Frazers Darstellung der magischen und religiösen Anschauungen der Menschen ist unbefriedigend: sie läßt diese Anschauungen als *Irrtümer* erscheinen. […] Schon die Idee, den Gebrauch—etwa die Tötung des Priesterkönigs—erklären zu wollen, scheint mir verfehlt. Alles, was Frazer tut, ist, sie zu Menschen, die so ähnlich denken wie er, plausible zu machen. Es ist sehr merkwürdig, daß alle diese Gebräuche endlich sozusagen als Dummheiten dargestellt werden. Nie wird es aber plausible, daß die Menschen aus purer Dummheit all das tun" (Wittgenstein 1993, 118).

13 Perhaps a more expressive translation would end with "by mistake." Original: "Frazer wäre im Stande zu glauben, daß ein Wilder aus Irrtum stirbt" (Wittgenstein 1993, 130).

14 Original: "Der Unsinn ist hier, daß Frazer es so darstellt, alt hätten diese Völker eine vollkommen falsche (ja wahnsinnige) Vorstellung vom Laufe der Natur, während sie nur eine merkwürdige Interpretation der Phänomene besitzen. D.h., ihre Naturkenntnis, wenn sie sie niederschrieben, würde von der unsern sich nicht *fundamental* unterscheiden. Nur ihre *Magie* ist anders" (1993, 140).

15 "Nur *beschreiben* kann man hier und sagen: so ist das menschliche Leben" ("Here one can only *describe* and say: this is what human life is like") Wittgenstein (1993, 120-1).

16 "Frazer ist viel mehr savage, als die meisten seiner savages … " ("Frazer is much
    more savage than most of his savages … ") (Wittgenstein 1993, 130–1).

17 I take it that this is one of Cioffi's important observations—that it makes little sense
    to insist that the practitioners will *never* be able to justify their practice; the point is
    rather that they need not do it, that the practice makes demanding for justification
    awkward.

18 This would obviously require an extended discussion, and it depends on how one
    reads "functioning." Note, for example, that the thread of literature dealing with the
    psychotic-like characteristic of some "new religious movements" implies that whole
    communities can be infected by delusions. These cases are indeed problematic
    and cover a number of rather different instances, from suicidal sects, to benign
    communal life. In the best situations, the striking thing to notice is that, despite
    voicing bizarre convictions, members do *not* appear ill. Or, as psychiatrists would
    rather put it, they remain *functional*. Even a society of the mad, to the extent that it
    is a society, may not be itself mad; it may even prove healing.

19 Original: "Frères humains, laissez-moi vous raconter comment ça s'est passé. On
    n'est pas votre frère, rétorquerez-vous, et on ne veut pas le savoir. Et c'est bien vrai
    qu'il s'agit d'une sombre histoire, mais édifiante aussi, un véritable conte moral,
    je vous l'assure. Ça risque d'être un peu long, après tout il s'est passé beaucoup de
    choses, mais si ça se trouve vous n'êtes pas trop pressés, avec un peu de chance vous
    avez le temps. Et puis ça vous concerne: vous verrez bien que ça vous concerne"
    (Littell 2006).

20 Unfortunately this English edition sometimes deviates from the original: "Zumal
    da Ilias und Odyssee, die am Anfang alles Griechischen stehen, unmittelbar zu uns
    sprechen und uns stark anrühren, übersehen wir leicht, wie grundverschieden von
    dem uns Gewohnten bei Homer alles ist" (Snell 1946/2011, 7).

    Perhaps a better way to render the last part would be: "how radically different
    from what is familiar to us is everything in Homer."

21 Original: "[D]ie Griechen haben nicht nur mit Hilfe eines schon vorweg gegebenen
    Denkens nur neue Gegenstände (etwa Wissenschaft und Philosophie) gewonnen
    und alte Methoden (etwa ein logisches Verfahren) erweitert, sondern haben, was
    wir Denken nennen, erst geschaffen … " (1946/2011, 7).

22 "die uns entfernteste und fremdeste Stufe des Griechentums" (Snell 1946/2011, 12).

23 This way of putting it has little to do with psychology, but refers to a cultural
    heritage which has come to inform the meaning of the Western concept of
    thought.

24 Original: "Wenn im Folgenden etwa behauptet wird, die homerischen Menschen
    hätten keinen Geist, keine Seele und infolgedessen auch sehr viel anderes noch
    nicht gekannt, ist also nicht gemeint, die homerischen Menschen hätten sich
    noch nicht freuen oder nicht an etwas denken können und so fort, was absurd
    wäre; nur wird dergleichen eben nicht als Aktion des Geistes oder der Seele

interpretiert: in *dem* Sinn gab es noch keinen Geist und keine Seele. [...] Natürlich war "etwas" da, das an der Stelle dessen stand, was die späteren Griechen als Geist oder Seele auffaßten—in dem Sinn hatten die homerischen Griechen natürlich Geist und Seele—, nur wäre es verwaschenes, unprägnantes Gerede, wenn man ihnen deswegen Geist und Seele zuspräche: denn Geist, Seele usw. "sind" nur im Selbstbewußtsein" (Snell 1946/2011, 10).

25 See Snell (1953—chapters 1, 10).

26 See Jaynes (1976/2000, 73–4). This view naturally led Jaynes to speculate further about hallucinated voices we have clear evidence about in "normal" and clinical settings. This is not the only instance of theoretical construction in which a certain kind of civilization and schizophrenia intersect, though it usually happens in antipsychiatric writings.

27 See especially the Introduction (1–18).

28 See e.g. 1976/2000, 84–5, where Jaynes tries, and, I think, fails, to convey the experience of the bicameral man by analogy with the "absent-minded driver," *minus* whatever conscious thoughts the driver might have while absent-mindedly driving: "Now simply subtract that consciousness and you have what a bicameral man would be like." *How*, one might want to ask.

29 Original: "Dahinter steht allerdings die Überzeugung, daß dies Fremde uns trotz allem verständlich ist, das heißt, daß wir das so Ausgegrenzte doch mit lebendigem Sinn erfüllen, obwohl wir diesen Sinn nicht mit unserer Sprache greifen können. Zumal, wenn es sich um Griechisches handelt, brauchen wir in diesem Punkt nicht allzu skeptisch zu sein ... " (Snell 1946/2011, 10).

30 "The scheme of relationship and the conclusion being the essential things in thinking, that kind of mind-stuff which is handiest will be the best for the purpose. Now words, uttered or unexpressed, are the handiest mental elements we have. Not only are they very *rapidly* revivable, but they are revivable as actual sensations more easily than any other items of our experience. Did they not possess some such advantage as this, it would hardly be the case that the older men are and the more effective as thinkers, the more, as a rule, they have lost their visualizing power and depend on words. This was ascertained by Mr. Galton to be the case with members of the Royal Society. The present writer observes it in his own person most distinctly" (James 1890/1983).

31 Contrary to what is claimed by Russell Goodman in his discussion of James and Wittgenstein: "Strangely enough, there is an obvious objection to James that Wittgenstein does not make: the Ballard case does not support James's claim that thought is possible without language because Ballard already *has* language" (2004, 127).

32 On this, see Schulte (2003, 8–9), Goodman (2004), Hacker (2010, 278).

33 Ballard is mentioned in other notes, too—for example in *Zettel* (Wittgenstein 1998, § 109)/*RPP* II (Wittgenstein 1990b, § 214).

34 Original: "Bist du sicher, daß dies die richtige Übersetzung deiner wortlosen
    Gedanken in Worte ist?—möchte man fragen. Und warum reckt diese Frage—die
    doch sonst gar nicht zu existieren scheint—hier ihren Kopf hervor? Will ich sagen,
    es täusche den Schreiber sein Gedächtnis?—Ich weiß nicht einmal, ob ich *das* sagen
    würde. Diese Erinnerungen sind ein seltsames Gedächtnisphänomen—und ich
    weiß nicht, welche Schlüsse auf die Vergangenheit des Erzählers man aus ihnen
    ziehen kann!" (Wittgenstein 1953/2009, § 342).

35 *Suppose* we read his autobiography thus; Ballard's notes support this reading, but, as
    already noted, they remain irreducibly ambiguous.

36 See also Hanfling (2001, 156) for similar observations.

37 Original: "[D]a würden wir bloß die Köpfe schütteln und müßten seine Worte für
    eine seltsame Reaktion ansehen, mit der wir nichts anzufangen wissen. (Es wäre
    etwa, wie wenn wir jemand im Ernste sagen hörten: 'Ich erinnere mich deutlich,
    einige Zeit vor meiner Geburt geglaubt zu haben, … ') Jener Ausdruck des Zweifels
    gehört nicht zu dem Sprachspiel; aber wenn nun der Ausdruck der Empfindung,
    das menschliche Benehmen, ausgeschlossen ist, dann scheint es, ich *dürfe* wieder
    zweifeln. Daß ich hier versucht bin, zu sagen, man könne die Empfindung für etwas
    andres halten, als was sie ist, kommt daher: Wenn ich das normale Sprachspiel mit
    dem Ausdruck der Empfindung abgeschafft denke, brauche ich nun ein Kriterium
    der Identität für sie; und dann bestünde auch die Möglichkeit des Irrtums"
    (Wittgenstein 1953/2009, §288).

38 Even if *thinking* is often treated together with other psychological concepts—for
    example Wittgenstein (1998, §113, 1990a, §129, 1990b, §35)—it also has a place
    in other themes, for example language, calculation and logic. Thinking is not
    special in Wittgenstein's earlier sense of "metalogical" (see Hacker 2010, 282ff),
    nonetheless: "Die Begriffe des Glaubens, Erwartens, Hoffens, sind einander weniger
    artfremd, als sie dem Begriff des Denkens sind" ("The concepts of believing,
    expecting, hoping are less different in kind from one another than they are from
    the concept of thinking") Wittgenstein (1953/2009, §574). See also Wittgenstein
    (1990b, §12). This observation is continuous with another aspect of this concept's
    complexity, that of the "scattered" character of thought (Wittgenstein 1998, §110)
    which makes for a difficult presentation: "Was muß der Mensch nicht alles tun,
    damit wir sagen, er *denke*!" ("What a lot of things a man must do in order for us to
    say he *thinks*!")(Wittgenstein 1990a, §563).

39 In question is the aligning of the mental with the "inner" and with privacy, but
    Rorty sometimes goes further than that, see e.g. note#16, p. 109: "[W]e can save
    Wittgenstein's epistemological insights, which center around the impossibility
    of learning the meaning of words without antecedent 'stage-setting,' without
    getting caught up in a hostility to privacy which led Wittgenstein to the edge of
    behaviorism and which led some of his followers over the edge."

40 "Wittgenstein rejects the possibility of a scientific psychology; that is, any theory that purports to explain behavior in terms of inner mental causes" (Williams 1999, 242). As this stands, it seems to amount to a rejection of *a certain kind* of scientific psychology—Williams targets in this text cognitive psychology à la Fodor and Stich. But it is quite clear that a more ambitious skepticism is read by Williams in Wittgenstein, that a rejection of scientific psychology *simpliciter* is in view.

41 Ironically, one is reminded here of a characteristically Fodorian footnote: "The scientific method as I have come to understand it: *Try not to say anything false; try to keep your wits about you*" (Fodor 2008, 4).

42 Original: "Die Begriffe der Psychologie sind eben Begriffe des Alltags. Nicht von der Wissenschaft zu ihren Zwecken neu gebildete Begriffe, wie die der Physik und Chemie" (Wittgenstein 1990b, §62).

Chapter 5

1 See e.g. Darwin's comment on insanity in animals, and his reference to Lindsay (1896, 79). I was led to Lindsay while reading Laurel Braitman's *Animal Madness* (2014).

2 Also some (Southern) European peoples, and even some peripheral British communities.

3 *Mutatis mutandis*, if one happens to have Humean inclinations—"From this standpoint, Kant looks like a desperate reactionary" (McDowell 1998, 175).

4 For an overview, see Maher (2012).

5 Or "cultivating the human" (*Bildung zum Menschen*), as Herder called it (Gadamer 2006, 8).

6 See the reference in the next chapter to Michael Tomasello's book of the same title.

7 Here, I borrow from Tumulty (2008).

8 Or: "Perceptual sensitivity to the environment need not amount to awareness of the outer world, I have been defending the claim that awareness of the outer world can be in place only concomitantly with full-fledged subjectivity. Somewhat similarly, feelings of pain or fear need not amount to awareness of an inner world. So we can hold that animal has no inner world without representing it as insensate and affectless" (McDowell 2000, 119).

Chapter 6

1 I was led to this particular manuscript after seeing a similar illustration used by David Lindberg (2007, 332, Fig. 13.5).

2   And not only medicine. Jacobi used his prominent position in pediatrics to demand progressive social reforms. How children were treated had a decisive impact on the capacity of the United States (his adoptive country) to fulfill its destiny of "humanizing and civilizing the scum of all the inferior races and nationalities" (1909, 51). I have written more about Jacobi in Tudorie (2017).

3   Original: "La variété d'intonations qu'il acquiert, indique chez lui une délicatesse d'impression et une délicatesse d'expression supérieures.—Par cette délicatesse il est capable d'idées générales.—Nous ne faisons que l'aider à les saisir en lui suggérant nos mots.—Il y accroche des idées sur lesquelles nous ne comptions pas et généralise spontanément en dehors et au-delà de nos cadres. Parfois il invente non seulement le sens du mot, mais le mot lui-même.—Plusieurs vocabulaires peuvent se succéder dans son esprit, par l'oblitération d'anciens mots que des nouveaux mots remplacent.—Plusieurs significations peuvent se succéder pour lui autour du même mot qui reste fixe.—Plusieurs mots inventés par lui sont des gestes vocaux naturels.—Au total, il apprend la langue déjà faite, comme un vrai musicien apprend le contrepoint, comme un vrai poète apprend la prosodie; c'est un génie original qui s'adapte à une forme construite pièce à pièce par une succession de génies originaux; si elle lui manquait, il la retrouverait peu à peu ou en découvrirait une autre équivalente" (Taine 1876).

4   The full quote will be instructive: "I believe it will deepen our understanding of social phenomena generally and help our research in the social sciences if we get a clearer understanding of the nature and the mode of existence of social reality. We need not so much a philosophy *of* the social sciences of the present and the past as we need a philosophy *for* the social sciences of the future."

5   As I try to summarize and evaluate Searle's views on this issue, the following abbreviations will be used: CIaA = "Collective Intentions and Actions"—page numbers refer to the reprint (Searle 2002, 90–105); CoSR = *The Construction of Social Reality*; SO = "Social Ontology: The Problem and Steps toward a Solution" (2007), MSW = *Making the Social World*.

6   Especially actions that can *only* be performed by groups. Searle's favorite examples are moves in team sports or the performance of complex musical pieces like symphonies.

7   E.g. "But there are also forms of collective intentionality in such things as believing and desiring. I might, for example, as a member of a religious faith, believe something only as part of our believing it, as part of our faith. I might, as part of a political movement, desire something as a part of our desiring it" (2010, 43).

8   The examples are Searle's (2007, 19).

9   *Mutatis mutandis* for the "by way of" operator.

10   Searle presents such a counterexample for the reductive analysis given by Tuomela and Miller. In their view, subject A "we-intends" to do X amounts to:

A intends to do his part of X.

A believes that the preconditions of success obtain, especially he believes that the other members of the group will (or at least probably will) do their parts of X.

A believes that there is a mutual belief among the members of the group to the effect that the preconditions of success mentioned in 2 above obtain.

11 I follow Bratman here, but note that this claim is in fact problematic. What would it take for a plan to be complete? The answer could not point to a "reasonable" level of detail; that would be a rephrasing of the question. A charitable reading may point to at least some situations when we explicitly *leave room* for further happenings, but to describe even this as "incompleteness" may be misleading.

12 Vs. being merely conduct-conducive. Again, here I merely present Bratman's views, and only to get the case for shared intention going. This should not be read as accepting Bratman's theory of intention, but as a charitable setting of circumstances for evaluating, next, what the developmentalists do with Bratman's account.

13 On the contrary. For example, Bratman notes that animals show signs of impressive coordination—with their own previous actions and with others—but they *cannot* be said to plan. "[S]tructures of planning agency of the sort I am trying to describe are basic and, perhaps, *distinctive* aspects of our agency. Many animals, human and nonhuman, are purposive agents—agents who pursue goals in light of their representations of the world. But we—*normal adult human agents in a modern world*—are not merely purposive agents in this generic sense. Our agency is typically embedded in planning structure" (Bratman 1999b, 5—emphasis added). Also: "A tiger hunting her prey may exhibit wonderfully coordinated activity without being capable of such planning. But for creatures like us—as Donagan says, 'creatures … of will'—planning is an important coordinating mechanism" (Bratman 1999f, 114).

14 About the view described below, Bratman says: "Such shared intention is primarily a psychological—rather than primarily a normative—phenomenon" (1999f, 128). This is in reference to Margaret Gilbert's insistence on *obligations* intrinsic to shared agency, but it also fits nicely my methodological point. Bratman's also offers an adequate name for what I am avoiding for the reasons stated above in his recent texts: "normative emergence."

15 Bratman argues for sufficient conditions, not for necessary ones. He notes in a number of places that, for all he says, shared intention might be "multiply realizable."

16 "[J]ust the ordinary predictability of ordinary agents" (Bratman 1999c, 155).

17 See Tomasello, Carpenter, and Liszkowski (2007) for an emphatic statement of this preference.

18 The translation is mine. Original: "Wir sehen uns weder veranlasst, jede dieser Konzeptionen zurückzuweisen, noch zwischen ihnen wählen zu müssen, weil die

dort vertretenen Ansichten an verschiedenen Stellen der evolutionären und Entwicklungstheorie auf angemessene Weise zur Anwendung kommen können. […] Uns scheint gerade Bratmans Konzeption angemessen, um die frühen Stadien dieser Entwicklung zu beschreiben, in denen Individuen versucht sind, einander auf rekursive Weise zu begreifen. Allerdings geht Searle recht in der Annahme, dass im Leben heutiger erwachsener Menschen die für Normen und Institutionen konstitutive gemeinsame Bezugnahme *qua primitivum* auf den Plan tritt und man nicht auf das rekursive, mentale Hin-und-Zurück Einzelner angewiesen ist. Jedenfalls hoffen wir—angesichts des dezidierten Ziels, evolutionäre und ontogenetische Sequenzen zu rekonstruieren—auf eklektische Weise unterschiedliche theoretische Versatzstücke kombinieren zu können, anstatt einen Gewinner in der Debatte um die angemessene Konzeption gemeinsamer Intentionalität küren zu müssen."

Chapter 7

1   "[C]linicians and even scientists attempting to discover genetic or neural underpinnings of disease have all too often reified the disorders listed in DSM-IV-TR as 'natural kinds.' This reification of DSM diagnostic entities has, in turn, created historical inertia in rethinking the nature and classification of psychiatric disorders" (Hyman 2003, xix).

Note that there is a *progression* of skepticism in these samples. Even if the critics are correct in saying that DSM categories are not arrived at by following the regular scientific (~causal) route, this methodological point does not *by itself* exclude the possibility that DSM diagnosis locks on "natural kinds." Indeed, systematic co-occurrence of symptoms is something to be explained, and (certain yet unknown) common causes constitute a natural explanatory candidate. So far, the criticism could only affirm that one does not have *sufficient* reasons to bet on the DSM system, even if there *are* some reasons. The criticism goes further, however, when it is suggested that DSM categories *could not* overlap with causally identified disease entities, and that consequently medical research based on these categories goes nowhere. I am not insisting on this distinction at this point, but it must be kept in mind, since it will resurface in the following.

2   For a sample of the public discussions elicited immediately after the publication of the DSM-5, see Board (2013), Belluck and Carey (2013), Friedman (2013), Greenberg (2013), and Hacking (2013).

3   Consider, to give an example that does not question the DSM framework itself, the considerable commotion caused by the modifications of the autism category in the new edition of the manual. Some have suggested that the aim has been

a definitional "cure" for the epidemic of autism in the United States, one which costs insurance companies and public education agencies fortunes. The autism bar has now been raised. Moreover, and typical for DSM *modus operandi*, a whole subcategory, which was just becoming a pop cultural icon, the Asperger syndrome, has disappeared from the new classification. Understandably, Aspies may feel confused, and one may wonder whether such a situation could be in the cards for, say, diabetics. For a brief presentation, see Carey (2012).

4   The translation is sometimes contested, because the original refers to an ill person, not to an illness. This might matter given that whether this was a case of mental illness (delusion, psychosis) is sometimes disputed—more so in any case than the idea that Schreber was in some sense a sufferer.

5   But only, perhaps, if one does not take into account the (hard to adjudicate) possibility that some mystical writings coming from undiagnosed individuals are in fact manifestations of psychotic delusion.

6   The entire third chapter, which discussed family history, was withdrawn from publication, probably by family members (Santner 1996, 35, Dinnage 2000, xxiii). In the autumn of 1900, Schreber's psychiatrist at Sonnenstein, Guido Weber, while advising a court against his patient's release, had this to say about the *Memoirs*: "When one looks at the content of his writings, and takes into consideration the abundance of indiscretions relating to himself and others contained in them, the unembarrassed detailing of the most doubtful and aesthetically impossible situations and events, the use of the most offensive vulgar words, etc., one finds it quite incomprehensible that a man otherwise tactful and of fine feeling could propose an action which would compromise him so severely in the eyes of the public, were not his whole attitude to life pathological, and he unable to see things in their proper perspective, and if the tremendous overvaluation of his own person caused by lack of insight into his illness had not clouded his appreciation of the limitations imposed on man by society" (quoted in Santner 1996, 80).

7   Schreber-*père* was a celebrity too—see below.

8   Note, however, that this is the same Flechsig about whom the historian Edward Shorter writes as follows: "Two giants in the study of neuroanatomy and cerebral localization opened university clinics in the 1880s: Paul Flechsig in Leipzig in 1882 and Eduard Hitzig in Halle in 1885. [...] Both men had immense achievements. Both were also terrible clinicians. [...] Emil Kraepelin, who worked briefly as a resident under Flechsig until leaving in disgust, recalled Flechsig as being completely uninterested in learning about patients or their problems" (1997).

9   See below for qualification.

10 Original: "Es gibt nun eine weit energischere und erfolgreichere Art der Abwehr, die darin besteht, dass das Ich die unerträgliche Vorstellung mitsamt ihrem Affekt verwirft und sich so benimmt, als ob die Vorstellung nie an das Ich herangetreten wäre" (1894/1925, 303).

11 It is, indeed, a more solid, if less interesting, example, in the sense that Freud actually attempted to treat this patient. Frau P is a person, not a literary character, a distinction Freud often ignored.

12 Original: "Bei Paranoia wird der Vorwurf auf einem Wege, den man als *Projektion* bezeichnen kann, verdrängt, indem das Abwehrsymptom des Misstrauens gegen andere errichtet wird" (1896/1925, 385).

13 Original: "An der Symptombildung bei Paranoia ist vor allem jener Zug auffällig, der die Benennung *Projektion* verdient. Eine innere Wahrnehmung wird unterdrückt, und zum Ersatz für sie kommt ihr Inhalt, nachdem er eine gewisse Entstellung erfahren hat, als Wahrnehmung von außen zum Bewußtsein. Die Entstellung besteht beim Verfolgungswahn in einer Affektverwandlung; was als Liebe innen hätte verspürt werden sollen, wird als Haß von außen wahrgenommen. Man wäre versucht, diesen merkwürdigen Vorgang als das Bedeutsamste der Paranoia und als absolut pathognomonisch für dieselbe hinzustellen, wenn man nicht rechtzeitig daran erinnert würde, daß 1. die Projektion nicht bei allen Formen von Paranoia die gleiche Rolle spielt und 2. daß sie nicht nur bei Paranoia, sondern auch unter anderen Verhältnissen im Seelenleben vorkommt, ja, daß ihr ein regelmäßiger Anteil an unserer Einstellung zur Außenwelt zugewiesen ist" (Freud 1911, 417–18).

14 E.g. "[W]e are in point of fact driven by experience to attribute to homosexual wishful phantasies an intimate (perhaps an invariable) relation to this particular form of disease" (Freud 1958).

15 Original: Das Interesse des praktischen Psychiaters an solchen Wahnbildungen ist in der Regel erschöpft, wenn er die Leistung des Wahnes festgestellt und seinen Einfluß auf die Lebensführung des Kranken beurteilt hat; seine Verwunderung ist nicht der Anfang seines Verständnisses. Der Psychoanalytiker bringt von seiner Kenntnis der Psychoneurosen her die Vermutung mit, daß auch so absonderliche, so weit von dem gewohnten Denken der Menschen abweichende Gedankenbildungen aus den *allgemeinsten und begreiflichsten* Regungen des Seelenlebens hervorgegangen sind, und möchte die Motive wie die Wege dieser Umbildung kennenlernen. In dieser Absicht wird er sich gerne in die Entwicklungsgeschichte wie in die Einzelheiten des Wahnes vertiefen (1911, 365— emphasis added).

16 Original: "Wir befinden uns also auch im Falle Schreber auf dem wohlvertrauten Boden des Vaterkomplexes. Wenn sich dem Kranken der Kampf mit Flechsig als ein Konflikt mit Gott enthüllt, so müssen wir diesen in einen infantilen Konflikt mit dem geliebten Vater übersetzen, dessen uns unbekannte Einzelheiten den Inhalt des Wahns bestimmt haben. Es fehlt nichts von dem Material, das sonst durch die Analyse in solchen Fällen aufgedeckt wird, alles ist durch irgendwelche Andeutungen vertreten" (Freud 1911, 406).

17 One of a series of sadomasochistic-looking orthopedic contraptions aimed at correcting the posture of children.

18 From the open letter to Flechsig with which Schreber begins his book.

19 On the paranoid fear of brainwashing and thoroughly changing individuals by Communist psycho-magic, see Staub (2011, especially chapter 3, II).

20 John Greenwood notes that this was also a time of conceptual change in American social psychology, an "asocial" view focused on controlled experiments at the individual level becoming dominant (2004, chapter 9).

21 A somewhat hypocritical orthodoxy, as most are. To use an example other than those revolving around the Schreber case, here is one documented by Edward Shorter: "In 1908, Ferenczi became keen on treating Frau M., who suffered from paranoia. Yet first Ferenczi sought the Professor's opinion: Did Freud think she needed to be treated in an institution, or would an outpatient basis suffice? Freud replied, 'I've seen Frau M. She has frank paranoia, and probably is beyond the border of treatability; still, you can have a go at it and learn from her at all events. Her brother-in-law, who is accompanying her and is a doctor, is an ass. He will probably advise something other than what I've proposed. I demanded that she enter the Budapest [private] asylum and there let herself be treated by you'" (1997).

22 Shorter again: "Generations of American mothers had to suffer unwarranted reproaches as 'schizophrenogenic mothers' to use Fromm-Reichmann's notorious phrase after her writings on this subject began to appear in 1948" (1997). See also Healy (2002, 141).

23 Here is the first (August 1, 1960):
    "Dr. R. I. Dung
    Ward D-16
    Ypsilanti State Hospital
    My dear husband,
    I have been aware on Channel 1 that you have been waiting for me to visit for you a very long time. If the good Lord permits I will visit you at the Ypsilanti State Hospital on Ward D-16 on this Thursday at 1 o'clock.

    Sincerely,
    Madame Dr. R. I. Dung" (Rokeach 2011, 201–2).

24 But see the note on the DSM controversies at the beginning of this chapter.

25 This seems the correct way to put it, despite various delimitations—for example the one from the zeal of the schizophrenogenic mother theory (see Bentall 2003, chapter 12).

26 See also Bentall (1994/2019, 2020).

27 There are many other similar remarks, for example: "For Jaspers, the empathetic attitude of the psychiatrist towards the patient functions as a kind of diagnostic test. If the empathy scanner returns the reading 'ununderstandable' the patient

is psychotic and suffering from a biological disease. However, behaviours and experiences may vary in degree according to how amenable they are to empathy. By not empathizing hard enough, we may fail to recognize the intelligible aspects of the other person's experiences. Moreover, once we have decided that the patient's experiences are unintelligible, we are given an apparent licence to treat the patient as a disordered organism, a malfunctioning body that we do not have to relate to in a human way" (Bentall 2003).

28 "My own view is that most psychiatric diagnoses are about as scientifically meaningful as star signs … " (Bentall 2010, 110).

29 The last two paragraphs are adapted from my review of *Doctoring the Mind* (Tudorie 2011).

30 The triad refers roughly to impairments in socialization, communication, and imagination.

31 See e.g. Abu-Akel and Shamay-Tsoory (2013), Kronbichler et al. (2017), Bechi et al. (2018), Vass et al. (2018), Thibaudeau et al. (2021).

32 It is worth looking at the whole paragraph: "Despite this negative evidence, I don't think we should give up on Chris Frith's theory. Indeed, there is obviously something *theory-of-mind-ish* about persecutory delusions, which inevitably involve mistaken assumptions about the intentions of other people. It is as if the paranoid person can make inferences about the beliefs and attitudes of other people but, for some reason, reaches the wrong conclusions about what those beliefs and attitudes are." One wonders how being able to infer is compatible with *often* arriving at the wrong conclusions. The answer, as per above, is the usual "shift" theory (compare: redshift)—the whole structure of inference is derailed by external forces, but it remains *internally intact* as it is derailed.

33 I refer the reader to the ongoing DSM-5 debate mentioned at the beginning of this chapter.

34 See Andreasen (2001) for an example of optimism; for a more nuanced history of antipsychotic medication, see Healy (2002). For parallel examples of being favorable to, versus skeptical about medication and medicalization in the case of depression, see Kramer (2005) vs. Horwitz and Wakefield (2007).

35 Note that this is the same point made by Insel—see the beginning of the chapter—when he opposes reliability to validity.

36 For a discussion of the effects of medical training, but also of the "coaching" of patients, see Borch-Jacobsen (2009).

37 See Burns (2007, 50–1). Bentall, as documented above, also favors a dimensional perspective.

38 This is one of the places where the contrast with Bentall helps. A committed dimensional approach would be more radical, since it would imply the bankruptcy of the Kraepelinian effort to systematize long-term observation into categories, and to continuously refine the definitions of these categories.

39 Only suggested in this fragment, but explicitly discussed later in the text—see below.

40 For some emphatic statements to this effect, see Frith (2007).

41 E.g. "diagnosis has implications about aetiology"; "'Explaining' schizophrenia inevitably involves saying something about cause" (Frith 1992, 7, 33).

42 The use of "dys" instead of "dis" suggests, as explained in Stephan, Friston, and Frith (2009), that there is not only *lack* of connectivity, for example, between frontal and parietal regions of the brain, but also that there is *mis*connection.

43 Frith, Morton, and Leslie (1991, 433) describe the triad thus: "(1) impairment in socialization (a specific impairment in the quality of reciprocal interactions); (2) impairment in communication (a delay in language acquisition and poor use of verbal and non-verbal means of communication); and (3) impairment in imagination (a lack of spontaneous pretend play)."

44 Frith himself says that the proposal uses a "doubtless over-inclusive framework" (1992, 133).

45 This theory explains that when an action plan is about to be executed, a copy of it is sent to brain structures that register sensory consequences. The sensory effect of the action is thus anticipated. Corollary discharge refers to this copy forwarding. In plain words, we are not surprised by our own actions; anticipating their sensory fallout is supposedly what allows us to recognize them as *our* actions. Introducing the notion of self-monitoring, Frith says that corollary discharge is a form of self-monitoring (1992, 74).

46 Here Frith draws on the work on relevance by Sperber and Wilson (1986/1996).

47 Compare: "Inferring mental states has become routine in many situations and achieved the status of a direct perception. If such a system goes wrong, then the patient will continue to 'feel' and 'know' the truth of such experiences and will not easily accept correction" (Frith 1992, 122).

Conclusion

1 And there are others, contemporary, for example, the beautiful grisaille began by Girolamo da Treviso in 1525 in the Saraceni chapel of Saint Petronio Basilica in Bologna (Campani et al. 2010, Presciutti 2019).

References

Abu-Akel, Ahmad, and Simone G. Shamay-Tsoory. 2013. "Characteristics of Theory of Mind Impairments in Schizophrenia". In *Social Cognition in Schizophrenia. From Evidence to Treatment*, edited by David L. Roberts and David L. Penn, 196–214. Oxford University Press.

American Psychiatric Association. 2000. *Diagnostic and Statistical Manual of Mental Disorders. Fourth Edition Text Revision (DSM-IV-TR)*. American Psychiatric Association.

Amidon, Stephen and Thomas Amidon. 2011. *The Sublime Engine: A Biography of the Human Heart*. Rodale.

Anand, Kanwaljeet J.S., Jacob V. Aranda, Charles B. Berde, ShaAvhrée Buckman, Edmund V. Capparelli, Waldemar Carlo, Patricia Hummel, C. Celeste Johnston, John Lantos, Victoria Tutag-Lehr, Anne M. Lynn, Lynne G. Maxwell, Tim F. Oberlander, Tonse N.K. Raju, Sulpicio G. Soriano, Anna Taddio, and Gary A. Walco. 2006. "Summary Proceedings from the Neonatal Pain-Control Group". *Pediatrics* 117 (Supplement 1): S9–S22. doi: 10.1542/peds.2005-0620C.

Anand, Kanwaljeet S., and Paul R. Hickey. 1987. "Pain and Its Effects in the Human Neonate and Fetus". *The New England Journal of Medicine* 317 (21):1321–9.

Anand, Kanwaljeet S., and Frank M. Scalzo. 2000. "Can Adverse Neonatal Experiences Alter Brain Development and Subsequent Behavior?" *Biology of the Neonate* 77 (2):69–82.

Andreasen, Nancy C. 2001. *Brave New Brain: Conquering Mental Illness in the Era of the Genome*. Oxford, New York: Oxford University Press.

Ariès, Philippe. 1960. *L'Enfant et la vie familiale sous l'Ancien Régime*. Paris: Plon.

Baillargeon, Renée, Rose M. Scott, and Zijing He. 2010. "False-belief Understanding in Infants." *Trends in Cognitive Sciences* 14 (3):110–18. doi: https://doi.org/10.1016/j.tics.2009.12.006.

Baron-Cohen, S. 2004. *Essential Difference: Male and Female Brains and the Truth about Autism*. Basic Books.

Baron-Cohen, Simon. 2002. "The Extreme Male Brain Theory of Autism." *Trends in Cognitive Sciences* 6 (6):248–54. doi:http://dx.doi.org/10.1016/S1364-6613(02)01904-6.

Baron-Cohen, Simon, Alan M. Leslie, and Uta Frith. 1985. "Does the Autistic Child Have a 'Theory of Mind'?" *Cognition* 21 (1):37–46. doi:http://dx.doi.org/10.1016/0010-0277(85)90022-8.

Bateson, Gregory. 1969/1987. "Double Bind." In *Steps to an Ecology of Mind. Collected Essays in Anthropology, Psychiatry, Evolution, and Epistemology*, 199–204. Jason Aronson Inc. Original edition.

Bateson, Gregory, Don D. Jackson, Jay Haley, and John H. Weakland. 1956/1987. "Toward a Theory of Schizophrenia". In *Steps to an Ecology of Mind. Collected Essays in Anthropology, Psychiatry, Evolution, and Epistemology*, 153–70. Jason Aronson Inc. Original edition.

Bechi, Margherita, Marta Bosia, Giulia Agostoni, Marco Spangaro, Mariachiara Buonocore, Laura Bianchi, Federica Cocchi, Carmelo Guglielmino, Antonella Rita Mastromatteo, and Roberto Cavallaro. 2018. "Can Patients with Schizophrenia Have Good Mentalizing Skills? Disentangling Heterogeneity of Theory of Mind". *Neuropsychology* 32 (6):746.

Beiser, Frederick C. 2011. *The German Historicist Tradition*. Oxford University Press.

Belluck, Pam, and Benedict Carey. 2013. "Psychiatry's Guide Is Out of Touch with Science, Experts Say". *The New York Times*, May 6. http://www.nytimes. com/2013/05/07/health/psychiatrys-new-guide-falls-short-experts-say. html?pagewanted=all.

Bentall, Richard. 2004. "Abandoning the Concept of Schizophrenia. The Cognitive Psychology of Hallucinations and Delusions". In *Models of Madness. Psychological, Social and Biological Approaches to Schizophrenia*, edited by John Read, Loren Mosher and Richard Bentall, 195–208. Brunner—Routledge.

Bentall, Richard. 2010. *Doctoring the Mind. Why Psychiatric Treatments Fail*. Penguin Books.

Bentall, Richard P. 1994/2019. "Cognitive Biases and Abnormal Beliefs: Towards a Model of Persecutory Delusions". In *The Neuropsychology of Schizophrenia*, edited by Anthony S. David and John C. Cutting, 337–60. Psychology Press.

Bentall, Richard P. 2003. *Madness Explained. Psychosis and Human Nature*. Allen Lane - Penguin.

Bentall, Richard P. 2020. "The Role of Early Life Experience in Psychosis". In *Psychotic Disorders: Comprehensive Conceptualization and Treatments*, edited by Carol A. Tamminga, Jim van Os, Elena Ivleva and Ulrich Reininghaus, 406–14. Oxford University Press.

Berbiguier, Alexis-Vincent-Charles Berbiguier. 1821. *Les Farfadets, ou tous les démons ne sont pas de l'autre monde*. 3 vols. Vol. 1. Gueffier.

Berlin, Isaiah. 1980. "Does Political Theory Still Exist?" In *Concepts and Categories. Philosophical Essays*, edited by Isaiah Berlin, Henry Hardy and Bernard Williams (intro.), 143–72. Oxford University Press.

Bhatia, Sunil. 2017. *Decolonizing Psychology: Globalization, Social Justice, and Indian Youth Identities*. Oxford University Press.

Biemel, Walter. 1968. "Einleitung des Herausgebers". In *Phänomenologische Psychologie*, edited by Edmund Husserl, xiii–xxviii. Martinus Nijhof.

Blanchard, Pascal, Gilles Boëtsch, and Nanette Jacomijn Snoep, eds. 2011. *L'invention du sauvage*: Actes Sud. Musée du quai Branly.

Board, Editorial. 2013. "Shortcomings of a Psychiatric Bible". *The New York Times*, May 11. http://www.nytimes.com/2013/05/12/opinion/sunday/shortcomings-of-a-psychiatric-bible.html.

Bolton, Derek, and Jonathan Hill. 2003. *Mind, Meaning, and Mental Disorder: The Nature of Causal Explanation in Psychology and Psychiatry*. Second ed. Oxford University Press.

Borch-Jacobsen, Mikkel. 2000. "How a Fabrication Differs from a Lie". *London Review of Books* 22 (8), April 13. https://www.lrb.co.uk/the-paper/v22/n08/mikkel-borch-jacobsen/how-a-fabrication-differs-from-a-lie.

Borch-Jacobsen, Mikkel. 2009. *Making Minds and Madness. From Hysteria to Depression*. Cambridge University Press.

Borch-Jacobsen, Mikkel, and Sonu Shamdasani. 2012. *The Freud Files: An Inquiry into the History of Psychoanalysis*. Cambridge University Press.

Bouveresse, Jacques. 2008. "Wittgenstein's Critique of Frazer". In *Wittgenstein and Reason*, edited by John Preston, 1–20. Blackwell.

Braitman, Laurel. 2014. *Animal Madness. How Anxious Dogs, Compulsive Parrots, and Elephants in Recovery Help Us Understand Ourselves*. Simon & Schuster.

Brandom, Robert. 2009a. "How Analytic Philosophy Has Failed Cognitive Science". In *TAP-2009. Towards an Analytic Pragmatism. Proceedings of the Workshop on Bob Brandom's Recent Philosophy of Language*, edited by Cristina Amoretti, Carlo Penco and Federico Pitto, 121–33. University of Genoa, Department of Philosophy.

Brandom, Robert. 2009b. *Reason in Philosophy: Animating Ideas*. Harvard University Press.

Bratman, Michael E. 1992. "What Is Intention?" In *Intentions in Communication*, edited by Philip R. Cohen, Jerry Morgan and Martha E. Pollack, 15–32. MIT Press.

Bratman, Michael E. 1999a. "Davidson's Theory of Intention". In *Faces of Intention. Selected Essays on Intention and Agency*, edited by Michael Bratman, 209–40. Cambridge University Press.

Bratman, Michael E. 1999b. *Faces of Intention: Selected Essays on Intention and Agency*. Cambridge University Press.

Bratman, Michael E. 1999c. "I Intend That We *J*". In *Faces of Intention. Selected Essays on Intention and Agency*, edited by Michael Bratman, 142–61. Cambridge University Press.

Bratman, Michael E. 1999d. *Intention, Plans, and Practical Reason*. Center for the Study of Language and Information.

Bratman, Michael E. 1999e. "Shared Cooperative Activity". In *Faces of Intention. Selected Essays on Intention and Agency*, edited by Michael Bratman, 93–108. Cambridge University Press.

Bratman, Michael E. 1999f. "Shared Intention". In *Faces of Intention. Selected Essays on Intention and Agency*, edited by Michael Bratman, 109–29. Cambridge University Press.

Bratman, Michael E. 2010a. "Acting Over Time, Acting Together". Presentation at the August 2010 Collective Intentionality Conference, Basel, Switzerland, August.

Bratman, Michael E. 2010b. "Agency, Time, and Sociality". APA Presidential Address, Pacific Division, San Francisco, April 2.

Bratman, Michael E. 2020. "Tomasello on 'we' and the Sense of Obligation". *Behavioral and Brain Sciences* 43:e62. doi: 10.1017/S0140525X19002383.

Broome, Matthew R, and Lisa Bortolotti. 2009. "Mental Illness as Mental: In Defence of Psychological Realism". *Humana Mente* 11:25–43.

Bruner, Jerome. 1990. *Acts of Meaning*. Harvard University Press.

Bukowski, Charles. 2006. *Factotum*. HarperCollins e-books.

Burge, Tyler. 2018. "Do Infants and Nonhuman Animals Attribute Mental States?" *Psychological Review* 125 (3):409.

Burns, Jonathan. 2007. *The Descent of Madness. Evolutionary Origins of Psychosis and the Social Brain*. Routledge.

Burnside, Kimberly, Vivianne Severdija, and Diane Poulin-Dubois. 2020. "Infants Attribute False beliefs to a Toy Crane". *Developmental Science* 23 (2):e12887. doi: https://doi.org/10.1111/desc.12887.

Butter, Michael, and Peter Knight. 2020. *Routledge Handbook of Conspiracy Theories*. Routledge.

Callaghan, Tara, Henrike Moll, Hannes Rakoczy, Felix Warneken, Ulf Liszkowski, Tanya Behne, and Michael Tomasello. 2011. "Early Social Cognition in Three Cultural Contexts". *Monographs of the Society for Research in Child Development* 76 (2):1–142.

Campani, Elisa, Antonella Casoli, Maria Elena Darecchio, Francesca Paccagnella, and Paolo Zannini. 2010. "Saint Petronio Basilica in Bologna (Italy): A Case Study on a XVI Century Mural Ppainting". *Nuovo Cimento Della Societa Italiana Di Fisica B-Basic Topics in Physics* 125 (2):219–41.

Canetti, Elias. 1981. *Crowds and Power*. Translated by Carol Stewart. Continuum.

Carey, Susan. 2009. *The Origin of Concepts, Oxford Series in Cognitive Development*. Oxford University Press.

Carey, Benedict. 2012. "New Definition of Autism Will Exclude Many, Study Suggests". *The New York Times*, January 19. http://www.nytimes.com/2012/01/20/health/research/new-autism-definition-would-exclude-many-study-suggests.html?pagewanted=all&_r=0.

Carpenter, Malinda, Michael Tomasello, and Tricia Striano. 2005. "Role Reversal Imitation and Language in Typically Developing Infants and Children with Autism". *Infancy* 8 (3):253–78.

Cavell, Stanley. 1979/1999. *The Claim of Reason. Wittgenstein, Skepticism, Morality, and Tragedy*. Oxford University Press.

Cerbone, David R. 2000. "How To Do Things with Wood: Wittgenstein, Frege and the Problem of Illogical Thought". In *The New Wittgenstein*, edited by Alice Crary and Rupert Read, 293–314. Routledge.

Chomsky, Noam. 1969. "The Menace of Liberal Scholarship". *The New York Review of Books*, January 2.

Chomsky, Noam. 1971. "The Case against B.F. Skinner". *The New York Review of Books*, December 30.

Chomsky, Noam. 2000. *New Horizons in the Study of Language and Mind*. Cambridge University Press.

Churchland, Paul M. 1996. *The Engine of Reason, the Seat of the Soul. A Philosophical Journey into the Brain*. MIT Press.

Cioffi, Frank. 1998. *Wittgenstein on Freud and Frazer*. Cambridge University Press.

Clair, Jean, ed. 2005. *Mélancolie. Génie et folie en Occident*. Gallimard, Réunion des Musées Nationaux, Staatliche Museen zu Berlin.

Clarke, Arthur C. 2012. *Rendezvous with Rama*. Orion.

Clifford, William Kingdon. 1877/2021. *The Ethics of Belief*. Good Press.

Cobb, Matthew. 2020. *The Idea of the Brain*. Findaway World, LLC.

Cole, Bruce. 2018. *Titian and Venetian Painting, 1450–1590*. Routledge.

Collingwood, Robin George. 1935/1999. "Reality as History". In *The Principles of History and Other Writings in Philosophy of History*, edited by Robin George Collingwood, 170–208. Oxford University Press.

Collingwood, Robin George. 1948. "Psychology as the Pseudo-Science of Thought". In *Philosophical Essays, Volume II. An Essay on Metaphysics*, edited by Robin George Collingwood, 112–21. Oxford University Press.

Collingwood, Robin George. 1992. *The Idea of History*. Oxford University Press. Original edition, 1946.

Collingwood, Robin George. 1999. "The Principles of History". In *The Principles of History and Other Writings in Philosophy of History*, edited by Robin George Collingwood, 1–113. Oxford University Press.

Coltheart, Max, and Martin Davies, eds. 2000. *Patologies of Belief, Readings in Mind and Language*. Blackwell.

Comar, Philippe. 2005. "André-Pierre Pinson". In *Mélancolie. Génie et folie en Occident* edited by Jean Clair, 260. Gallimard, Réunion des Musées Nationaux, Staatliche Museen zu Berlin.

Conant, James. 1991. "The Search for Logically Alien Thought: Descartes, Kant, Frege, and the Tractatus". *Philosophical Topics* 20 (1):115–80.

Conant, James. 2000. "Elucidation and Nonsense in Frege and Early Wittgenstein". In *The New Wittgenstein*, edited by Alice Crary and Rupert Read, 174–217. Routledge.

Condorcet, Marie Jean Antoine Nicolas de Caritat. 1793–94/1822. *Esquisse d'un tableau historique des progrès de l'esprit humain; suivie de réflexions sur l'esclavage des nègres*. Masson et fils.

Condorcet, Marie Jean Antoine Nicolas de Caritat. 1795. *Outlines of an Historical View of the Progress of the Human Mind*. J. Johnson.

Currie, Gregory. 2000. "Imagination, Delusion and Hallucinations". In *Pathologies of Belief*, edited by Max Coltheart and Martin Davies, 167–82. Blackwell.

Darwin, Charles. 1896. *The Descent of Man and Selection in Relation to Sex*. John Murray.

Darwin, Charles Robert. 1877. "A Biographical Sketch of an Infant". *Mind* 2 (7):285–94.

Davidson, Donald. 1963/2001. "Actions, Reasons, and Causes". In *Essay on Actions and Events*, edited by Donald Davidson, 1–19. Oxford University Press.

deMause, Lloyd. 1975. "The Evolution of Childhood". In *The history of childhood*, edited by Lloyd deMause, 1–73. Harper & Row.

Dilthey, Wilhelm. 1883. *Einleitung in die Geisteswissenschaften für das Studium der Gesellschaft und der Geschichte*. Duncker & Humblot.

Dilthey, Wilhelm. 1883/1990. *Gesammelte Schriften I. Band. Einleitung in die Geisteswissenschaften: Versuch einer Grundlegung für das Studium* der Gesellschaft und der Geschichte, I. Band. Ninth ed. B.G. Teubner.

Dilthey, Wilhelm. 1894/1990. "Ideen über eine beschreibende und zergliedernde Psychologie". In *Gesammelte Schriften V. Band. Die Geistige Welt: Einleitung in die Philosophie des Lebens; Hälfte 1, Abhandlungen zur Grundlegung der Geisteswissenschaften*, edited by Wilhelm Dilthey, 139–240. B.G. Teubner.

Dilthey, Wilhelm. 1977. *Descriptive Psychology and Historical Understanding*. Translated by Richard M. Zaner and Kenneth L. Heiges. Edited by Rudolf A. Makkreel. Martinus Nijhoff.

Dilthey, Wilhelm. 1989. *Introduction to the Human Sciences*. Translated by Michael Neville, Jeffrey Barnouw, Franz Schreiner and Rudolf A. Makkreel. Princeton University Press.

Dinnage, Rosemary. 2000. "Introduction". In *Memoirs of My Mental Illness*, edited by Daniel Paul Schreber, Ida Macalpine and Richard A. Hunter, xi–xxiv. New York Review Books.

Dörrenberg, Sebastian, Hannes Rakoczy, and Ulf Liszkowski. 2018. "How (Not) to Measure Infant Theory of Mind: Testing the Replicability and Validity of Four Nonverbal Measures". *Cognitive Development* 46:12–30.

Dray, William H., and W.J. van der Dussen. 1999. "Editors' Introduction". In *The Principles of History and Other Writings in Philosophy of History*, edited by Robin George Collingwood, xiii–lxxxvii. Oxford University Press.

Dray, William. 1957. *Laws and Explanation in History*. Oxford University Press.

Droysen, Johann Gustav. 1882. *Grundriss der Historik*. Third revised ed. Veit & Comp.

Duffin, Jacalyn. 1999. *History of Medicine: A Scandalously Short Introduction*. University of Toronto Press.

Fanon, Frantz. 1952. *Peau noire, masques blancs*. Éditions du Seuil.

Fanon, Frantz. 2002. *Les damnés de la terre*. La Découverte.

Festinger, Leon, Henry W. Riecken, and Stanley Schachter. 2008. *When Prophecy Fails. A Social and Psychological Study of a Modern Group that Predicted the Destruction of the World*. Edited by Elliot Aronson. Pinter & Martin. Original edition, 1956.

First, Michael B. 2012. "Comments: The National Institute of Mental Health Research Domain Criteria (RDoC) Project: Moving towards a Neuroscience-based Diagnostic Classification in Psychiatry". In *Philosophical Issues in Psychiatry II: Nosology*, edited by Kenneth S. Kendler and Josef Parnas, 12–18. Oxford University Press.

Fodor, Jerry. 2008. *LOT 2. The Language of Thought Revisited*. Oxford University Press.

Foucault, Michel. 1972. *Histoire de la folie à l'âge classique*. Gallimard.

Foucault, Michel. 1975. *Surveiller et punir. Naissance de la prison*. Gallimard.

Foucault, Michel. 2006. *History of Madness*. Translated by Jonathan Murphy and Jean Khalfa. Routledge.

Frazer, James George. 1890/2009. *The Golden Bough. A Study of Magic and Religion*. The Floating Press. Original edition, 1890.

Frege, Gottlob. 1893. *Grundgesetze der Arithmetik. I. Band*. Hermann Pohle.

Frege, Gottlob. 1964. *The Basic Laws of Arithmetic. Exposition of the System*. Translated by Montgomery Furth. Edited by Montgomery Furth. University of California Press.

Freud, Sigmund. 1894/1925. "Die Abwehr-Neuropsychosen". In *Gesammelte Schriften, I*, edited by Sigmund Freud, 290–305. Internationaler Psychoanalytischer Verlag.

Freud, Sigmund. 1896/1925. "Weitere Bemerkungen über die Abwehr-Neuropsychosen". In *Gesammelte Schriften, I*, edited by Sigmund Freud, 363–87. Internationaler Psychoanalytischer Verlag.

Freud, Sigmund. 1911. "Psychoanalytische Bemerkungen über einen autobiographisch beschriebenen Fall von Paranoia (Dementia paranoides)". In Gesammelte Schriften, VIII, edited by Sigmund Freud, 355–435. Internationaler Psychoanalytischer Verlag.

Freud, Sigmund. 1958. "Psycho-analytic Notes on an Autobiographical Account of a Case of Paranoia (*Dementia Paranoides*) " In *The Standard Edition of the Complete Psychological Works of Sigmund Freud, XII*, edited by James Strachey, 9–82. The Hogarth Press and the Institute of Psycho-Analysis.

Freud, Sigmund. 1962a. "Further Remarks on the Neuro-Psychoses of Defence". In *The Standard Edition of the Complete Psychological Works of Sigmund Freud, III*, edited by James Strachey, 162–85. The Hogarth Press and the Institute of Psycho-Analysis.

Freud, Sigmund. 1962b. "The Neuro-Psychoses of Defence". In *The Standard Edition of the Complete Psychological Works of Sigmund Freud, III*, edited by James Strachey, 45–68. The Hogarth Press and the Institute of Psycho-Analysis.

Freud, Sigmund. 1966. "Draft H. Paranoia". In *The Standard Edition of the Complete Psychological Works of Sigmund Freud, I*, edited by James Strachey, 206–12. The Hogarth Press and the Institute of Psycho-Analysis.

Friedman, Richard A. 2013. "The Book Stops Here". *The New York Times*, May 20. http://www.nytimes.com/2013/05/21/health/the-dsm-5-as-a-guide-not-a-bible.html?_r=2&.

Frith, Christopher. 1996. "Neuropsychology of Schizophrenia: What Are the Implications of Intellectual and Experimental Abnormalities for the Neurobiology of Schizophrenia?". *British Medical Bulletin* 52 (3):618–26.

Frith, Christopher D. 1992. *The Cognitive Neuropsychology of Schizophrenia*. Lawrence Erlbaum Associates.

Frith, Christopher D. 2007. *Making Up the Mind. How the Brain Creates Our Mental World*. Blackwell.

Frith, Christopher D., Sarah-Jayne Blakemore, and Daniel M. Wolpert. 2000. "Explaining the Symptoms of Schizophrenia: Abnormalities in the Awareness of Action". *Brain Research Reviews* 31 (2000):357–63.

Frith, Uta, John Morton, and Alan M. Leslie. 1991. "The Cognitive Basis of a Biological Disorder: Autism". *Trends in Neurosciences* 14 (10):433–8. doi:http://dx.doi. org/10.1016/0166-2236(91)90041-R.

Fromm-Reichmann, Frieda. 1948. "Notes on the Development of Treatment of Schizophrenics by Psychoanalytic Psychotherapy". *Psychiatry* 11 (3):263–73.

Gadamer, Hans-Georg. 2006. *Truth and Method*. Second revised ed. Continuum. Original edition, 2004. Reprint, 2006.

Gardiner, Patrick. 1952/1978. *The Nature of Historical Explanation*. Oxford University Press.

Geertz, Clifford. 2001. "Imbalancing Act: Jerome Bruner's Cultural Psychology". In *Jerome Bruner. Language, Culture and Self*, edited by David Bakhurst and Stuart G. Shanker, 19–30. Sage.

Gergely, György, Harold Bekkering, and Ildikó Király. 2002. "Rational Imitation in Preverbal Infants". *Nature* 415:755.

Gilbert, Margaret. 2007. "Searle and Collective Intentions". In *Intentional Acts and Institutional Facts. Essays on John Searle's Social Ontology*, edited by Savas L. Tsohatzidis, 31–48. Springer.

Gilbert, Margaret. 2009. "Shared Intention and Personal Intentions". *Philosophical Studies: An International Journal for Philosophy in the Analytic Tradition* 144 (1):167–87.

Goodman, Russell B. 2004. *Wittgenstein and William James*. Cambridge University Press.

Gräfenhain, Maria, Tanya Behne, Malinda Carpenter, and Michael Tomasello. 2009. "Young Children's Understanding of Joint Commitments". *Developmental Psychology* 45 (5):1430–43.

Graham-Dixon, Andrew. 2004. "ITP 216: The Miracle of the Speaking Babe by Titian". https://www.andrewgrahamdixon.com/archive/itp-216-the-miracle-of-the-speaking-babe-by-titian.html.

Greenberg, Gary. 2013. "The Rats of N.I.M.H". *Elements*, May 16. http://www.newyorker. com/online/blogs/elements/2013/05/the-scientific-backlash-against-the-dsm.html.

Greenberg, Joanne. 1964/2009. *I Never Promised You a Rose Garden: A Novel*. St. Martin's Press.

Greenwood, John D. 2004. *The Disappearance of the Social in American Social Psychology*. Cambridge University Press.

Greenwood, John D. 2009. *A Conceptual History of Psychology*. McGraw-Hill.

Hacker, P. M. S. 1993. *Wittgenstein. Meaning and Mind. Exegesis §§ 243–427, Analytical Commentary on the Philosophical Investigations*. Blackwell.

Hacker, P. M. S. 2000. *Wittgenstein. Mind and Will, Analytical Commentary on the Philosophical Investigations*. Blackwell.

Hacker, P. M. S. 2001a. "Developmental Hypotheses and Perspicuous Representations: Wittgenstein on Frazer's *Golden Bough*". In *Wittgenstein: Connections and Controversies*, edited by P. M. S. Hacker, 74–97. Oxford University Press.

Hacker, P. M. S. 2001b. "Wittgenstein and the Autonomy of Humanistic Understanding". In *Wittgenstein: Connections and Controversies*, edited by P. M. S. Hacker, 34–73. Oxford University Press.

Hacker, P. M. S. 2001c. *Wittgenstein: Connections and Controversies*. Oxford University Press.

Hacker, P. M. S. 2007. "The Relevance of Wittgenstein's Philosophy of Psychology to the Psychological Sciences". Conference on Wittgenstein and Science, Leipzig.

Hacker, P.M.S. 2010. "The Development of Wittgenstein's Philosophy of Psychology". In *Mind, Method and Morality Essays in Honour of Anthony Kenny*, edited by P. M. S. Hacker and J. Cottingham, 275–305. Oxford University Press.

Hacking, Ian. 2013. "Lost in the Forest". *London Review of Books* 35 (15), August 2013. https://www.lrb.co.uk/the-paper/v35/n15/ian-hacking/lost-in-the-forest.

Hanfling, Oswald. 2001. "Thinking". In *Wittgenstein: A Critical Reader*, edited by Hans-Johann Glock, 138–55. Blackwell.

Hanganu-Bresch, Cristina. 2019. "Public Perceptions of Moral Insanity in the 19th Century". *The Journal of Nervous and Mental Disease* 207 (9):805–14.

Hanganu-Bresch, Cristina, and Carol Berkenkotter. 2019. *Diagnosing Madness: The Discursive Construction of the Psychiatric Patient, 1850–1920*. University of South Carolina Press.

Hansen, Julie V. 1996. "Resurrecting Death: Anatomical Art in the Cabinet of Dr. Frederik Ruysch". *The Art Bulletin* 78 (4):663–80. doi: 10.1080/00043079.1996.10786711.

Hartwell, Carol Eadie. 1996. "The Schizophrenogenic Mother Concept in American Psychiatry". *Psychiatry* 59 (3):274–97.

Haskell, Ebenezer. 1869. *The Trial of Ebenezer Haskell, in Lunacy, and His Acquittal before Judge Brewster, in November, 1868 Together with a Brief Sketch of the Mode of Treatment of Lunatics in Different Asylums in This Country and in England, with Illusrations, Including a Copy of Hogarth's Celebrated Painting of a Scene in Old Bedlam, in London, 1635*. Ebenezer Haskell.

Healy, David. 2002. *The Creation of Psychopharmacology*. Harvard University Press.

Hepach, Robert, and Felix Warneken. 2018. "Editorial Overview: Early Development of Prosocial Behavior: Revealing the Foundation of Human Prosociality". *Current Opinion in Psychology* 20:iv–viii.

Hill, Elisabeth, and Uta Frith. 2004. "Understanding Autism: Insights from Mind and Brain". In *Autism: Mind and Brain*, edited by Uta Frith and Elisabeth Hill, 1–19. Oxford University Press.

Horwitz, Allan V., and Jerome C. Wakefield. 2007. *The Loss of Sadness. How Psychiatry Transformed Normal Sorrow into Depressive Disorder*. Oxford University Press.

Hyman, Steven E. 2003. "Foreword". In *Advancing DSM. Dilemmas in Psychiatric Diagnosis*, edited by Katharine A. Phillips, Michael B. First and Harold Alan Pincus, xi–xxi. American Psychiatric Association.

Hyman, Steven E. 2010. "The Diagnosis of Mental Disorders: The Problem of Reification". *Annual Review of Clinical Psychology* 6 (1):155–79. doi:10.1146/annurev.clinpsy.3.022806.091532.

Ingram, David. 1989. *First Language Acquisition. Method, Description, and Explanation.* Cambridge University Press.

Insel, Thomas. 2011. "Improving Diagnosis through Precision Medicine". *NIMH Director's Blog*, November 15. http://www.nimh.nih.gov/about/director/2011/improving-diagnosis-through-precision-medicine.shtml.

Insel, Thomas. 2013. "Transforming Diagnosis". *NIMH Director's Blog*, April 29. http://www.nimh.nih.gov/about/director/2013/transforming-diagnosis.shtml.

Jacob, Pierre. 2020. "What Do False-Belief Tests Show?" *Review of Philosophy and Psychology* 11 (1):1–20. doi: 10.1007/s13164-019-00442-z.

Jacobi, Abraham. 1889. "Introductory". In *Cyclopaedia of the Diseases of Children Medical and Surgical*, edited by J.M. Keating, 1–10. J.B. Lippincott Company.

Jacobi, Abraham. 1909. "The Relations of Pediatrics to General Medicine". In *Collectanea Jacobi. Dr. Jacobi's Works. Collected Essays, Addresses, Scientific Papers and Miscellaneous Writings of A. Jacobi*, edited by William J. Robinson, 41–53. The Critic and Guide Company.

James, William. 1890/1983. *The Principles of Psychology*. Edited by George A. Miller. Harvard University Press.

James, William. 1892a. "A Plea for Psychology as a 'Natural Science'". *The Philosophical Review* 1 (2):146–53. doi: 10.2307/2175743.

James, William. 1892b. "Thought before Language: A Deaf-Mute's Recollections". *The Philosophical Review* 1 (6):613–24.

James, William. 1892/2001. *Psychology: The Briefer Course*. Dover Publications.

Jaspers, Karl. 1913/1973. *Allgemeine Psychopathologie*. Ninth ed. Springer.

Jaspers, Karl. 1997. *General Psychopathology*. Translated by J. Hoenig and Marian W. Hamilton. Edited by Paul R. McHugh. Vol. I. Johns Hopkins University Press.

Jaynes, Julian. 1976/2000. *The Origin of Consciousness in the Breakdown of the Bicameral Mind*. Houghton Mifflin Co. A Mariner Book. Original edition, 1976.

Kern, Andrea, and Henrike Moll. 2017. "On the Transformative Character of Collective Intentionality and the Uniqueness of the Human". *Philosophical Psychology* 30 (3):319–37.

Klibansky, Raymond, Erwin Panofsky, and Fritz Saxl. 1979. *Saturn and Melancholy. Studies in the History of Natural Philosophy, Religion, and Art*. Kraus Reprint.

Köhler, Wolfgang. 1947/1992. *Gestalt Psychology. An Introduction to New Concepts in Modern Psychology*. Liveright. Original edition, 1970.

Kramer, Peter D. 2005. *Against Depression*. Penguin.

Kronbichler, Lisa, Melanie Tschernegg, Anna Isabel Martin, Matthias Schurz, and Martin Kronbichler. 2017. "Abnormal Brain Activation during Theory of Mind Tasks in Schizophrenia: A Meta-Analysis". *Schizophrenia Bulletin* 43 (6):1240–50. doi: 10.1093/schbul/sbx073.

Ladd, George Trumbull. 1892. "Psychology as So-Called 'Natural Science'". *The Philosophical Review* 1 (1):24–53. doi: 10.2307/2175528.

Langdon, Robyn, and Max Coltheart. 2000. "The Cognitive Neuropsychology of Delusions". In *Pathologies of Belief*, edited by Max Coltheart and Martin Davies, 183–216. Blackwell.

Lee, Young-eun, and Felix Warneken. 2020. "Children's Evaluations of Third-party Responses to Unfairness: Children Prefer Helping over Punishment". *Cognition* 205:104374.

Leslie, Alan M. 1987. "Pretense and Representation: The Origins of 'Theory of Mind'". *Psychological Review* 94 (4):412–26.

Leslie, Alan M. 1992. "Pretense, Autism, and the Theory-of-mind Module". *Current Directions in Psychological Science* 1 (1):18–21.

Leslie, Alan M, and Laila Thaiss. 1992. "Domain Specificity in Conceptual Development: Neuropsychological Evidence from Autism". *Cognition* 43 (3):225–51.

Levelt, Willem J. M. 2013. *A History of Psycholinguistics: The Pre-Chomskyan Era*. Oxford University Press.

Lindberg, David C. 2007. *The Beginnings of Western Science. The European Scientific Tradition in Philosophical, Religious, and Institutional Context, Prehistory to A.D. 1450*. Second ed. University of Chicago Press.

Lindsay, William Lauder. 1876. "Mind in Plants". *Journal of Mental Science* 21 (96):513–32. doi: 10.1192/bjp.21.96.513.

Lindsay, William Lauder. 1877. "The Pathology of Mind in the Lower Animals". *Journal of Mental Science* 23 (101):17–44. doi: 10.1192/bjp.23.101.17.

Lindsay, William Lauder. 1879. *Mind in the Lower Animals in Health and Disease*. Vol. I. *Mind in Health*: C. Kegan Paul & Co.

Liszkowski, Ulf, Malinda Carpenter, Tricia Striano, and Michael Tomasello. 2006. "12- and 18-Month-Olds Point to Provide Information for Others". *Journal of Cognition and Development* 7 (2):173–87.

Littell, Jonathan. 2006. *Les Bienveillantes*. Gallimard

Littell, Jonathan. 2009. *The Kindly Ones*. Translated by Charlotte Mandell. Harper.

Liu, Shari, Tomer D Ullman, Joshua B Tenenbaum, and Elizabeth S Spelke. 2017. "Ten-month-old Infants Infer the Value of Goals from the Costs of Actions". *Science* 358 (6366):1038–41.

Lothane, Zvi. 1998. "Pour la defense de Schreber. Meurtre d'âme et psychiatrie. Postscriptum 1993". In *Schreber Revisité. Colloque de Cerisy*, edited by Daniel Devreese, Zvi Lothane and Jacques Schotte, 11–30. Presses Universitaires de Louvain.

Lothane, Zvi. 2010. "The Legacies of Schreber and Freud". *JEP—European Journal of Psychoanalysis, Humanities, Philosophy, Psychotherapies* 1 (30):17–78.

Ludwig, Kirk. 2007. "Foundations of Social Reality in Collective Intentional Behavior". In *Intentional Acts and Institutional Facts. Essays on John Searle's Social Ontology*, edited by Savas L. Tsohatzidis, 49–71. Springer.

Maher, Chauncey. 2012. *The Pittsburgh School of Philosophy: Sellars, McDowell, Brandom*. Routledge.

Makkreel, Rudolf A. 1975/1992. *Dilthey: Philosopher of the Human Studies*. Princeton University Press.

Makkreel, Rudolf A. 2012. "Wilhelm Dilthey". In *The Stanford Encyclopedia of Philosophy*, edited by Edward N. Zalta. https://plato.stanford.edu/archives/sum2012/entries/dilthey/.

Makkreel, Rudolf A., and Frithjof Rodi. 1989a. "Introduction to Volume I". In *Introduction to the Human Sciences*, edited by Wilhelm Dilthey, 3–43. Princeton University Press.

Makkreel, Rudolf A., and Frithjof Rodi. 1989b. "Preface to All Volumes". In *Introduction to the Human Sciences*, edited by Wilhelm Dilthey, xiii–xv. Princeton University Press.

Marr, David. 1982. *Vision. A Computational Investigation into the Human Representation and Processing of Visual Information*. W.H. Freeman and Company.

Mayes, Rick, and Allan V. Horwitz. 2005. "DSM-III and the Revolution in the Classification of Mental Illness". *Journal of the History of the Behavioral Sciences* 41 (3):249–67. doi: 10.1002/jhbs.20103.

McDowell, John. 1998. *Mind, Value, and Reality*. Harvard University Press.

McDowell, John. 2000. *Mind and World*. Harvard University Press.

McDowell, John. 2002. "Knowledge and the Internal Revisited". *Philosophy and Phenomenological Research* 64 (1):97–105.

Merivale, Charles. 1879. *My Experiences in a Lunatic Asylum. By a Sane Patient*. Chatto and Windus.

Messaggero. 2017. *Saint Anthony's Miracles—The Speaking Infant*. https://www.youtube.com/watch?v=beGF5LK5B5w.

Meyer, Catherine, ed. 2005. *Le livre noire de la psychanalyse. Vivre, penser et aller mieux sans Freud*. Les Arènes

Miguens, Sofia, ed. 2020. *The Logical Alien. Conant and His Critics*. Harvard University Press.

Mill, John Stuart. 1872/2006. *Collected Works. A System of Logic, Ratiocinative and Inductive, Books IV–VI, Appendices*. Edited by R.F. McRae. Vol. VIII. Liberty Fund.

Miller, George A. 1956. "The Magical Number Seven, Plus or Minus Two: Some Limits on Our Capacity for Processing Information". *Psychological Review* 63 (2):81–97.

Miller, George A. 1983. "Introduction". In *The Principles of Psychology*, edited by William James, ix–xxi. Harvard University Press.

Moll, Henrike. 2016. "Tension in the Natural History of Human Thinking". *Journal of Social Ontology* 2 (1):65–73.

Moll, Henrike, and Michael Tomasello. 2007. "Cooperation and Human Cognition: The Vygotskian Intelligence Hypothesis". *Philosophical Transactions of the Royal Society B* 362 (1480):639–48.

Moll, Henrike, Ryan Nichols, and Jacob L. Mackey. 2021. "Rethinking Human Development and the Shared Intentionality Hypothesis". *Review of Philosophy and Psychology* 12 (2):1–12, 453–64.

Morton, John. 2004. *Understanding Developmental Disorders. A Causal Modelling Approach*. Blackwell.

Murphy, Jeffrie G. 1972. "Moral Death: A Kantian Essay on Psychopathy". *Ethics* 82 (4):284–98.

The New York Times. 1992. "Study Backs Deep Anesthesia for Babies in Surgery". *The New York Times*, January 2. http://www.nytimes.com/1992/01/02/us/study-backs-deep-anesthesia-for-babies-in-surgery.html.

NIMH. 2011. "NIMH Research Domain Criteria (RDoC). Draft 3.1". http://www.nimh.nih.gov/research-priorities/rdoc/nimh-research-domain-criteria-rdoc.shtml.

Okazaki, Sumie, E. J. R. David, and Nancy Abelmann. 2008. "Colonialism and Psychology of Culture". *Social and Personality Psychology Compass* 2 (1):90–106. doi: https://doi.org/10.1111/j.1751-9004.2007.00046.x.

Onians, Richard Broxton. 1951/2000. *The Origins of European Thought*. Cambridge University Press.

Onishi, Kristine H., and Renée Baillargeon. 2005. "Do 15-Month-Old Infants Understand False Beliefs?" *Science* 308 (5719):255–8. doi: 10.1126/science.1107621.

Pattinson, Damian, and Maria Fitzgerald. 2004. "The Neurobiology of Infant Pain: Development of Excitatory and Inhibitory Neurotransmission in the Spinal Dorsal Horn". *Regional Anesthesia and Pain Medicine* 29 (1):36–44.

Perner, Josef. 1991. *Understanding the Representational Mind*. MIT Press.

Piaget, Jean. 1971. *Genetic Epistemology*. W. W. Norton & Company.

Pollock, Linda A. 1983. *Forgotten Children: Parent-child Relations from 1500 to 1900*. Cambridge University Press.

Poulin-Dubois, Diane, Hannes Rakoczy, Kimberly Burnside, Cristina Crivello, Sebastian Dörrenberg, Katheryn Edwards, Horst Krist, Louisa Kulke, Ulf Liszkowski, Jason Low, Josef Perner, Lindsey Powell, Beate Priewasser, Eva Rafetseder, and Ted Ruffman. 2018. "Do Infants Understand False Beliefs? We Don't Know yet – A Commentary on Baillargeon, Buttelmann and Southgate's Commentary". *Cognitive Development* 48:302–15. doi: https://doi.org/10.1016/j.cogdev.2018.09.005.

Presciutti, Diana Bullen. 2019. "Miracles in Monochrome: Grisaille in Visual Hagiography". *Art History* 42 (5):862–91.

Putnam, Hilary. 2000. "Rethinking Mathematical Necessity". In *The New Wittgenstein*, edited by Alice Crary and Rupert Read, 218–31. Routledge.

Putnam, Hilary. 2001. *Representation and Reality*. MIT Press. Original edition, 1988.

Quine, Willard Van Orman. 1986. *Philosophy of Logic*. Second ed. Harvard University Press.

Raffaele, Paul. 2006. "Sleeping with Cannibals". *Smithsonian Magazine*.

Rakoczy, Hannes. 2003. "The Development of Performing and Understanding Pretend Play: A Cultural Learning Perspective". Unpublished doctoral dissertation, Der Fakultät für Biowissenschaften, Pharmazie und Psychologie der Universität Leipzig.

Rakoczy, Hannes. 2008a. "Collective Intentionality and Uniquely Human Cognition". In *Learning from Animals? Examining the Nature of Human Uniqueness*, edited by E. Neumann-Held and L. Röska-Hardy, 105–21. Psychology Press.

Rakoczy, Hannes. 2008b. "Pretence as Individual and Collective Intentionality". *Mind & Language* 23 (5):499–517.

Rakoczy, Hannes, and Michael Tomasello. 2007. "The Ontogeny of Social Ontology: Steps to Shared Intentionality and Status Functions". In *Intentional Acts and Institutional Facts. Essays on John Searle's Social Ontology*, edited by Savas L. Tsohatzidis, 113–37. Springer.

Rakoczy, Hannes, Felix Warneken, and Michael Tomasello. 2008. "The Sources of Normativity: Young Children's Awareness of the Normative Structure of Games". *Developmental Psychology* 44 (3):875–81.

Robinson, Daniel N. 1995. *An Intellectual History of Psychology*. Third ed. University of Wisconsin Press.

Rokeach, Milton. 2011. *The Three Christs of Ypsilanti*. Edited by Rick Moody. New York Review Books.

Rorty, Richard. 1980. *Philosophy and the Mirror of Nature*. Princeton University Press.

Ryle, Gilbert. 1949. *The Concept of Mind*. Hutchinson's University Library. Original edition, 1949. Reprint, 1951.

Sacks, Oliver. 1999. *Awakenings*: Vintage Books.

Sagan, Carl. 2016. *Contact*. Simon & Schuster.

Saks, Elyn R. 2007. *The Center Cannot Hold. A Memoir of My Schizophrenia*. Virago.

Santner, Eric L. 1996. *My Own Private Germany. Daniel Paul Schreber's Secret History of Modernity*. Princeton University Press.

Sass, Louis A. 1994. *The Paradoxes of Delusion. Wittgenstein, Schreber, and the Schizophrenic Mind*. Cornell University Press.

Schatzman, Morton. 1971. "Paranoia or Persecution: The Case of Schreber". *Family Process* 10 (2):177–207. doi: 10.1111/j.1545-5300.1971.00177.x.

Schmidt, Marco F. H., and Michael Tomasello. 2012. "Young Children Enforce Social Norms". *Current Directions in Psychological Science* 21 (4):232–6.

Schreber, Daniel Paul. 2000. *Memoirs of My Mental Illness*. Translated by Ida Macalpine and Richard A. Hunter. Edited by Rosemary Dinnage. New York Review Books.

Schulte, Joachim. 2003. *Experience and Expression. Wittgenstein's Philosophy of Psychology*. Oxford University Press.

Scobel, Gert, and Michael Tomasello. 2008. "Interview by Gert Scobel with Michael Tomasello on 3SAT". [Video]. http://video.google.com/videoplay?doc id=8933367116959974563#.

Scott, Rose M., and Renée Baillargeon. 2017. "Early False-belief Understanding". *Trends in Cognitive Sciences* 21 (4):237–49.

Seabrook, John. 2008. "Suffering Souls. The Search for the Roots of Psychopathy". *The New Yorker*, November 10.

Searle, John R. 1983. *Intentionality, an Essay in the Philosophy of Mind*. Cambridge University Press.

Searle, John R. 1990/2002. "Collective Intentions and Actions". In *Consciousness and Language*, edited by John R. Searle, 90–105. Cambridge University Press. Original edition, 1990.

Searle, John R. 1995. *The Construction of Social Reality*. Free Press.

Searle, John R. 1999. *Mind, Language and Society: Philosophy in the Real World*. Basic Books.

Searle, John R. 2002. *Consciousness and Language*. Cambridge University Press.

Searle, John R. 2003a. *Minds, Brains, and Science*. Harvard University Press. Original edition, 1984.

Searle, John R. 2003b. *Rationality in Action*. MIT Press.

Searle, John R. 2007. "Social Ontology: The Problem and Steps toward a Solution". In *Intentional Acts and Institutional Facts. Essays on John Searle's Social Ontology*, edited by Savas L. Tsohatzidis, 11–28. Springer.

Searle, John R. 2008. *Freedom and Neurobiology: Reflections on Free Will, Language, and Political Power*. Columbia University Press.

Searle, John R. 2010. *Making the Social World*. Oxford University Press.

Shaftesbury, A.A.C.E. 1708. *A Letter Concerning Enthusiasm, to My Lord *****. J. Morphew.

Shanker, Stuart. 1998. *Wittgenstein's Remarks on the Foundations of AI*. Routledge.

Shorter, Edward. 1997. *A History of Psychiatry: From the Era of the Asylum to the Age of Prozac*. John Wiley & Sons.

Skinner, Burrhus F. 1957. *Verbal Behavior, the Century Psychology Series*. Appleton-Century-Crofts.

Skinner, Burrhus F. 1963. "Behaviorism at Fifty". *Science*, May 31, 951–8.

Skinner, Burrhus F. 1971. *Beyond Freedom and Dignity*. Penguin Books.

Skinner, Burrhus F. 2005a. *Walden Two*. Hackett Publishing Company. Original edition, 1948.

Skinner, Burrhus F. 2005b. "Walden Two Revisited". In *Walden Two*, edited by Burrhus F. Skinner, v–xvi. Hackett Publishing Company. Original edition, 1976.

Smith, Barry C. 2003. "John Searle: From Speech Acts to Social Reality". In *John Searle*, edited by Barry C. Smith, 1–33. Cambridge University Press.

Smith, Barry, and Joëlle Proust. 1999. "Cognitive Theories of Mental Illness". *The Monist* 82 (4).

Snell, Bruno. 1946/2011. *Die Entdeckung des Geistes. Studien zur Entstehung des europäischen Denkens bei den Griechen*. Vandenhoeck & Ruprecht.

Snell, Bruno. 1953. *The Discovery of the Mind. The Greek Origins of European Thought*. Translated by T.G. Rosenmeyer. Harvard University Press.

Sperber, Dan, and Deirdre Wilson. 1986/1996. *Relevance. Communication and Cognition*. Second ed. Blackwell.

Staub, Michael E. 2011. *Madness Is Civilization. When the Diagnosis Was Social, 1948–1980.* University of Chicago Press.

Stephan, Klaas E., Karl J. Friston, and Chris D. Frith. 2009. "Dysconnection in Schizophrenia: From Abnormal Synaptic Plasticity to Failures of Self-monitoring". *Schizophrenia Bulletin* 35 (3):509–27. doi: 10.1093/schbul/sbn176.

Sterelny, Kim. 2003. *Thought in a Hostile World: The Evolution of Human Cognition.* Blackwell.

Stich, Stephen P. 1983. *From Folk Psychology to Cognitive Science. The Case against Belief.* MIT Press.

Stich, Stephen P., and Shaun Nichols. 2003. "Folk Psychology". In *The Blackwell Guide to Philosophy of Mind*, edited by Stephen P. Stich and Ted A, 235–55. Warfield. Blackwell.

Stroud, Barry. 1965/2002. "Wittgenstein and Logical Necessity". In *Meaning, Understanding, and Practice. Philosophical Essays*, edited by Barry Stroud, 1–16. Oxford University Press.

Taine, Hippolyte. 1876. "L'acquisition du langage chez les enfants et dans l'espèce humaine". *Revue Philosophique de la France et de l'Étranger* (1):5–23.

Taine, Hippolyte. 1877. "M. Taine on the Acquisition of Language by Children". *Mind* 2 (6):252–9.

Thibaudeau, Élisabeth, Caroline Cellard, Mélissa Turcotte, and Amélie M. Achim. 2021. "Functional Impairments and Theory of Mind Deficits in Schizophrenia: A Meta-analysis of the Associations". *Schizophrenia Bulletin* 47 (3):695–711.

Thomason, Krista K. 2021. "The Philosopher's Medicine of the Mind: Kant's Account of Mental Illness and the Normativity of Thinking". In *Kant on Morality, Humanity, and Legality: Practical Dimensions of Normativity*, edited by Ansgar Lyssy and Christopher Yeomans, 189–206. Springer International Publishing.

Thornton, Tim. 2000. "Mental Illness and Reductionism: Can Functions be Naturalized?" *Philosophy, Psychiatry, & Psychology* 7 (1):67–76.

Titchener, Edward Bradford. 1914. "On 'Psychology as the Behaviorist Views It'". *Proceedings of the American Philosophical Society* 53 (213):1–17. doi: 10.2307/984126.

Tomasello, Michael. 1999. *The Cultural Origins of Human Cognition.* Harvard University Press.

Tomasello, Michael. 2008. *Origins of Human Communication.* MIT Press.

Tomasello, Michael. 2009. *Why We Cooperate.* MIT Press.

Tomasello, Michael. 2010. "Human Culture in Evolutionary Perspective". In *Advances in Culture and Psychology*, edited by Gelfand Michele J., Chiu Chi-yue and Hong Ying-yi, 5–51. Oxford University Press.

Tomasello, Michael. 2011. "Human Culture in Evolutionary Perspective". In *Advances in Culture and Psychology*, edited by Michele J. Gelfand, 5–51. Oxford University Press.

Tomasello, Michael. 2014. *A Natural History of Human Thinking.* Harvard University Press.

Tomasello, Michael. 2016. *A Natural History of Human Morality*. Harvard University Press.

Tomasello, Michael. 2018. "How Children Come to Understand False beliefs: A Shared Intentionality Account". *Proceedings of the National Academy of Sciences* 115 (34):8491–8. doi: 10.1073/pnas.1804761115.

Tomasello, Michael. 2019. *Becoming Human: A Theory of Ontogeny*. Belknap Press.

Tomasello, Michael. 2020. "Response to: Rethinking Human Development and the Shared Intentionality Hypothesis". *Review of Philosophy and Psychology* 12 (2):465–8.

Tomasello, Michael, and Amrisha Vaish. 2013. "Origins of Human Cooperation and Morality". *Annual Review of Psychology* 64:231–55.

Tomasello, Michael, and Hannes Rakoczy. 2003. "What Makes Human Cognition Unique? From Individual to Shared to Collective Intentionality". *Mind & Language* 18 (2):121–47. doi: 10.1111/1468-0017.00217.

Tomasello, Michael, and Henrike Moll. 2010. "The Gap is Social: Human Shared Intentionality and Culture". In *Mind the Gap. Tracing the Origins of Human Universals*, edited by Peter M. Kappeler and Joan B. Silk. Springer.

Tomasello, Michael, and Henrike Moll. 2011. "Replik auf die Kommentare". *Deutsche Zeitschrift für Philosophie* 59 (1): 164–9.

Tomasello, Michael, Ann Cale Kruger, and Hilary Horn Ratner. 1993. "Cultural Learning". *Behavioral and Brain Sciences* 16 (3):495–511. doi:10.1017/S0140525X0003123X.

Tomasello, Michael, Malinda Carpenter, Josep Call, Tanya Behne, and Henrike Moll. 2005. "Understanding and Sharing Intentions: The Origins of Cultural Cognition". *Behavioral and Brain Sciences* 28 (5):675–91. doi:10.1017/S0140525X05000129.

Tomasello, Michael, Malinda Carpenter, and Ulf Liszkowski. 2007. "A New Look at Infant Pointing". *Child Development* 78 (3):705–22.

Tudorie, George. 2011. "The Return of Antipsychiatry Notes on Richard Bentall's Doctoring the Mind". *Philobiblon: Transylvanian Journal of Multidisciplinary Research* 16 (2): 589–97.

Tudorie, George. 2013. "Margins of Psychology". Central European University. unpublished doctoral dissertation.

Tudorie, George. 2017. "The Child in Early Paediatrics and Developmental Psychology: Abraham Jacobi and Charles Darwin". In *Exploring Communication through Qualitative Research*, edited by Corina Daba-Buzoianu, Monica Bîră, Alina Duduciuc and George Tudorie, 152–79. Cambridge Scholars Publishing.

Tudorie, George. 2021. "'So Don't You Lock up Something/That You Wanted to See Fly'. What Story for Asylum Psychiatry?" *Romanian Journal of Communication and Public Relations* 23 (1):71–9.

Tumulty, Maura. 2008. "Diminished Rationality and the Space of Reasons". *Canadian Journal of Philosophy* 38 (4):601–30.

van de Roemer, Gijsbert M. 2009. "From Vanitas to Veneration: The Embellishments in the Anatomical Cabinet of Frederik Ruysch". *Journal of the History of Collections* 22 (2):169–86. doi: 10.1093/jhc/fhp044.

Van Prooijen, Jan-Willem. 2018. *The Psychology of Conspiracy Theories*. Routledge.

Vanderschraaf, Peter, and Giacomo Sillari. 2009. "Common Knowledge". http://plato. stanford.edu/archives/spr2009/entries/common-knowledge/.

Vass, Edit, Zita Fekete, Viktória Simon, and Lajos Simon. 2018. "Interventions for the Treatment of Theory of Mind Deficits in Schizophrenia: Systematic Literature Review". *Psychiatry Research* 267:37–47. doi: https://doi.org/10.1016/j. psychres.2018.05.001.

Velleman, J. David. 1997. "How to Share an Intention". *Philosophy and Phenomenological Research* 57 (1): 29–50.

von Wright, Georg Henrik. 2007. "Humanism and the Humanities". *e-Journal Philosophie der Psychologie* 9. http://www.phps.at/texte/WrightG1.pdf.

Wang, Esmé Weijun. 2019. *The Collected Schizophrenias: Essays*. Graywolf Press.

Warneken, Felix. 2006. "The Origins of Helping and Cooperation". Doctoral dissertation, Der Fakultät für Biowissenschaften, Pharmazie und Psychologie, Universität Leipzig.

Warneken, Felix. 2018. "How Children Solve the Two Challenges of Cooperation". *Annual Review of Psychology* 69:205–29.

Warneken, Felix, Frances Chen, and Michael Tomasello. 2006. "Cooperative Activities in Young Children and Chimpanzees". *Child Development* 77 (3):640–63.

Watson, John B. 1913/1994. "Psychology as the Behaviorist Views It". *Psychological Review* 101 (2):248–53.

Watson, John B. 1916. "Behavior and the Concept of Mental Disease". *The Journal of Philosophy, Psychology and Scientific Methods* 13 (22):589–97. doi: 10.2307/2012555.

Watson, John B. 1917. "Does Holt Follow Freud?" *The Journal of Philosophy, Psychology and Scientific Methods* 14 (4):85–92. doi: 10.2307/2012952.

Williams, Meredith. 1999. *Wittgenstein, Meaning and Mind. Toward a Social Conception of Mind*. Routledge.

Winch, Peter. 1964. "Understanding a Primitive Society". *American Philosophical Quarterly* 1 (4):307–24.

Winn, Philip. 2000. "The Biological Basis of Schizophrenia". In *Biological Psychiatry*, edited by E. Edward Bittar and Neville Bittar, 233–61. JAI Press Inc.

Wittgenstein, Ludwig. 1953/2009. *Philosophical Investigations*. Translated by G. E. M. Anscombe, P. M. S. Hacker and Joachim Schulte. Fourth revised ed. Wiley-Blackwell.

Wittgenstein, Ludwig. 1990a. *Remarks on the Philosophy of Psychology. Bemerkungen über die Philosophie der Psychologie*. Translated by G.E.M. Anscombe. Vol. I. Basil Blackwell. Original edition, 1980.

Wittgenstein, Ludwig. 1990b. *Remarks on the Philosophy of Psychology. Bemerkungen über die Philosophie der Psychologie*. Translated by C.G. Luckhardt and M.A.E. Aue. Vol. II. Basil Blackwell. Original edition, 1980.

Wittgenstein, Ludwig. 1993. *Philosophical Occasions*. Hacket Publishing Co.

Wittgenstein, Ludwig. 1998. *Zettel*. Translated by G.E.M. Anscombe. Basil Blackwell.

Wittgenstein, Ludwig. 1999. *Last Writings on the Philosophy of Psychology*. Translated by C.G. Luckhardt and Maximilian A.E. Aue. Vol. II. Blackwell. Original edition, 1992.

Wolpert, Lewis. 1992. *The Unnatural Nature of Science. Why Science Does Not Make (Common) Sense*. Harvard University Press.

Woods, Angela. 2011. *The Sublime Object of Psychiatry: Schizophrenia in Clinical and Cultural Theory*. Oxford University Press.

Zaibert, Leo. 2003. "Intentions, Promises, and Obligations". In *John Searle*, edited by Barry C. Smith, 52–84. Cambridge University Press.

Index

Lightning Source UK Ltd.
Milton Keynes UK
UKHW020807230622
404821UK00003B/223

9 781350 155121